Conquer and Colonize

STEVENSON'S REGIMENT AND CALIFORNIA

CONQUER
AND
COLONIZE

Donald C. Biggs

Presidio Press

SAN RAFAEL • CALIFORNIA

PRESIDIO PRESS
1114 Irwin Street
San Rafael, CA 94901

Library of Congress Cataloging in Publication Data

Biggs, Donald C
    Conquer and colonize.

    Bibliography: p.
    Includes index.
    1. California—History—1846-1850.   2. New York
Infantry.   1st Regt., 1846-1848.   3. United States—
History—War with Mexico—1845-1848—Regimental histories
—New York Infantry—1st.   4. Stevenson, Jonathan Drake,
1800-1894.   I. Title.
F864.B6   979.4'03   77-73564
ISBN 0-89141-023-6

Library of Congress Catalog Card Number 77-073564

ISBN 0-89141-023-6

Printed in the United States of America

For Bernice who helped

Contents

Acknowledgments xi
Introduction xv

Part One: INCEPTION   1

ONE   Divine Providence and the Pacific Shore ... 3
TWO   James K. Polk: His Plans for California 15
THREE   Volunteers for California 23
FOUR   Raising the Regiment 35
FIVE   The Nature of a Regiment:
        Pioneers in the Cause 49
SIX   Motivation: Providence Plus
        a Golden Jesus 59
SEVEN   Departure from New York 69

Part Two: PROGRESS   77

EIGHT   Bound for California 79
NINE   The Best Friends of California 87
TEN   Deployment 93
ELEVEN Colonel Mason and the North 105
TWELVE Fraternity in the South 115

vii

Part Three: ISSUE   129

THIRTEEN   Peace and the Golden Lure 131
FOURTEEN   At the Mines 141
FIFTEEN   Toward Local Control: The San Francisco
            Guards and Legislative Assembly 155
SIXTEEN   Growing Up with the Country: The
            Constitutional Convention and Statehood .177
SEVENTEEN   Outlaws, Hounds, and Filibusters 197
EIGHTEEN   Businessmen and "Pioneers" 211
NINETEEN   Colonel Stevenson 223
TWENTY   The Issue 233

Bibliographical Essay 241
Index 257

Illustrations

Disturnell's Map of Alta California 10
The Regiment on Governors Island 42
Presentation of the Bibles 51
Cartoon Depicting the Regiment's Departure 65
The "California Grand March" 72
Handwritten Letter by James K. Polk 73
San Francisco in 1846-1847 94-95
Encampment of Company I in Monterey 101
Monterey in 1848 109
En Route to the Gold Fields 142
Col. Jonathan D. Stevenson 225

Acknowledgments

As with any project for which the research has been both extensive and so prolonged as for this account of Colonel Stevenson and his regiment, one contracts virtually numberless debts while making and enjoying the acquaintance and benefitting from the assistance of many generous people. Particularly I would like to acknowledge and tender thanks for the patience and aid of my two daughters and two sons and of Bernice Prince Biggs, to whom this book is properly dedicated. She contributed good counsel and the more tedious typewriting, as well as companionship and hardihood, tramping through many a Mother Lode cemetery, regimental volunteers' list in hand.

To list all who have been helpful in my research is an impossibility, but my sincere thanks go to each one.

The genesis of this work in its present form, emphasizing as it does the broader American social issues involved, occurred first under the prompting of a wise man, a good friend, and an alluring teacher, the late Professor Tremaine McDowell, Director of the Program in American Studies at the University of Minnesota. Another of his devotees and a successor in his rôle in that program, Professor Mary C. Turpie, contributed years of encouragement and weeks of solace in trying and now memorable times. To her, special thanks. Professors McDowell and Turpie aided in securing for me a Carnegie Corporation Fellowship under which this work was begun and which was of immense aid. Much of the actual writing was accomplished in the freedom afforded by a fellowship generously granted and more generously renewed by the Del Amo Foundation of Los Angeles and Madrid and by two of the Foundation's trustees, Don Eugenio Cabrero and the Marqués de Villa-Alcazar.

The professional staffs of many federal and state military and civil agencies and archives, invariably cooperative, will welcome the conclusion of this endeavor, only completed with their aid and assistance. Learned and imaginative friends in historical agencies in many states have shown exceeding kindness and have saved me from many an error. I single out the New-York Historical Society (and Dr. James Heslin), the California Historical Society (especially James Abajian and Mrs. Maude K. Swingle and a former staff member there, Dr. Edwin H. Carpenter, now of the Huntington Library), The Society of California Pioneers, and county societies in both New York and California.

Over the years such luminaries in California studies as Henry C. Carlisle, Sr., George L. Harding, Colonel Fred B. Rogers, Dr. Frank L. Fenton, and the Rev. Maynard Geiger, O.F.M.—whose advice is no longer available but whose works stand as their monuments—have served as friends and guides.

Allies in the Bancroft Library of the University of California, Berkeley; the Huntington Library, San Marino; the Department of Special Collections of the University of California, Los Angeles; the New York Public Library; and the public libraries of Bath and Alfred, New York, have helped immensely.

The number of direct and collateral descendants of volunteers in the regiment who have been cooperative is almost legion, but two warrant special mention—Miss Mary I. Vincent of Springfield, Missouri, the granddaughter of Sgt. Joshua S. Vincent of Company I, and the late Palmer B. Hewlett of San Francisco, the son of Lt. Palmer B. Hewlett of Company I. The lives of the Hewletts, father and son, the one beginning in New York, both ending in California, spanned an astonishing 145 years, from the presidency of James Monroe to that of Lyndon B. Johnson.

One noteworthy night in northern Spain, in Pamplona, Miss Eleanor McClatchy of Sacramento read an early version of the first chapters of this study, and by her enthusiasm, which has remained undiminished, stimulated its completion. John Langellier of the Presidio Army Museum, San Francisco, read the completed work and deemed the history of President Polk's successful experiment worthy of publication. To these and other friends and colleagues such as José Tomás Carrió, John Carden Campbell, Dr. John A. Hussey, David Forsberg, and Kenneth M. Johnson, I express my great appreciation.

Donald C. Biggs

San Francisco, California
June 17, 1977

Introduction

On Governors Island, New York, in September, 1846, Rev. Dr. John McVickar addressed a regiment of New York Volunteers about to set sail for California. The chaplain gave each man a Bible and a message. In the regiment, he told them, he saw "an organized body of armed citizens who go forth alike to conquer and to colonize, and who bid adieu to their country and to their homes, with the professed understanding that they return not, but are to find alike their dwellings and their graves in a far distant land."

The regiment's "main object in view," as Secretary of War Marcy had declared in his general orders, was the military occupation of California, an enormous and little known but presumably valuable province of Mexico, with whom the United States was at war. But Marcy and the president he served, James K. Polk, clearly had further objectives in mind, one of them being the permanent acquisition of California. The regiment had been raised under peculiar and secret terms. These volunteers were to have been carefully selected, not exclusively for military experience or aptitude, but for good habits, variety of occupation, and the desire to remain in California. In addition, the men were not enlisted for a fixed time but "for the war."

In March, 1847, the transport ships *Thomas H. Perkins*, *Loo Choo*, and *Susan Drew* sailed into the harbor of San Francisco with these 599 volunteers, under the command of Colonel Jonathan D. Stevenson. By this time the key coastal

xv

points were in the hands of naval and land forces of the United States. For the next eighteen months, reinforced by 237 additional recruits from New York, the regiment garrisoned nine posts in Upper California and two in Lower California. When official word arrived of the Treaty of Guadalupe Hidalgo, ending the Mexican War, Stevenson's men were mustered out, in August, September and October of 1848. But, while every other regiment raised in the United States to fight the Mexican War was returned at government expense to its original place of muster, Stevenson's Regiment was mustered out in California.

From the beginning Stevenson's Regiment was controversial. Opponents of the Mexican War saw in the regiment an instrument of blatant imperialism, of immoral and un-American conquest. Proponents of the war, the majority, held the prevailing public opinion that territorial American expansion was not only right but divinely inspired in fulfilling America's manifest destiny. Stevenson and his men thus became moral agents in a glorious and righteous cause. Rev. Dr. McVickar was the first to overlook the military nature of the regiment, and he represented a point of view that most historians have since taken. Of the regiment as a military armament, he said, "I look not at it and speak not of it." Instead, he spoke of "the transplanted germ of American freedom [striking] its roots deep on the shores of the broad Pacific."[1]

Throughout its service in California, Stevenson's Regiment was by far the largest single body of United States troops stationed there, and its influence was felt. American freedom, at least American sovereignty, was indeed transplanted, partly by the volunteers. It became apparent soon after their discharge that the men had put down deep roots in the community. Gold had been discovered in California in January 1848, and in a year's time the population almost doubled to 26,000. By the end of 1849, the population had soared to about 115,000. Far from being absorbed into the enormous gold-seeking population, Stevenson's men contributed to the state's development in diverse ways and at critical moments. But, because of association with the opportunism of the Gold Rush, and because the misconduct of some volunteers tarnished the reputation of the entire unit, Stevenson's Regiment has not been highly regarded. Yet the records show that no other single body of men contributed so much in California's formative years. Their influence is observable almost to the end of the century.

The significant role of Stevenson's Regiment in California can be seen in its frequent and prominent mention in books and articles published during these years. In 1849, and for a few years after, the commonest type of book written about California was the emigrants' guide to the gold regions. One of the most interesting was a remarkable little book entitled, *The Emigrants' Guide to the Gold Mines. Three Weeks in the Gold Mines, or Adventures with the Gold-Diggers of California, in August, 1848, together with Advice to Emigrants, with full Instructions upon the best Methods of Getting There, Living, Expenses, etc. etc., and a Complete Description of the Country, With a Map, and Illustrations.* Published in New York late in 1848, it was one of the first guides to appear and the first of many fraudulent ones. The author, Henry I. Simpson, identifies himself as a member of Stevenson's Regiment, and three times in the first four pages he refers to the regiment, stating that he had come to California with the unit in 1847. There was, however, no Henry I. Simpson in Stevenson's Regiment. The author undoubtedly believed that such an assertion would add credibility, convincing readers that he had an intimate knowledge of northern California and its people.

Forty-five years later Stevenson's Regiment had not been forgotten. In 1893 the short story, "Gambler's Gulch," by Judge T. E. Jones, appeared in the June issue of *The Californian Illustrated Magazine*, a general-interest magazine of photographs, articles, and local-color fiction, published in San Francisco. The story tells of a hard-luck miner who settled in Weaverville, Trinity County, California, in 1854, after five years of unsuccessful prospecting. In a Weaverville monte parlor he meets his long-lost sweetheart from New York, and in a melodramatic episode, he learns that his beloved Adele is the wife of a debauched professional gambler named Castro. After the accidental death of the mustáchioed Castro and when the prospector's new claim has become "a successful venture," he invites the widow Adele Castro to share his life. She accepts. Gambler's Gulch is a fortunate place after all.

What is of interest in this tale is the prospector's background. He and Adele had grown up in a village in the state of New York, picking wild strawberries together, walking hand-in-hand home from school. But there were problems.

Her people were well to do—mine very poor. I realized this as I grew to manhood. . . . I left our humdrum place to better myself, and put myself in a position to be worthy of her. When I got to New York, Stevenson was just forming his California Regiment. I was only a boy in years, but I lied about my age, was accepted and came here.[2]

Jones's use of the name of the regiment lent verisimilitude to the tale. The young man of the story had not come to California as a mere argonaut and adventurer in the Gold Rush. That he had come for opportunities to improve his station is implied by his membership in Stevenson's "California Regiment." The author knew that the readers would understand this implication, as by 1893 the regiment had become legendary in California. In those forty-five years after their discharge, the influence of Stevenson's men was felt throughout the growing state of California.

Most of the ex-volunteers had headed straightaway to the gold fields, some before, some just after being mustered out. Some found death instead of gold. No fewer than seventeen of the men drowned in treacherous Sierra Nevada rivers. Others died violently, some killed by Indians. A number died of cholera and other diseases common to the river valleys and mining camps. A few became rich there. But in gold country, fortunes could be made in many ways: the men founded towns, built houses, opened stores, went into trading, published mining-camp newspapers. About one hundred spent the rest of their lives in the Mother Lode.

Most who went to the gold fields did not stay long—a few weeks, a few months, a few years. Back in the supply centers and coastal cities (often back to the ones where they had served), the men opened businesses, followed their professions and trades, and performed the services for which they were trained (and some for which they were not trained). A dozen were elected alcaldes, the chief municipal and district magistrates in the period before statehood. Some men founded, printed and wrote for newspapers. Some wrote books, a few of them exceedingly good books. Some of the men farmed on the 160 acres of bounty land each received on request from the government. Some acquired enormous ranches. Some speculated in California farming land and in city building lots. Some built homes and hotels and theaters.

In the period September 1848 to September 1849, with uncertainty about California's political status and resistance to continued military government, ex-volunteers led movements in San Francisco and Sacramento to organize militia and provide civil government for those cities. They agitated for a convention to produce the constitution necessary for statehood; and when that convention met, seven volunteers were elected delegates, one-seventh of the total number.

Stevenson's men also became congressmen and state senators and assemblymen (almost thirty of the ex-volunteers for one or more terms), judges and justices of the peace, sheriffs and U.S. marshals; and one became a warden of San Quentin Prison. Some, on the other side of the law, were imprisoned, hanged, or shot.

California's first filibuster was an ex-volunteer. Eight men went with William Walker to Nicaragua, most of them to die there. Others followed gold and silver rushes throughout the western world: to the Comstock, to Australia, to the Fraser River.

A large number of the men served in the Civil War—most for the Union, a few for the Confederacy. An extraordinary number achieved field-officer rank; many became generals.

Many did nothing illustrious, but settled down in California to lead inconspicuous lives. And some of them, of course, returned to New York at the very first opportunity. By and large, Stevenson's Regiment and the rôle of the men in it have been neglected or misunderstood. The actual accomplishments speak for themselves.

NOTES

1. John McVickar, *Rev. Dr. M'Vickar's Address to the California Regiment* (New York: n.p., 1846), 3-4.
2. Judge T. E. Jones, "Gambler's Gulch," *The Californian Illustrated Magazine*, IV (1893), 123.

Conquer and Colonize

Governors Island, New York, 1846

PART ONE

INCEPTION

Chapter One

Divine Providence and the Pacific Shore

I N THE MID-1840s a great many people expected the
United States to find itself in possession of California.
Most of them anticipated that New Mexico would also
be brought into the fold. Some even thought that ultimately all of Mexico, or all the continent, would—and should
because of reciprocal benefits—become part of the United
States. This kind of expansionism became known as "Manifest
Destiny"; James K. Polk and Stevenson's Regiment were decidedly part of it.

Manifest Destiny, as carefully analyzed and described by
Frederick Merk, meant "expansion, prearranged by Heaven,
over an area not clearly defined."[1] It envisioned the United
States as a continental republic of confederated states. Government would be representative; society, classless; religious
worship, free. Land acquisition would be easy; trade, free.
States and peoples destined to be delivered from whatever
former state would share all these blessings and many more.

3

Natural resources would be beneficially used for the general good and backward peoples regenerated. The United States, in turn, was destined to become the greatest nation on earth, as it was already the most benevolent, and to control half the commerce of the world, particularly that of the Orient.

Growing out of the period of continued economic distress after 1837, which saw the birth of numerous reform movements, and broadcast by the rather new, immensely popular penny press, the doctrines of Manifest Destiny were powerful attractions to the young and eager. There was something grand and solemn, expansive yet exclusive, in marching right out with Congressman William F. Giles of Maryland who, on the floor of the House early in 1847, stated that

we shall gain territory, and must gain territory, before we shut the gates of the temple of Janus. We must have it. We must march right out from ocean to ocean. . . . We must march from Texas straight to the Pacific ocean and be bounded only by its roaring wave. We must admit no other government to any partition of this great territory. It is the destiny of the white race, it is the destiny of the Anglo-Saxon race; and, if they fail to perform it, they will not come up to that high position which Providence, in his mighty government, has assigned them.[2]

This kind of continentalist expansionism was common sentiment as was the related notion of the innate superiority of the Anglo-Saxon.

As Congressman Giles marched from ocean to ocean, he would be treading on foreign soil, and critics knew the word for that. Conquest, however divinely clothed, was still conquest, and they thought it an unworthy ideal for an administration or for an individual, if he were an American.

Early in 1847 the American Peace Society, headquartered in Boston, offered a $500 prize for the best book-length review of the Mexican War "on the principles of Christianity and an enlightened statesmanship." Abiel Abbot Livermore won the competition, and the society published his *The War With Mexico Reviewed* in 1850. In this remarkably good book, Livermore returned repeatedly to one point—the self-deception involved in pleading for Manifest Destiny:

Prompt excuses have been discovered for this boa-constrictor appetite of swallowing states and provinces, in the glory of free institutions, the blessings of civil and religious liberty, and the extension of our industrial and commercial system. Alas! we have thus discovered opiates to lull our consciences when they were uneasy, and tonics to invigorate our ambition when it was halting.

These tonics fed a kind of lust, and "the god Terminus," Livermore wrote, "is an unknown deity in America."[3]

The literature of Stevenson's Regiment demonstrates how the "opiates" worked (and also just when they wore off) and what effect the "tonics" had. After the war, one of the company captains, John B. Frisbie, wrote:

Sometimes, thinking upon the acquisition of Texas, California, New Mexico—while Mexico was innocent, had done nothing to justify war, we were suffering no grievances on her account, yet she was an obstacle to progress. She was holding possession of territory that was barren to the world.[4]

This concept of immoral possession of land without use of the land became an important one when Manifest Destiny touched California.

Almost the entire complex of Manifest Destiny ideas and ideals appears in a poem by a regimental poet aboard one of the transport ships between Valparaiso and San Francisco in February 1847. Dated February 25 and signed simply with the initials W. M., "Columbia's Greeting to California" was read—and parodied—aboard the ship and was later printed in San Francisco newspapers.

California, awake! arise! 'tis time to sleep no more,
The bright warm sun is even now the mountains peeping o'er;
Awake! the night is speeding fast, the clouds have passed away,
Already break the first faint beams of the fast coming day,
And yet, though dark and heavy night has shrouded o'er the mind,
Fair nature in material things has bounteous been and kind.
Thy sleep was in defiance of each rich and saving boon,
A dull and deep Siesta, 'neath the broad full light of noon!
But now the waking hour is nigh, we come to set thee free,
We come as doth the else unfruitful sea,

To speed upon thy bosom, the barks of wealth and peace,
To multiply a thousand fold the bounteous land's increase;
We come to bring thee blessings rare, which freedom's age hath
shed,
Outgushing rich and plenteous as a mighty river head;
We come to scatter then abroad, rich seed, which sown, shall be,
Productive of a happy race, a people wise and free.
Columbia sends her people on a message unto thee,
She would that you were happy, she would that ye were free;
Receive from her, her people, receive from her, her laws,
Receive from her the spirit of His great and glorious cause,
And when the Future shall mature, what now receives its birth,
When California stands among the mighty powers of earth,
When knowledge, freedom, and the arts, have bro't forth glorious
fruit,
Each rivaling the other in one common grand pursuit.
Then, Californians, pause to think, who brought these blessings rare,
Think who it was first pealed the note of freedom on the air,
And you will learn with heartfelt praise, to bless the happy day,
When freedom took its westward flight to California.[5]

"Columbia's people" were very well armed when they went to
set California "free."

Indeed, most statements of Manifest Destiny, from whatever source, were utterly cheerless. Humor normally had no
part in the earnest business, but W.M.'s grandiloquence occa-
sioned an unusual reply from a poet aboard the *Loo Choo*,
Private Roderick Morrison. In the narrative poem "The Volunteer's Vision," Morrison dozes off while the ship is becalmed in the South Pacific and dreams of California. And
what dreams! The sights and scenes of fair California are not
so fair at all. He sees ". . . a rude and rocky tract in such a
situation / A picture bold, and glaring it—of perfect desola-
tion." Most melancholy in the miserable scenery is "a kind of
human creature" who turns out to be the sole survivor of the
New York Volunteers. When the creature speaks, the imagery
is familiar:

O California! Wake! Arise! Thy sun has tumbled down;
But on my soul its glorious rays have done me up quite brown!
Of all the humbugs on the earth, I reckon you the latest—

And though you're last—you're not the least, but certainly the
greatest!
When first I landed here I thought a Paradise to see;
But oh! my luck! you have turned out—a wilderness to be.[6]

While Morrison was having good fun and certainly did
expect to find a perfect paradise in California, the truth is
evident that he could neither have located nor described the
place, except very generally. None of the volunteers had ever
been to California. What they knew of it they had read in
newspapers and in a few books.

Granted, American contact with California had begun
early in the century. Sea otter and fur-seal hunters explored
the area until about 1820, followed by whalers and general
traders lured by the lucrative hide-and-tallow trade of the
next two decades. Out of that trade came letters about California from ship captains and supercargoes which were
printed in New York and Boston newspapers in the 1830s. A
more influential and more accurate account was Richard
Henry Dana's *Two Years Before the Mast.* The book was published in 1840 when most of the future volunteers were but
fifteen and sixteen years old. Many of the volunteers who
kept journals or wrote letters home had read Dana. On the
voyage and later in California, they repeatedly referred to the
book, and there was a copy on two of the three transport
ships that carried the men around the Horn. Most of the
volunteers' information on California was of the coastal area
Dana described, particularly the ports of San Francisco, Monterey, and San Diego, and also the town of Santa Barbara.

Reports of the region appeared after the United States
government expeditions to the Pacific Coast—the Slacum expedition sent to Oregon and San Francisco Bay in 1836 by
Jackson, and the Wilkes expedition in 1841 sent by Van
Buren—but the reports of these expeditions had little popular effect. The second western expedition of John Charles
Frémont, overland, took him to Oregon and into northern
California in 1843 and 1844. His report, printed by order of
both houses of Congress in 1845, became the principal popular source of information about the West. From Frémont one

learned more about the coast and harbors and also something about California's central valley and that part of California east of the Sierra Nevada, although this was still vague. While the book had four maps, they were general, with boundaries poorly defined. A reader could not determine where California stopped and New Mexico began.[7]

Some of the volunteers had read Frémont, but many more had read the letters that appeared increasingly in eastern newspapers through the 1840s. Some of these were written by Thomas Oliver Larkin, an American resident of Monterey since 1832, and others by John Marsh, a pioneer doctor in the San Francisco Bay region. Still others were written by the overland immigrants who had begun to come into California in 1841. These letters in newspapers were responsible for the reputation of California.

Stevenson's volunteers were devoted to newspapers. They even produced their own on one of the ships that carried them to California. First mention of the *Fish Market Reporter* appeared in Sergeant Joshua S. Vincent's "Log-Book" on December 15, 1846, when the *Susan Drew* was approaching Cape Horn. A prospectus had appeared, pasted on a board hung up by the main hatch: "It is to give the latest news from California—from the States—Lat. and Lon.—the Markets Tales Poetry Scandal &c." The prospectus was signed by Obadiah Dolphin, Zachariah Flounder, Sephomiah Blackfish and Ezekiel Sheepshead.[8] In the first number the editors addressed their patrons:

The "universal Yankee nation" has been styled by envious and malignant Foreigners [a] grasping and avaricious dollar and cent prop—indifferent to aught else besides the acquisition of *Dimes*. We do not make mention of this to deny it . . . We do it merely to give our definition of the Yankee Race—Viz: A Newspaper reading Republic.[9]

For the next two weeks, until the Cape Horn weather grew altogether too rough, the newspaper appeared regularly. On December 18 the *Reporter* had something to say about the volunteers and California:

We're like the minstrel boy and we're going to the wars way off in a distant clime where the New York sun don't shine and stars can't be seen without a Telescope and where it's so hot shoe leather's no use, or so cold that if I was speaking there I should be knee deep in froze up eloquence, and there's impenetrable forests, unscalable rocks, insurmountable mountains, impassable rivers and unfathomable frog ponds and there's Indians who ride Mammoths, dance with bears and claw tigers to pieces with their finger nails, and Anaconda's live there which will swallow a Regiment and chase the baggage wagons for a dainty, and there's bloody Mexicans who shoot copper bullets 20 of em almost as good as one American. So you see you're going to no Cainaan [sic] flowing with milk and honey but to California.[10]

When the volunteers arrived in California, they would indeed find more of everything than they had expected—greater distances, more extremes in climate and topography, exotic people living strangely. If no domesticated mammoths or tigers or anacondas inhabited the area, at least there really were Mexicans.

The mention of the Mexicans in this selection from the *Fish Market Reporter* is unusual. More often than not in 1846, the fact that California was Mexican territory went unacknowledged.

California was and had been under Mexican rule for twenty-five years. For centuries before the Mexican Revolution of 1821, it had been Spanish. Only in the 1... fifty years of that time, however, after 1769, had Upper California been at all settled, and then only the few ports and the narrow coastal plain. California had been part of the borderlands of New Spain, a missionary and military fringe, occupied late and only out of fear of Russian and British designs on the area. California was a defensive outpost and was treated as such; its status was second or third class. As a consequence, and because of the great distance from the capital in Mexico and the difficulty of supply, California's ties to its mother country were not strong. Decrees from Mexico City were not always acknowledged and put into effect, and officials from the capital were not always welcome.

ALTA (UPPER) CALIFORNIA IN 1847

Part of John Disturnell's "Mapa de los Estados Unidos de Méjico," that attached to the Treaty of Guadalupe Hidalgo, February 2, 1848. This treaty marked the conclusion of the Mexican War and transferred title of California to the United States. Mexican Upper California included the present-day states of California, Nevada, Arizona, Utah, and parts of Colorado and New Mexico. (Courtesy Bancroft Library, Berkeley.)

To settle California, Spain had used its time-proven frontier institutions: the mission, the presidio, and the pueblo. In its fifty years in Upper California, Spain gradually but systematically occupied the coastal margin of the area. Twenty-one missions were founded by the Franciscans between San Diego in the south and Sonoma in the north. Four permanent presidios, or military garrisons, were established—at San Diego, Santa Barbara, Monterey, and San Francisco. Three pueblos, for civilian colonization, were created, at Los Angeles in the south and at San Jose and Branciforte (Santa Cruz) in the north.

Under the Republic of Mexico, the presidios and pueblos were maintained, but the missions were secularized in the mid-1830s and their lands confiscated. Mexican immigration was encouraged and foreign immigration was generally permitted under certain conditions. Under the Mexicans there was some interest and activity in the central valleys of the Sacramento and San Joaquin rivers, and some lands were granted there, but the concentration of population remained along the coast.

No interest whatsoever was shown in that vast area of Upper California east of the Sierra Nevada. The best cartographic authority for the boundaries is John Disturnell's "Map of Mexico," the revised edition of 1847, which was used by the makers of the Treaty of Guadalupe Hidalgo. Disturnell shows Alta California from the Pacific, south of the Oregon line easterly to a point about 250 miles east of the Great Salt Lake. On this map the eastern boundary roughly parallels the upper courses of the Rio Grande from north of Taos to El Paso. Chihuahua, Sonora, and Baja California form the southern boundary. The area thus consisted of the present states of California, Nevada, Utah, and Arizona, as well as portions of Colorado and New Mexico.[11]

Most of the portion of Upper California east of the Sierra was unpopulated except for Indians. According to Bancroft's estimates, the foreign male population of Upper California in 1840 was 380. Of these a number were Americans who had married Mexican women, become Catholics, and gone into business or ranching. By the beginning of 1846, with 7,000 of some Spanish blood in California, the foreign male population was 680, of whom most were Americans who had come to California overland beginning in 1841.[12] These immigrants did not follow the pattern of remaining along the coast. Rather, they settled in the interior valleys to farm. They had come to stay, and, isolated as they chose to be, these people were less amenable and less susceptible to control by Mexico's California officials. The officials were properly apprehensive. Just ten years earlier Texas had become an independent republic.

From the Mexican capital to the Department of California, beginning in April 1845, came repeated warnings of imminent war and invasion by forces of the United States, with orders to take all precautions to resist.[13]

NOTES

1. Frederick Merk, *Manifest Destiny and Mission in American History* (New York: Alfred A. Knopf, 1963), 24. Much of this section is influenced by Professor Merk's penetrating study.

2. U.S., Congress, *Congressional Globe*, 29th Cong., 2d sess., Feb. 11, 1847, 387.

3. Abiel Abbot Livermore, *The War with Mexico Reviewed* (Boston: The American Peace Society, 1850), 12-13.

4. John B. Frisbie, "Reminiscences" (MS), 1884, 3.

5. Francis D. Clark, *The First Regiment of New York Volunteers* (New York: George S. Evans & Co., 1882), 68. Signing himself "W.M.," the poet is unknown. He may have been Walter Murray, private in Company A aboard the *Loo Choo*.

6. Roderick M. Morrison, "The Volunteer's Vision," 2-4. Reproduced from a facsimile of the original manuscript presented to Barry & Patten in San Francisco, in 1863, by James H. Adams. Adams was a private in Company A, as was Morrison.

7. U.S., Congress, Senate, *Report of the exploring expedition to the Rocky Mountains in the year 1842, and to Oregon and north California in the years 1843-44*, by John Charles Frémont, Ex. Doc. 174, 28th Cong., 2d sess., 1845.

8. Joshua S. Vincent, "Log-Book," (MS), Dec. 15, 1846. These gentlemen predicted in their first number, Dec. 17, 1846, that "when Homer, Milton and Shakespeare shall have become names that were," their own names would live in tale and song, "and the volumes of the 'Reporter' will be as precious as the 'Sybilline leaves.' " In the latter they were correct. Other than the long quotation in Vincent's journal (strongly suggesting that he did part or all of the writing), and references in the journals of other men on the ship, nothing has come down to us of *The Fish Market Reporter.* It was undoubtedly handwritten, as there is no evidence of a press on the ship.

9. *Ibid.*, Dec. 17, 1846.

10. *Ibid.*, Dec. 18, 1846.

11. John Disturnell, Map of Mexico (rev. ed., 1847) in George P. Hammond, ed., *The Treaty of Guadalupe Hidalgo* (Berkeley: Friends of the Bancroft Library, 1949).

12. Hubert Howe Bancroft, *History of California*, vol. 5 (vols. 5 to 7—San Francisco: The History Company, 1886-1890), 524-25; Robert E. Riegel, *America Moves West*, Rev. ed. (New York: Henry Holt and Company, 1947), 375.

13. Bancroft, vol. 4 (vols. 1 to 4—San Francisco: A. L. Bancroft & Company, 1884-1886), 600-1.

Chapter Two

James K. Polk:
Plans for California

ON MAY 11, 1846, President James K. Polk sent Congress a message asking for recognition of the existing state of war between the United States and Mexico. At the same time he asked to have placed at his disposition the means of vigorously prosecuting the war to hasten the restoration of peace. The accompanying war bill provided for an appropriation of ten million dollars, permitted the use of the army and the navy, and authorized the service of fifty thousand volunteers. Despite its controversial preamble, which assigned to the Republic of Mexico all blame for the hostilities, the war bill was passed by the House on May 11, and the House bill by the Senate the next day. On May 13 the president signed the act recognizing and providing for the prosecution of the existing state of war.

On that same day, May 13, two related events occurred that would prove important to the yet unformed and unnamed California regiment. During the morning General Winfield Scott and Secretary of War William L. Marcy called on President Polk with a plan for the requisition of the fifty thousand war-time volunteers authorized by Congress. The president quickly approved this measure. During the meeting of the cabinet in the evening, however, Polk was obliged to overrule and reprove his secretary of state, James Buchanan, for some strange and uncharacteristic proposals. To the president's astonishment, in the draft of his memorial to foreign governments, Buchanan had proposed to explain that the United States did not go to war to dismember Mexico but only to defend United States territory to the boundary at the Rio Grande del Norte. Specifically, the secretary disclaimed any intention on the part of the United States to acquire New Mexico or California. Not to so state, Buchanan argued, would bring certain war with England and probably with France, for neither power would stand by and allow the annexation of California by the United States. With the support of every other member of the cabinet, Polk was resolute. He would not tolerate the intervention of any European power on this continent, nor would he consider—or at least not publicize—predetermined conditions for peace. Moreover, he wrote:

> Sooner than give the pledge he [Buchanan] proposed, that we would not if we could fairly and honorably acquire California or any other part of the Mexican Territory which we desired, I would let the war which he apprehended with England come and would take the whole responsibility.[1]

At the close of the discussion, Polk himself drafted a short statement to substitute for the offending paragraph on dismembering Mexico, acquiring California, and setting the Rio Grande as the ultimate boundary. Polk wrote, "We go to war with Mexico solely for the purpose of conquering an honorable peace."[2] It appeared that such a peace, once "conquered," would require the acquisition of at least California by the United States.

Polk's determination to acquire California was no secret. It was understood by Congress, assumed by many of the voters who had elected him, and was best known in the cabinet, where plans for acquisition were discussed and approved in 1845. Polk's strategy for obtaining California was threefold. During his first year and a half in office the president worked concurrently on all three plans: (1) to purchase California outright, (2) to encourage revolution among Mexican Californians, who would then seek admission to the Union, and (3) to seize California forcibly in the event of a war and to be in possession of it at the conclusion of that war. Should all three fail, patient waiting (but not by Polk) would probably see the prize won through steady American immigration and the "Texas game." Heavily infiltrated by Americans, Mexican Texas had declared itself independent in 1836. Recognized as an independent republic, Texas was formally annexed to the United States in one of President Tyler's last acts in 1845, after the election and just before the inauguration of Polk.

Polk was not the first president of the United States to try to buy California. Routinely associated at first with the desirable acquisition of Texas and the settlement of boundary disputes in the quarter century after 1820, the acquisition of California became more and more a part of American diplomacy. Acting for President James Monroe, Secretary of State John Quincy Adams had tried to secure California in the early 1820s, as he did again as president in early 1827. Andrew Jackson unsuccessfully attempted the purchase of California in the first year of his administration, 1829, and periodically thereafter, an effort he renewed with vigor in 1835 and yet again in 1837, shortly before leaving office. If not consistently pursued, interest in the cession of California was still maintained through the administrations of Van Buren and Tyler.

To this same end, Polk sent John Slidell as a commissioner to Mexico in the fall of 1845. In negotiating the Texas boundary dispute, Slidell was authorized to offer five million dollars for the cession of New Mexico. For California, "money would be no object," the secretary of state wrote in his instructions.[3] Mexican hostility toward the United States for the annexation of Texas prevented negotiations, however. Slidell was not even received.

Polk's second plan was to acquire California through the efforts of the Mexican Californians once they had asserted their independence from Mexico. The president's chief instrument here was Monterey's Thomas Larkin. Larkin fully believed that the Californians could voluntarily be induced to transfer their allegiance to the United States. In 1843 he had been appointed United States consul in the previous administration, and the appointment was regularly renewed through 1848. Larkin had been a good choice as consul. He was a prosperous merchant, knew everyone of influence in California, and was discreet and generally esteemed. While initially his principal work as consul was lending assistance to sick and destitute American seamen, more and more often he was called upon for information on California. Through 1845 he wrote long letters to the State Department and in October of that year was appointed a confidential agent. His duties were to report on any British and French plans involving California and to continue to encourage a sense of independence in the Californians. Once free of Mexico, they should be persuaded to unite their country with the United States.

Larkin wrote letters not only to the State Department but also to newspapers in Massachusetts and New York. In these he gave details about the country, the people, and the opportunities abounding, and, in addition, he never failed to sound the alarm about British interest in California. This interest he exaggerated into designs for imminent seizure. By the end of 1845 newspapers were writing to Larkin for news. In December the editors of both the *New York Herald* and the New York *Sun* pleaded for more of his valuable correspondence. The editor of the *Sun* wrote to him on December 24, 1845, saying that interest in California was especially great. "Just now there are strong opinions that California will be joined to the United States."[4]

This was no surprise. Strong opinions were already evident when President Polk delivered his first annual message to Congress on December 2, 1845. In the address he warned European nations against interference in the Americas, where nations were equally sovereign and independent. But he went even further, reasserting the Monroe Doctrine clearly and vigorously:

We must ever maintain the principle that the people of this continent alone have the right to decide their own destiny. Should any portion of them, constituting an independent state, propose to unite themselves with our Confederacy, this will be a question for them and us to determine without any foreign interposition.[5]

Polk was remembering Texas and thinking ahead to California. Should he be unable to buy California and should the Californians not assert their independence, the president could use still a third plan. It involved war, which seemed very likely to break out at any time.

The annexation of the Republic of Texas by Congress in March, 1845, had led to talk of war both in Washington and in Mexico City. Mexico had never recognized the independence of that republic, still considered Texas part of Mexico, and had threatened that annexation by the United States would be grounds for war. Formal diplomatic relations no longer existed between the two countries. There could be no doubt that the United States would win such a war, and anticipation of the indemnity Polk desired was only prudent.

The "prudent" preparations involved both land and naval forces. Once the Texan congress had ratified the terms of the resolution annexing Texas as a state, Polk sent troops under General Zachary Taylor into the disputed territory between the Nueces River and the Rio Grande. In July 1845 these forces concentrated at Corpus Christi on the Gulf of Mexico. Early in January 1846 they were ordered across the disputed area to the left bank of the Rio Grande. The preceding month Congress had taken the final action necessary to admit Texas as a state by extending the revenue system over the territory in question. It thus behooved the president to provide for the protection of American interests there. In April Taylor's forces engaged some Mexican forces on the "United States" side of the river. American lives were lost, and the war began.

While the United States had inherited claims (perhaps groundless) to the strip of land between the Nueces River and the Rio Grande, no such claims existed for California. Consequently, the president could only prepare for specific action in the Far West should hostilities actually begin.

Polk centered his plans on the navy. While not an exceptional fleet in 1845 and 1846, the Pacific Squadron of the United States Navy had steadily been strengthened since the late 1830s, as the British naval force in the Pacific had also been increased. Part of this American squadron under a different commander, Commodore Thomas ap Catesby Jones, had seized the port of Monterey in October 1842, to everyone's great embarrassment. The commodore had erroneously been informed that the United States and Mexico were at war and that California was being ceded to England. Presumably, his instructions were to forestall any such cession. While he retired in a few days with apologies, Commodore Jones had dramatically tipped the hand of the United States to Mexican officials. His "outrage" against a nation with whom the United States was at peace revealed nothing very startling, but, nonetheless, suggested something of interest to Washington: California was easy prey, and the Californians were generally indifferent.[6]

The incident had also revealed that the United States would not permit European intervention in California. But for all England's supposed interest in Upper California, the British in their men-of-war showed no concern. Larkin and the other eyewitnesses did not recognize the significance of this inaction. Since the British fleet off California was in every way superior to the American, England evidently did not care to risk war with the United States. Belief in British designs on California continued, however, and the foreign "peril" became even more common and more useful in politics after 1842.

In the spring of 1845 the U.S. Pacific Squadron was highly visible along the west coast of Mexico's mainland. Commanded by Commodore John D. Sloat, the squadron included the forty-four-gun frigates *Savannah*, *Constitution*, and *Congress*, four twenty-gun sloops of war and two transports.

As part of Polk's plan, if war broke out, the Pacific Squadron was to take California. On June 24, 1845, the secretary of the navy, George Bancroft, sent secret and confidential instructions to Commodore Sloat. "If you ascertain with certainty that Mexico has declared war against the United States," Bancroft wrote, "you will at once possess yourself of the port of San Francisco, and blockade or occupy such other ports as your force may permit." A closing paragraph to the letter attempted to anticipate any predatory implications.

The great distance of your squadron, and the difficulty of communicating with you, are the causes for issuing this order. The President hopes most earnestly that the peace of the two countries may not be disturbed. The object of the instructions is to possess you of the views of the government in the event of a declaration of war against the United States—an event which you are enjoined to do everything consistent with the national honor on your part, to avoid.[7]

The memory of Commodore Jones was still green.

On October 17, 1845, Bancroft confirmed the earlier instructions to Sloat. In this letter, Bancroft did not mention Mexico declaring war; he said Sloat was to act "in the event of hostilities." Perhaps that event was more likely, after all, with Taylor's army then poised at Corpus Christi.[8]

Nine months later, when hostilities had begun and Sloat was already in possession of the ports of Monterey and San Francisco, Bancroft again addressed him. The meaning could not be mistaken. In accord with its rights as a belligerent nation, Bancroft wrote,

the object of the United States . . . is to possess itself entirely of Upper California. . . . The object of the United States has reference to ultimate peace with Mexico; and if, at that peace the basis of the *uti possidetis* shall be established, the government expects, through your forces, to be found in actual possession of California.[9]

To Polk, California was indemnity for the past and security for the future.

NOTES

1.   Allan Nevins, *Polk: The Diary of a President* (New York: Longmans, Green and Co., 1929), 90-91.

2.   Philip Shriver Klein, *President James Buchanan* (University Park, Pa.: Pennsylvania State University Press, 1962), 186.

3.   *Ibid.*, 185.

4.   George P. Hammond, ed., *The Larkin Papers*, 10 vols., (Berkeley: University of California Press, 1951-1964), vol. 1, xi. Larkin's personal, official, and business correspondence and accounts were collected by Hubert Howe Bancroft, who relied heavily on it in writing his *History of California*. As edited by Hammond, there is no better single source for California in the period 1832-1846.

5.   James D. Richardson, ed., *Compilation of the Messages and Papers of the Presidents, 1789-1897, 11 vols.*, (53d Cong., 2d sess., H. Misc. Doc. No. 210 Washington: 1905-7), vol. 4, 301.

6.   Bancroft, *History of California*, vol. 4, 301.

7.   George Bancroft, Washington, to John D. Sloat, June 24, 1845, U.S. Gov. Doc. Ser. 520, p. 231.

8.   Bancroft, *History of California*, vol. 5, 195-96.

9.   Bancroft to Sloat, July 12, 1846, U.S. Gov. Doc. Ser. 520, p. 238. In international law the principle of *uti possidetis* grants to belligerents as absolute property the area in possession of each at the time of the establishment of peace.

Chapter Three

Volunteers for California

AFTER RECEIVING THE APPROVAL of the president on May 13, 1846, Secretary of War Marcy immediately proceeded to requisition the states for volunteer troops. Of the fifty thousand volunteers authorized by Congress in the war bill, the state of New York was asked to provide seven regiments of infantry, about 5,500 men. On May 28 Governor Silas Wright, as commander in chief of the state militia, issued General Orders from Albany through his adjutant general, R. E. Temple, for the enrollment of seven regiments of volunteers.[1] While these regiments were to be enrolled in just two weeks, by a deadline of June 15, they were only to be held in readiness to be mustered into the service, not mustered immediately.

Regiments, battalions, and companies of militia already organized and new, hastily formed voluntary associations would both be accepted. Applications from individuals would be accepted, too, and these volunteers would be formed into companies by the adjutant general as their numbers justified. The strength of each company would be seventy-seven men— one captain, one first lieutenant, one second lieutenant, four sergeants, four corporals, two musicians (one fifer, one drummer), and sixty-four private soldiers. Regiments would consist of ten such companies with three field officers in command—one colonel, one lieutenant colonel, and one major—with a small noncommissioned staff.

Governor Wright spelled out in detail the provisions of the New York constitution and legislative statutes governing militia, especially those relating to election of officers. We learn from a letter he wrote on May 28 to the secretary of war that he expected fully half of the required 5,500 men to have no prior militia experience.

After describing the proper organization of companies and regiments, the governor proceeded to the terms of service. Volunteers once mustered into the service of the United States would be subject to the rules and articles of war, would receive the same pay and allowances as regular army, would be armed by the United States when mustered, and would be required to serve either for twelve months or to the end of the war, depending upon their agreement at the time of muster. Privates and noncommissioned officers between the ages of fifteen and forty-five would be accepted.

Governor Wright concluded his General Orders with a trace of apprehension and a patriotic appeal:

> If the voluntary applications to the Adjutant General in pursuance of this order shall not be such by the 15th day of June next as to offer a reasonable certainty of promptly filling the seven regiments called for by the requisition of the President further measures will be then taken. . . . The Citizen Soldiery of New York have never been deaf to the call of their country for aid against a foreign enemy and until the spirit which animated our ancestors during the struggles of the Revolution shall be lost and the memory of the Niagara Frontier during the late war shall be obliterated such a call will not be unheeded by them. That call is now addressed to them.[2]

Silas Wright was apprehensive, with better reason than he then knew. He also disapproved of the war. In 1844, when a United States senator from New York, Wright had allied himself with Senator Thomas Hart Benton in voting against ratification of President Tyler's proposed treaty for the annexation of Texas. In the Senate he spoke vigorously against ratification. After his vote, in a campaign speech in Watertown, New York, he explained the reason to his constituents: "I believed that the treaty, from the boundaries that must be implied in it, embraced a country to which Texas had no claims, over which she had never asserted jurisdiction, and which she had no right to cede."[3]

Wright had other grievances, too. As a powerful and high-ranking Democrat, he had been a contender for the presidential nomination at the Democratic National Convention in Baltimore. Because of his identification with the anti-annexation faction, he had been passed over in favor of James K. Polk.[4] Silas Wright was not alone, since President Tyler was not renominated for the same reason and John C. Calhoun was scorned for his own special kind of factional association. The convention properly appraised the country's spirit of expansionism and correctly assumed the annexation of Texas to be an unbeatable issue. James K. Polk was the right man. Now Wright found himself obliged to raise New York troops (more than one-tenth of the total authorized by Congress) to fight Polk's war over the very boundary dispute that may have cost him the presidential nomination.

In a letter to the secretary of war on May 28, Governor Wright revealed his concern over raising seven regiments in New York. The governor requested further details about the requisition of troops and stated that he felt the quota for New York was too high. Marcy advised him to begin by assigning single organized companies to the existing six regiments of militia to bring them up to strength. This should be easy, Marcy suggested. The officials in Washington thought that incomplete regiments and companies would be glad to take measures to change their organization or increase their numbers. Again, the impression in Washington was that members of the New York militia certainly were "animated by the patriotic spirit which pervades the whole country."[5]

The governor had also asked Marcy about the payment of expenses for enrolling volunteers. There would be none, the secretary replied, since assembling the volunteers was unnecessary. More to the point, he admitted there was no provision for paying expenses until the volunteers were mustered. Wright had asked when that might be. Marcy replied:

With respect to the time when any of the Volunteers of New York or other Northern states will be mustered into service it is impossible to give any information. It depends altogether upon future events. As it affects these states the present measure is one of precaution only adopted with the view of having ready for immediate service a sufficient amount of force for any emergency that may arise. . . . The President would not be justified in causing any of the troops to be mustered until circumstances should require their immediate service.[6]

There is ample evidence in this and other letters written by Secretary Marcy that he thought the war would be a short one. Volunteers from northern states might never be needed. Requisitions on the governors of western, southwestern, and southern states were exceeding their quotas, and volunteers in prodigious numbers were assembling at Fort Leavenworth and at General Taylor's bases in Texas.[7]

The call-up of some of these New York volunteers did not, in fact, depend upon future events, as Marcy had supposed, but on past and current ones. The seizure of California ports by United States naval forces had already been ordered by the secretary of the navy, and the very day that he wrote his soothing letter to Governor Wright, June 3, Secretary Marcy had also written a confidential letter to Colonel Stephen Watts Kearny at Fort Leavenworth. While it was not prudent that it should become a matter of "public notoriety," Marcy wrote, "it has been decided by the President to be of the greatest importance, in the pending War with Mexico, to take the earliest possession of Upper California. An expedition with that view is hereby ordered, and you are designated to command it."[8]

Kearny had earlier been instructed to proceed to and seize the Mexican province of New Mexico. Now he was to accomplish that mission and press on to Upper California. His orders were to "assure the people of those provinces that it is the wish and design of the United States to provide for them a free government, with the least possible delay, similar to that which exists in our territories. . . . In your whole conduct you will act in such a manner as best to conciliate the inhabitants, and render them friendly to the United States." Kearny was also authorized to muster into service a body of Mormon volunteers to aid in the expedition against California.[9]

Two weeks later, on June 18, Marcy again wrote to Kearny. In those two weeks it had been decided to send one company of regular-army artillery with arms and provisions around Cape Horn to California. Also, Marcy revealed, "Arrangements are now on foot to send a regiment of volunteers by sea."[10] That would be Stevenson's Regiment.

Governor Wright's General Orders of May 28 calling for seven volunteer regiments were printed by New York City newspapers on May 29 and 30, with editorial comment generally favorable, and by weekly newspapers throughout the state of New York during the next week. The deadline for enlistment was June 15.

One of the communities that responded to the call was Bath, New York. In 1846, as it is today, Bath was the long-settled county seat of Steuben County. Center of a rich farming area in the Cohocton River valley about midway between Binghamton and Buffalo, Bath had a population of 1,500 and a weekly newspaper that prided itself on being the voice and conscience of Old Steuben. In existence for thirty years, *The Steuben Farmers' Advocate* was written, edited, and printed by Benjamin Smead, who had fought in the War of 1812. Smead was an expansionist and regularly pieced out his columns with news from a greater expansionist journal, the Albany *Argus*. While independent in some ways, Smead had urged the election of Polk in 1844 and had welcomed the annexation of Texas and its statehood in 1845. It was well known that England had designs on Texas, he repeatedly wrote. Benjamin Smead did not like England.

In the *Farmers' Advocate* of June 3, 1846, in column one on page three, the main news page, Benjamin Smead printed Governor Wright's General Orders in their entirety. Within a week there was response. On June 10, under the heading "Steuben Volunteers," this notice was published:

We, the undersigned, are authorized to raise a company of volunteers to be ready on the 15th day of June, 1846. All sound men disposed to enter their names as such, will come forward and place their names on the enlistment roll, or drop a line to us, and the roll will be sent to their residence for signature. The time is short to fill up the roll, and such as are willing to enter should make it known at once. After the Company shall be filled, they will then elect their Officers by ballot. Will the people of Old Steuben be deaf to their country's call? Or will they fill up one or two Companies in remembrance of their worthy name?

Dated June 8 at Bath, the notice was signed by Henry and John Magee.[11]

Benjamin Smead was gratified that the Magee boys (sons of the sheriff, Hugh Magee, Henry was twenty-one, John, eighteen) had been authorized by the governor to raise volunteers in the county, well known to be populated by "brave patriots." "We hope," he wrote, "to see at least one company quickly organized to represent *Old Steuben* under the flag of Maj. Gen. Taylor."

The Magee boys had asked for one or two companies from the county. Smead, somewhat more realistically, "hoped" for at least one company. But the deadline of June 15 passed —without notice—and the *Farmers' Advocate* of June 17 carried only this statement:

Volunteers for the Mexican War.—The 7 regiments of reserve to be raised in this state, were probably filled by the 15th. We wait the report. The patriotic enthusiasm of the South and West States will doubtless so shorten this bloody work, as may not require the North to partake in it.[12]

Smead was mistaken about the seven regiments being filled, but it is interesting that the provincial editor and the secretary of war were of one mind about the likelihood of a short war.

By June 24 still no news had been issued about the one
Steuben company—or two—and nothing was written of volunteers. By July 1 there was news. A company was organized,
"a fine full Company," Smead wrote, relieved. The company
existed through "the patriotic exertions of Sheriff Magee and
Sons," Smead said, not seeing the humor in it. On June 26 the
company had elected officers: William E. Shannon as captain;
Henry Magee, first lieutenant; Palmer B. Hewlett, second
lieutenant. When the newspaper later printed a complete list
of the men, the reason for the delay in raising the company
became clear. Old Steuben had not exactly sprung to arms.
While about half were from Steuben, the balance were from
Chemung and Yates counties.

There were further surprises, however. Once the company was organized and its officers commissioned, no orders
followed. Not one of the seven regiments Benjamin Smead
presumed were complete had been mustered into the service
and ordered to Mexico. Through the month of July, while
covering news of the war in Mexico, the *Farmers' Advocate*
maintained silence about Captain Shannon's company. It
appeared that the plowboys would still be on hand to harvest.
But when there was news, on July 29, it was startling. The
company would not be representing Old Steuben under the
flag of General Taylor. They were now "Volunteers for
California."

On June 26, 1846, the secretary of war had written the
following letter to Colonel Jonathan D. Stevenson, who had
been selected to lead the California regiment:

The President having determined to send a regiment of Volunteers
around Cape Horn to the Pacific to be employed in preventing
hostilities in Mexico, probably in Upper California, has authorized
me to say that if you will organize one on the conditions hereinafter
specified and tender its services it will be accepted. It is proper it
should be done with the approbation of the Governor of New York.

The President requests and indeed requires that great care
should be taken to have it composed of suitable persons, I mean
persons of good habits, as far as practicable of various pursuits and
such as would be likely to desire to remain at the end of the war
either in Oregon or any territory in that region of the globe which

may be then a part of the United States. The act of the 13th of May last authorizes the acceptance of Volunteers for twelve months or during the war with Mexico. The condition of the acceptance in this case must be a tender of services during the war and it must be explicitly understood that they may be discharged without a claim for returning home, wherever they may be serving at the termination of the war provided it is in the then territory of the United States or may be taken to the nearest or most convenient territory belonging to the United States and then discharged.

The men must be apprised expressly that their term of service is for the war and that they are to be employed on a distant service. It is however very desirable that it should not be publicly known or proclaimed that they are to go to any particular province of Mexico. On this point great caution is enjoined.

The communications to the officers and men must go so far as to remove all just ground of complaint that they have been deceived in the nature and place of service.

It is expected that the regiment will be in readiness to embark as early as the first of August next if practicable. Steps will be immediately taken to provide for transportation etc.[13]

This remarkably revealing document was to gain celebrity, to the chagrin of the administration. A letter authorizing a regiment for such a purpose was redolent of an offensive war, not the defensive war claimed by President Polk. Everything was there—the strange selection of men, the unusual terms, the secrecy. This letter revealed even more clearly than the orders to Kearny that the administration was determined on the permanent conquest of California.

Polk's knowledge of the Southwest was imperfect geographically and militarily, but he knew that it would be important to hold the desired Mexican territories at the end of the war. The navy had been ordered to take possession of San Francisco and either or both the ports of Monterey and Mazatlán, as the relatively small force might permit. Kearny's Army of the West would take and garrison New Mexico, and what companies could be spared would move on to California as soon as possible. The orders had been issued, but Polk did not expect Kearny's arrival in California before the spring of 1847. The Mormon Battalion was to follow on Kearny's heels and should be helpful in taking California but not in holding it; the Mormons had been mustered for twelve months only and their allegiance was at least questionable. In addition, one artillery company of the regular army would go to California by sea. All in all, the aggregate was too small. A sizable force was needed to put teeth in the occupation and give it permanence, a force that would arrive in California by the end of the year. The month was June, and it was doubtful that any overland party could reach the Pacific by year's end. The solution lay in a regiment raised in the East and sent to California by sea.

Events of the next two years were to justify the selection of Jonathan D. Stevenson to command this special regiment of New York volunteers. The manner of his selection is undocumented and shadowy, both because of the political nature of his appointment and the secrecy surrounding the regiment's destination. The reasons for his selection, however, seemed perfectly clear to the anti-war faction in Congress and in the press when, in early July, plans for the expedition were first announced. They became clearer later that month when Marcy's letter to Stevenson was made public at the request of Congress. One of the party faithful was being rewarded. Opponents of the war felt that, while the expedition itself was an outrage, a party hack was particularly unworthy to lead it.

Stevenson was a Democrat who had served in the lower house of the New York legislature and was an officer of the New York State Militia (and had been since 1833). He later wrote that he had served the party in 1838, preventing the stuffing of ballot boxes in Baltimore, and again in 1840, exposing fraudulent elections in New York City.[14]

Stevenson had been in Washington in the early 1820s on the staff of Daniel Tompkins, ex-governor of New York and vice-president under James Monroe. The possibility exists that he was acquainted with Polk and the other high-level Democrats with whom he was later to claim intimacy. He very likely knew the secretary of war, a former long-time governor of New York. The only certainty is a rather formal friendship with the influential Jacksonian Democrat Amos Kendall, with whom he corresponded.[15] Hubert Howe Bancroft was wary of extravagent political statements by and about Stevenson and in his *History of California* simply wrote, "It was in a conversation with Kendall about the Mormons that Stevenson claims to have first suggested the idea of sending a volunteer regiment to Cal."[16] The route through Amos Kendall to the secretary of war and the president is an altogether reasonable one. Stevenson knew Kendall and was in Washington in June. Like so many other solicitors for favors, he "found" himself there offering his services.

Thomas Crosby Lancey, who served on the U.S.S. *Dale* in the Mexican War and spent the balance of his life in San Francisco, later wrote this version of the origin of the regiment and selection of Stevenson to lead it. At the home of Amos Kendall,

. . . he [Stevenson] was introduced to a prominent Mormon, who had just secured permission from President Polk to organize a regiment at Council Bluffs to march to California under the command of a United States officer. During the conversation Colonel Stevenson remarked that he had heard much of California, and would like very much to go there. Mr. Kendall, in reporting the matter of the organizing of the Mormon regiment, incidentally mentioned that Colonel Stevenson was in the city, and also mentioned what he said relative to California. The President immediately said to Mr. Kendall: "See Colonel Stevenson, and tell him that if he is disposed to go to California I will give him authority to raise a regiment of New York volunteers."[17]

Stevenson's own elaborated version, written years after the events, appeared in the *San Francisco Examiner* in 1892. This was to be the only chapter of Stevenson's reminiscences ever to appear. He died two years later, and his memoirs, specified in his will as part of his estate, were burned in the San Francisco Fire of 1906. This chapter was little more than the ranting of a very old man who a year later was certified to be senile. Stevenson claimed that his influence had led to Polk's nomination for the presidency and that after the election Polk had made several appointments at his request and had offered him his choice of foreign posts. Stevenson wrote, "I told him I wanted nothing, unless the dispute with Great

Britain about the boundary amounted to war, and if so, I wanted a Colonel's commission and authority to raise a regiment, with which to fight John Bull." After the outbreak of the Mexican War, Stevenson went to see the president, who reportedly said to him

that he had been unable to arrange a war with England to suit my convenience, but he had a had a war with Mexico on hand. He asked me if I would take a Colonel's commission to fight against Mexico. I asked him where he would send me. "How would you like the Pacific?" he asked. I replied that California would just suit me. Then he gave me my commission.[18]

All this is nonsense and not characteristic of the president. In fact, Stevenson's commission came from the governor of New York and was not granted until July 31, 1846. Still, Stevenson's undoubted eagerness for a command and his willingness to go to California were opportune for President Polk.

NOTES

1. Silas Wright, General Orders, May 28, 1846, archives of the adjutant-general, state of New York, Albany.
2. *Ibid.*, 6-7.
3. Livermore, *The War With Mexico Reviewed*, 60-61.
4. Bernard DeVoto, *The Year of Decision: 1846*, (Boston: Little, Brown and Company, 1943), 7.
5. William L. Marcy, Washington, to Silas Wright, Albany, June 3, 1846, Record Group (hereinafter cited as RG) 393, Office of the Adjutant General of the United States, National Archives, Washington, D.C. (hereinafter cited as NA).
6. *Ibid.*
7. Dwight L. Clarke, *Stephen Watts Kearny, Soldier of the West* (Norman, Oklahoma: University of Oklahoma Press, 1961), 104-5; DeVoto, *Year of Decision*, 230-31.
8. Clarke, *Stephen Watts Kearny*, 394-97.
9. *Ibid.*
10. *Ibid.*, 398.
11. *The Steuben Farmers' Advocate*, June 10, 1846, 3.

12. *Ibid.*, June 17, 1846.
13. Marcy, Washington, to Col. J. D. Stevenson, New York City, June 26, 1846, RG 393, NA.
14. Jonathan D. Stevenson, *Memorial and Petition of Col. J. D. Stevenson of California* (San Francisco: J. R. Brodie & Co., 1886), 2-11.
15. Jonathan D. Stevenson, "Letter Books," 1836-1846, New-York Historical Society, New York City. In this period there are seven letters to Kendall reporting on political prospects, introducing friends, and asking modest favors. There is no correspondence between the two on the regiment or its command. Bernard DeVoto characterized Kendall as "the model of all Brain Trusters" and the "Man to See" in Washington in 1846. (*The Year of Decision*, 236.).
16. Bancroft, *History of California*, vol. 5, 472.
17. Thomas Crosby Lancey, untitled article, in Francis D. Clark, *The First Regiment of New York Volunteers*, 52. Lancey's material is generally untrustworthy. It is quite unlikely, as Bancroft assumed, that Lancey's information came from an unpublished narrative of Stevenson. Lancey was not in the regiment and was in no position to know the truth of what he presented as facts. He did not burden the artistry of his impressionistic article with any mention of his sources. The "prominent Mormon" would presumably have been Elder Jesse C. Little.
18. *San Francisco Examiner*, Jan. 1, 1892.

Chapter Four

Raising the Regiment

O N RECEIVING SECRETARY MARCY'S letter in New York City, Stevenson immediately sent a copy of it to the crusty governor of New York, formally requesting permission to raise such a regiment. In his request for approval, Stevenson stated that the lieutenant colonel and major of the regiment would be regular-army officers—West Point men, he hoped—holding their commissions from the United States, this at the suggestion of the secretary of war. In addition, as Marcy's letter had implied, Stevenson announced that he himself would command the regiment.

Governor Wright, who had already been contacted by the secretary of war, replied on July 1. Such a regiment might be raised as one of those requisitioned by the president, Wright stated, but the procedure was irregular. He reminded Stevenson that field officers of a militia regiment were to be elected, not appointed. Orders for the regiment had come from the highest authority, Governor Wright conceded, and the "unusual" nature of the regiment and its assignment might warrant a departure from the militia law. He and his adjutant general would prefer, however, that all commissions for the regiment come from the United States. Otherwise, he would insist that the regular-army officers also accept New York commissions. Since Stevenson had limited time, the governor advised him that companies now organized throughout the state would, in whole or in part, doubtless be willing to join such a regiment. The adjutant general could provide the names.[1]

The timing was perfect. Every Fourth of July militia officers in New York City gathered in the Governor's Room at the city hall. With the war just seven weeks old, this session was an animated and belligerent one. The newspapers reported the meeting in detail. Many speeches were given, including one by Jonathan Stevenson. Mentioning only briefly the glories of the Revolution and the valor of the American fighting men, Stevenson passed on to his sailor-father's impressment by the British and to his own contributions in the War of 1812. Thirteen years old, he had organized the schoolboys of New York to raise earthworks at the present site of the Battery. Now, in the present conflict with Mexico, he would serve again—on "a distant and perilous service." Then he announced the mission of the regiment, attributing the plan to the president and the secretary of war, and called for volunteers.

In doing so, he was indiscreet. Marcy had enjoined secrecy about the destination. Although Stevenson did not say that the regiment would go to California, he did say publicly that it would go by sea to "the Northwest Coast of Mexico," where the men would be discharged at the end of the war. That meant California. Everyone present must have guessed, including the newspapermen.[2] Stevenson may also have confided in reporters of two newspapers; all but the *New York Evening Post* assumed that the regiment was destined for California, but reporters for the *Herald* and the *Journal of Commerce* wrote that Stevenson had said it was "a California expedition."

The city's newspapers and those of the state were constant allies of Stevenson in recruiting volunteers. Some approved and some condemned, but the name and destination of the regiment were kept regularly before the public. The reporters called it "The California Expedition."

Among congressional critics of the Polk administration and the war, Representative George Ashmun of Massachusetts (a colleague of the like-minded John Quincy Adams) was one of the most censorious. A Whig, and violent in his hatred of slavery, Ashmun had denounced territorial expansion in any form well before the war. He had repeatedly spoken against the annexation of Texas and voted against it. When the war began, Ashmun spoke against recognizing it and was one of the fourteen members of the House who voted against the war bill.[3]

The newspaper publicity given the proposed California expedition gave Ashmun an opportunity. Indeed, the newspapers were the only source of information, for Congress had not been informed of plans to seize California, certainly not of plans to hold it permanently. Ashmun called for a documented report from the secretary of war on action ordered in the northern Mexican provinces. There were troubled minds among both Whigs and Democrats in the House, and the report was ordered. Marcy complied on July 17 with copies of his orders to General Kearny and his letter to Stevenson.

The orders to Kearny were suspicious, insisting as they did on conciliation of the Mexican population of California, but in the letter to Stevenson the object of the administration was transparent. The government had intended a war for conquest. "The mask is off," Ashmun said. "The veil is lifted." After analyzing the letter before the House, he summarized:

It is no longer pretended that our purpose is to repel invasion—to strike and defeat the military organizations which Mexico may set on foot to contend for the boundaries of Texas. The mask is off; the veil is lifted; and we see in the clearest characters invasion, conquest, and colonization emblazoned on our banners. We are no longer engaged in a defensive war; but we behold an expedition about to sail from New York to a distant region of the globe, which it cannot

possibly reach in less time than from four to six months, commanded by a mere political fortune-hunter of not the highest character,
and destined to accomplish the conquest and dismemberment of a
sister republic, whose weakness seems to make her a ready prey to
men whose pursuits are those of plunder![4]

The congressman then proceeded further to identify the
"mere political fortune-hunter." Of the Marcy letter, Ashmun
said,

It is addressed—not to an officer of the army whose habits and
education fit him for mere military service of the ordinary kind—
not to a man who has been distinguished by any public service in the
field—but to a mere political adventurer, who is only known to the
world as a partisan from the neighborhood of the Five Points and
the region where the Empire Club holds sway, and where the doctrine that "to the victors belong the spoils" is acknowledged and
practiced.[5]

Ashmun saw a full-scale filibustering expedition, with
mercenaries and a power-mad, politically ambitious leader.
There was no unanimity of opinion, however. While Ashmun's July 27th speech in the House was well reported by
anti-administration newspapers, other Washington and New
York editors were speaking in highest praise of the enterprise
and of the talents of the colonel commanding.

Against this background of controversy in the press, the
regiment was being formed. Stevenson had set up his headquarters at the state arsenal on White Street. The time was
short. The organizational problems were immense, and there
were prodigious uncertainties. The voyage around Cape
Horn would probably take five months but might take as long
as seven. The ships might or might not have the opportunity
to stop at Rio de Janeiro, Valparaiso, or Callao to take on
fresh provisions.

The conditions Stevenson would find in California on his
arrival could only be guessed. Attitudes of the Californians
varied. Through Larkin's confidential correspondence with
the secretary of state, the cabinet knew of sentiment both for
and against the United States. What effect the news of the
actual war would have was yet a question. It was not known if

the naval forces dispatched to take San Francisco and Monterey had arrived. As late as September 11, in detailed orders to Stevenson, Marcy could say only that it was probable that Monterey had been taken by the Pacific Squadron. The government had received "information which is deemed to be reliable, though not official," to that effect. It was almost certain that Kearny would not arrive in California before the regiment.

No one knew how long the war would last. The many months required for communication and supply meant that everything necessary for the regiment for at least a year must be carried on the ships—everything necessary for a forcible seizure and a peaceable occupation.

There were three, or perhaps four, ships to be chartered, and vast quantities of stores, equipment, ordnance, and ordnance equipment secured. Medical services were necessary for each ship. A uniform would have to be designed; grist and sawmills bought and disassembled. And there were ten companies of men to be enrolled and trained.

Beyond the letter of June 26 specifying men of good habits and varied pursuits, the secretary of war did not instruct Stevenson further about the selection of men for the regiment. The first need was for responsible recruiting officers. Most of the original recruiting officers for the companies raised in New York City had commissions in the U.S. Army or in the New York State Militia, and in many cases these individuals were later elected company officers. All were in their late twenties and thirties.

Enrollment for one company began July 1 in the Seventh Ward Democratic headquarters on Madison Street. By this date Stevenson had not received Governor Wright's authorization, and both the date and the place of enrollment suggest that politics was involved. Although at that point no public announcement of the expedition had been made, the enrollment form was headed "Col. Stevenson's Regiment for California."[6]

The necessity of haste, it appears, was the most influential consideration in the selection of recruiting officers, with

Stevenson accepting the services of the first mature men with army or militia experience who offered to raise companies. Soon after his arrival in California, Colonel Stevenson wrote General Kearny that "most of the Volunteer Officers were strangers to myself as well as the Department of War."[7] Friends of friends were probably welcome, but there is little evidence for the later charge that Stevenson influenced company elections and installed incompetent favorites over qualified men. Only one election was contested, that of the colonel's son to the captaincy of Company G.

Between July 6 and 10 recruiting offices were opened in hotels and public halls around the city, and three companies were enrolled in the White Street Arsenal. The newspapers did their work well, especially the *New York Herald*, informing interested readers of enrolling places. Stevenson's directions to his recruiting officers were evidently oral; no written instructions for the New York City companies have been found. Those instructions presumably would have been to enroll able-bodied men of diverse occupations who were willing to serve in California and to remain there after the war. Volunteers immediately began enlisting.

By July 11 Stevenson had accepted the offer of Governor Wright to include some of the companies already formed under his General Orders of May 28. The New York adjutant general, R. E. Temple, wrote to Stevenson on July 9 with the names of five captains whose companies were not assigned to regiments and with the news that one full company in Norwich and one then being enrolled in Albany expressly desired to be part of the California regiment.[8] On July 11 Stevenson wrote to William E. Shannon in Bath, Kimball H. Dimmick, in Norwich, and John B. Frisbie in Albany, offering their companies places in the regiment on three conditions. First, the men must agree to the terms set by the president and the secretary of war, which were presented to them in Marcy's words, not mentioning California. Stevenson significantly added that the men be unmarried and over eighteen years of age. Second, the recruiting officers would have to accept immediately, as time was short. Third, many of the men, "a good number," in those three companies were to be farmers.[9] Stevenson was trying to diversify the occupations represented in the regiment.

Most companies were rapidly filled, and some carelessly. By the end of the third week in July, the three companies from the interior of the state were part of the paper regiment, and the rolls of all the companies were filled. Elections had been held. The rolls and the names of elected officers were sent to the governor, who commissioned the officers on July 31.

On this date the captains of companies were the following:

Company A	Semour G. Steele	Company F	Francis J. Lippitt
Company B	James Turner	Company G	James Dirver
Company C	John E. Brackett	Company H	John B. Frisbie
Company D	Henry M. Naglee	Company I	William E. Shannon
Company E	Nelson Taylor	Company K	Kimball H. Dimmick

The secretary of war had hoped the regiment might embark on the first of August. That date proved impossible. On August 1, however, on Colonel Stevenson's orders, the seven New York City companies assembled at their places of enrollment, marched to the Battery, and were taken to Governors Island. These companies, the company from Albany, and the field officers and staff were mustered into the service of the United States by Colonel Bankhead, commandant. On the third of August Captain Shannon's company from Bath arrived and was mustered in. Captain Dimmick's company from Chenango County arrived on Governors Island August 4 and was mustered in August 5. For the first time—and for the last—the Seventh Regiment of New York Volunteers was close to strength.[10]

That Colonel Stevenson's was the first regiment certain of being called up, at least as much as the unusual nature of its assignment and its destination, helps explain the rapid filling of the enlistment rolls in New York City. For the same reasons men were readily available when replacements became necessary, as they did immediately.

Front-page woodcut from James Gordon Bennett's pro-regimental *New York Herald*, August 10, 1846, ten days after the first volunteers were mustered and equipped and began training at Fort Columbus, Governors Island. (Courtesy California Historical Society, San Francisco.)

When the companies arrived on Governors Island and were mustered, it was clear that not all the men enrolled had reported at their places of rendezvous. Whereas company strength was to have been seventy-seven men, some companies were ten, fifteen, and twenty men short. Medical examinations had not been given at the time of enrollment, so officers could anticipate some discharges for medical reasons. Recruits were steadily enrolled and mustered. Just as steadily, there were desertions. Some men lost enthusiasm in the routine of drill on Governors Island and in the boredom of waiting for embarkation. All soon discovered that discipline was to be rigid, which some had not expected.

Most of the volunteers who kept journals of their adventures in Stevenson's Regiment did not begin writing until they were at sea, so there are few records of events on the island. One private, however, Walter Murray of Company A, did keep a daily journal, which was later included in his "Narrative of a California Volunteer." Many pages were devoted to the Governors Island period, which had indeed been memorable. Murray was most impressed by the hard work (he had been detailed to cook), the discipline, as well as the confusion. He expressed a low opinion of the recruits enrolled as replacements who appeared to him a rough element.[11]

A close look at muster records on Governors Island reveals the continuous struggle to maintain the total organization at regimental strength. Captain Francis Lippitt's Company F is a good example. The enlisting officers had been Henry S. Carnes, who was a lieutenant of militia, and John S. Huddart. The rolls were filled at the White Street Arsenal in just three days. Of the seventy-eight men enrolled, seventeen did not report for mustering on August 1. By the muster of August 15, the places of sixteen had been filled from applicants at Fort Columbus, raising the total to seventy-seven. Although the company had been there two weeks, the men had not yet been given medical examinations. By August 31 Company F had lost thirteen more men, ten of whom had been replaced. Four had deserted. Seven had been discharged—three for medical reasons, one for legal reasons (the law had caught up with him), three on request as minors. By September 18, when the company was again mustered, thirty-one of the men had been recruited on Governors Island. Unfortunately, the eighteenth was payday, and each private soldier was paid $84, one year's clothing allowance, and six months' salary. Between September 18 and sailing on September 26, ten more men deserted.

Captain Lippitt's muster of October 31, at sea, showed 65 volunteers. The recruitment process had been difficult. He and his two lieutenants had enrolled a total of 140 men. Of the 65, just over fifty percent, 35 men, were of the original company. The greatest turnover had come in the men enrolled after August 1. Under these circumstances, enlisting men of varied pursuits and good habits was, to say the least, a matter of chance.

The recruiting experience of the other New York City companies was in every way similar. Of the companies raised in New York City, the following are the figures shown on musters of October 31, when the three ships of the transport fleet were at sea:

Company A	68	Company E	60
Company B	59	Company F	65
Company C	70	Company G	54
Company D	69		

Use of the musters of October 31 is not arbitrary. Musters were bimonthly, and, since the fleet had sailed September 26, the opportunity for desertion did not exist. Almost one hundred men had deserted in the eight days immediately preceding sailing.

The companies formed outside New York City fared no better. In Bath, Captain Shannon's Company I began assembling on July 20. On July 29, after three weeks of silence, Benjamin Smead had news in the *Steuben Farmers' Advocate* about the local company. He headed his long account "Volunteers for California":

Captain Shannon's Company, collected at this rendesvous [sic] in quick time from this and neighboring counties, is full. . . . We did not see a finer company in the last war—and their daring and patriotism in this enterprise, which will lead them a distance equal to half the circumference of the globe, are pretty sure pledges of their sincere devotion to the honor and interests of their country.[12]

Fine words indeed, but the pledges were not "pretty sure" at all.

On August 12 the *Farmers' Advocate* carried a list of the officers, noncommissioned officers, and privates who had enrolled, and Smead reported the arrival of the company and its mustering in at Governors Island. Three columns were devoted to news of the company and the regiment, including a long paraphrase of Colonel Stevenson's address to the men on August 5. Stevenson had praised the opportunities of California, to be the volunteers' "bounteous new home," and warned that each man should be prepared to die if necessary to insure that the blessings of liberty, law, and all free American institutions should flourish on the Pacific. Doubtless many men *would* die. California, Stevenson said, was believed to be in a state of insurrection. Editor Smead was obliged to conclude the article in an aggrieved tone:

We do not pretend to touch upon the brighter picture of their future fortunes presented by Col. S.; but are constrained to close this article with the mortifying record of those who, after a view of the innumerable bloodletting materials of the camp, and trembling like Belshazzar at the dark aspects of the Colonel's speech, soon found their bravery settle into their legs—when they *sloped*, leaving Capt. Shannon near $100 minus, paid by him for their passage and subsistence to visit the city.

Then followed a list of twelve who had "Backed Out at New York" and a list of ten who had "Backed Out at Bath." The latter list included the Steuben County sheriff's younger son, John Magee. No matter, Smead wrote, "Col. Stevenson forthwith found good men to supply the places of Capt. Shannon's defaulters; and indeed there were enough standing ready to embark in the enterprise to fill another regiment."[13]

Default and desertion plagued Captain Shannon and the captains of the other companies. The Magee brothers and Shannon had enrolled eighty-three men, and just one man short of a full company reached Governors Island. Ten had decided to remain at home, but Shannon had enrolled two in Geneva and one in Albany en route to New York City. By August 14, to show seventy-two men on his muster, Shannon had had to enroll sixteen privates at Fort Columbus. Only fifty-six from Bath remained. On August 31 Captain Shannon had seventy men. Two from Bath had been discharged and one transferred. Of six deserters between August 14 and 31, four had been from Bath.

In the muster of September 18, to show 79 in the company, Captain Shannon had so far enrolled a total of 114 men. One had been transferred, 12 discharged, and 22 had deserted. At sea on October 31, Company I was 10 men short, at a strength of 67. On the day of sailing 11 desertions had occurred, 4 of them men from Bath. At that date only 26—a mere thirty percent—remained of the original company enrolled in Steuben and neighboring counties. A few had been discharged formally, but most had "backed out." Company I lost a higher percentage of men than any other company on Governors Island.

Captain Kimball H. Dimmick enrolled Company K in Norwich, just north and west of the Catskills in central New York. Norwich was the county seat of Chenango County. An attorney, Dimmick was thirty-one years old and captain in the New York militia. A native of Connecticut, he had grown up in Chenango County where he had been first a printer before reading law. Although poor, he was locally rather prominent, and was a Democrat. He enrolled some members of his reserve militia company and filled the rolls in two weeks with men from Norwich and Chenango County, and others from neighboring Otsego, Cortland, Madison, and Delaware counties. Captain Dimmick arrived at Governors Island on August 4 with fifty-eight men. When the regiment sailed on September 26, Company K lacked just eight men. But only half of those sixty-nine who sailed, thirty-eight men, had been enrolled originally in Norwich.

Company H, with fifty-six men, arrived at Governors Island from Albany on August 1. By August 15 Captain John B. Frisbie had enrolled an additional twenty-one men to fill the company. Two weeks later company strength was reduced to seventy-four, of whom forty-eight were from Albany. By September 18 eight more of the original company had been lost by desertion or discharge. By September 26 Company H showed fifty-seven men, of whom thirty-four were from Albany. There had been the staggering total of twenty desertions in the week after payday.

In its first two months, Stevenson's Regiment, from every point of view, had been troubled. These organizational problems had not been lost on the New York press. The newspapers not in sympathy with the war saw in the difficulties of the regiment a good opportunity to underline their principal objections. The war was unnecessary and unjust, a war of conquest, and the first step of that conquest—the occupation of California—was to be taken by political hacks and undesirables. Horace Greeley's *New York Tribune* hopefully predicted from the middle of July that the regiment would never sail. And, at the end of August, the regiment still had not left Governors Island. The *Tribune* reported that Colonel Stevenson had chartered four ships for the voyage, but "as things look now, one will be amply sufficient, unless he sails very soon. . . . it [the regiment] will fall to pieces of itself, most likely."[14]

As regularly as the *Tribune*, the *Journal of Commerce*, and the *Morning Courier and Enquirer* exposed the organizational problems with delight, the *New York Herald*, the *Sun*, and the *Evening Post* defended. On September 14 the *Herald* countered some of the criticism in an editorial:

Much has been said, and much unjustly, relative to the organization of the regiment, and many have been the sneering remarks thrown out, predicting that a corporal's guard would be all remaining by the time that the day appointed for embarkation came round. The present actual condition and force of the regiment is the best answer to all such aspersions.

This long editorial, full of half-truths and falsification, reported the men contented and ready to start and concluded with this prodigy of an understatement: "The fifteen or twenty of them that . . . left the regiment could well be spared."[15] The correct figure was closer to five hundred!

NOTES

1. Wright, Albany, to Stevenson, New York City, July 1, 1846, Office of Adjutant General, State of New York, Albany.

2. Stevenson's speech and the newsworthy plans for the regiment were reported in the *New York Herald* and the *New York Evening Post* on July 5; in the New York *Sun*, the New York *Journal of Commerce*, the *New York Morning Courier and Enquirer*, the *New York Morning News*, and the *New York Tribune* on July 6.

3. William Jay, *A Review of the Causes and Consequences of the Mexican War* (Boston: Benjamin B. Mussey & Co., 1849), 171. Jay's book was probably written for the American Peace Society competition.

4. U.S., Congress, *Congressional Globe*, 29th Cong., 1st sess., July 27, 1846, 809.

5. *Ibid.* The "Five Points" was the section including Mulberry, White, Bayard, and Baxter streets in New York City.

6. Enrollment Forms, Company E, First Regiment of New York Volunteers (1846-1848), RG 94, NA. Although the first company with rolls opened specifically for the regiment, this company was not the first filled. Four companies preceded it.

7. Stevenson, on board *Thomas H. Perkins*, Harbor of San Francisco, to Brig. Gen. S. W. Kearny, Monterey, March 18, 1847, RG 393, NA.

8. R. E. Temple, Albany, to Stevenson, New York City, July 9, 1846, Office of Adjutant General, Albany.

9. J. D. Stevenson, "Letter Book," July 11, 1846.

10. Stevenson's was the first volunteer regiment from New York to go to the Mexican War. Six other regiments were partially organized under the militia laws before the end of July, and Governor Wright numbered the regiments and commissioned their commanding officers despite his earlier objections about regimental organization. Stevenson's was the seventh regiment, and he thus had the least seniority of the seven colonels. The governor himself knew something about politics.

Only one of the other regiments was ever fully organized, the First Regiment of Col. Ward Burnett. In December 1846, while Stevenson's Regiment was at sea bound for California, Burnett's regiment was mustered, the whole being an amalgamation of the six regiments. After a few months' training, Burnett and his men sailed for Tampico and saw service at Vera Cruz and the City of Mexico under General Scott. In 1847 the Department of War ordered Gov. John Young, who succeeded Silas Wright, to change the designations. As of Feb. 28, 1848, Stevenson's became the First Regiment of New York Volunteers and thereafter was so mustered.

11. Hon. Walter Murray, "Narrative of a California Volunteer," (MS), Bancroft Library, University of California, Berkeley.

12. *The Steuben Farmers' Advocate*, July 29, 1846.

13. *Ibid.*, Aug. 12, 1846.

14. *New York Tribune*, Aug. 29, 1846.

15. *New York Herald*, Sept. 14, 1846.

Chapter Five

The Nature of a Regiment: Pioneers in the Cause

O N SEPTEMBER 6, 1846, the *New York Herald* editorialized on "The California Expedition. Its Object and Purpose." For readers of that article, a number of basic assumptions were necessary to follow the argument. Chief among them was the acceptability of a war of conquest. Only the briefest mention was given to the undoubted desirability of California, and it was assumed that the United States was destined to claim the Far West.

The rich and beautiful region of California will without doubt come into formal possession of the United States, without any further fighting for it. Far removed as it is from our seat of Government, inhabited in a measure by a half-civilized people, it will be absolutely necessary, if we intend to hold it, that military possession be taken of it, and that a territorial government be established there, and what is the class who, under such circumstances, are best fitted to do this?

49

The editor then answered his own question. Not mere soldiers for such a mission. Certainly not politicians, who could only theorize and were utterly impractical. No, those who should take possession of California were

the sound, hardy mechanics of our country—the men whose hands know useful labor. . . . The hard-handed, honest laborer, the farmer, the blacksmith, the tailor, the shoemaker, the hatter, the carpenter, the mason; these are men under whose auspices a country rich in soil, healthy in climate, and possessing local advantages of a rare nature, will grow up and flourish. Precisely of this class are the men whom our Government are about sending to California . . . a fortnight more will probably find these pioneers in the cause of the advancement of human freedom, civilization and prosperity, on their way to the land of their hopes and future prospects. Arrived there, they will cause the *"wilderness to bud and blossom as the rose tree,"* and plant the standard of the American Government and enterprise upon the soil of California.[1]

The *Herald*'s ideal of "the mechanic" as the agent best adapted for this great mission is but an elaboration of Marcy's "suitable persons of good habits and various pursuits." (Like Dr. McVickar in his farewell address to the troops, the *Herald* notably ignored the military aspect of the regiment. Conquest —the "conquered peace" in Polk's words—thus was much more palatable.) Five days after this editorial appeared, the secretary of war sent Colonel Stevenson detailed instructions for the conduct of the regiment once in California. The people were to be conciliated. He wrote, "They should be made to feel that we come as deliverers."[2]

Who were these sound, hardy mechanics, soon to be pioneers and, willy-nilly, deliverers? We have seen how difficult it was to keep, if not to catch, a regiment. The ten companies sailing for California were not the same ten companies recruited in August. No more than half the original regiment remained, and there had been enormous turnover in the later recruits. But a kind of refinement, a selection, was inherent in this process. Those recruits with the least interest did not bother to go to Governors Island. The men who were mustered in, and the later recruits, had almost two months

THE SCENE OF THE PRESENTATION OF BIBLES TO THE NEW YORK LEGION, OR CALIFORNIA REGIMENT.

Front-page woodcut, *New York Herald*. Colonel Stevenson, center left, receives his gift Bible ("upon which Liberty has its foundation") from the Rev. Dr. John McVickar, chaplain of Governors Island, with the admonition that he and his troops "should go not only with the sword, but with the olive branch of peace." (Courtesy California Historical Society, San Francisco.)

for second thoughts. Almost one hundred would desert at the gangplank, as it were. With opportunities for desertion abounding, it would be safe to conclude that those who did sail, wanted to sail. If they did not in every case especially want to go to California, they were still willing and even anxious to leave New York. They were, after all, volunteers.

Within the uniformity of their status as volunteers, the men showed tremendous diversity in all other respects. Information from the rolls, musters, returns, and desertion forms permits the reconstruction in rough fashion of the occupational and social structure of the regiment. As source material, all these documents leave much to be desired. In particular, the enrollment forms vary widely in quality depending upon the care and patience exercised by the recruiting officers. Not all of them recorded place of birth or age, but the rolls do invariably include address, occupation, and signature of the volunteer. There is no problem of determining the age of those who sailed since ages were included on all later musters and returns. The enrollment forms are a major source of information, however, and a look at the documents completed for Captain Lippitt's Company F, raised in New York City, and for Captain Shannon's Company I, from Bath, is illuminating.

Company F

In the company of seventy-eight men first enrolled, sixty-six were from New York City, ten from Boston, one from New Bedford, and one from Albany. When the company sailed on September 26, of sixty-five men, fifty-three were from New York, eight from other cities, four from rural townships and counties. Company F was clearly urban.

Proportionally more of those over thirty years old and under twenty had been discharged or had deserted before sailing. The muster of October 31, at sea, showed no man in Company F under eighteen and only one over forty. Fourteen were in their late twenties and early thirties. Fifty were between eighteen and twenty-five years old, most of them twenty-one and twenty-two.

Of four illiterates whose marks were witnessed by the enrolling officers, only one sailed with the company.

Using both the muster of October 31 and the enrollment forms, it is possible to describe the occupational structure of the company. The captain, Francis Lippitt, was a lawyer. His two lieutenants were "gentlemen," and this classification was unique not only on the rolls of this company but of the entire regiment. The following were the occupations of the private soldiers:

Occupations: Company F (October 31, 1846)

Professions	*Metal Trades*
1 physician	1 brassfounder
1 surgeon	1 tinsmith
1 mechanical engineer	1 tin roofer
<u>1</u> chemist	1 coppersmith
4	<u>1</u> chainmaker
	5

"White-Collar" Occupations

8 clerks
2 merchants
<u>1</u> bookkeeper
11

Agriculture

5 farmers

Building Trades

4 carpenters
2 cabinetmakers
1 sashmaker
2 masons
<u>1</u> stonefinisher
10

Miscellaneous Trades and Services

6 butchers
2 bakers
2 tailors
1 hatter
1 hat presser
1 bootmaker
1 shoemaker
5 printers
2 bookbinders
1 furnaceman
1 perfumer
1 umbrella maker
1 clockmaker
2 boatmen
<u>2</u> oystermen
29

The makeup of this New York City company compares interestingly with the companies raised outside the city.

Company I

Captain Shannon's Company I from Bath had first been composed of more than half farmers and farm laborers, a total of forty-seven in a company of eighty-three. Twenty-four other occupations were represented among the balance of thirty-six. men. The proportion of agricultural workers did not remain high, however. By October 31, when only twenty-eight of the original company remained on the rolls, only eighteen of them were farmers and farm laborers. The occupations represented in Company I on October 31 were as follows:

Occupations: Company I (October 31, 1846)

Professions

2 lawyers
1 medical student
1 druggist
<u>1</u> surveyor
5

Metal Trades

3 blacksmiths
1 whitesmith
<u>1</u> tinsmith
5

"White-Collar" Occupations	*Miscellaneous Trades and Services*
2 merchants	3 printers
4 clerks	2 sailmakers
6	1 hunter
	1 drayman
Agriculture	2 butchers
	2 barbers
13 farmers	1 bookbinder
5 farm laborers	1 locksmith
18	1 millwright
	1 tailor
Building Trades	1 shoemaker
	1 ostler
3 carpenters	1 soldier
2 cabinetmakers	18
2 moulders	
2 plasterers	
1 varnisher	
2 masons	
3 painters	
15	

Comparing the composition of the two companies, certain observations can be made. Most conspicuously, Company I did not remain "rural." Just eighteen men were farm workers, under twenty-five percent of the total. While Company I contained fewer men with white-collar jobs and fewer performing miscellaneous services, both companies showed about the same number of different occupations and were reasonably representative of the balance of the regiment. Stevenson's Regiment was, in general, an urban regiment.

The age range of Captain Shannon's company was similar to that of Company F and also was representative of the entire regiment. On October 31, in Company I, one man was seventeen years old; one was forty-one. Some volunteers were in their late twenties or thirties, but fifty-two men were between eighteen and twenty-five, most of them between nineteen and twenty-one. The company captains were also young. Six were in their twenties, most in their mid-twenties, and four were in their early thirties. Colonel Stevenson at forty-six was —almost—the oldest man in the regiment. Private soldiers under fifteen and over forty-five were not to have been enrolled, but one, Stephen Harris, had joined the regimental staff as quartermaster sergeant on August 1. His age was given as forty-five; but, when he was discharged in California six months after arrival, his age was listed as fifty-six. Lieutenant William T. Sherman's order for his discharge was graphic: "Stephen Harris, Private in the 7 Regiment of N.Y. Volunteers, a decrepit old man, whose years and infirmities render him entirely unable to perform the duties of a soldier, is hereby honorably discharged."[3]

The only evidence of a general plan of recruiting by occupation is Colonel Stevenson's early decision to accept three companies raised outside New York City, in order to add a contingent of farmers. In theory, seven companies would be largely urban and three predominantly rural. Although circumstances precluded this plan, the occupations within the regiment were exceptionally diverse. No volunteer was engaged in any socially unacceptable occupation, it appears. If so, the fact was concealed. If there were politicians, that information was also concealed. The only minister was the regimental staff chaplain. Nine men were soldiers by occupation. There were a number of professional men, including two dozen lawyers and half that many doctors enrolled as privates, in addition to the three-man medical staff. There were also four dentists, but only one writer identified as such, no teachers, no architects, and, except for farm workers, extremely few laborers.

Except for records of later accomplishments, there is no index to the educational background of the volunteers. Few were illiterate; only nineteen could not sign their names. On the other hand, there were probably only a few with an education like Francis Lippitt. A graduate of Brown University, he had assisted Alexis de Tocqueville prepare notes for *Democracy in America*.[4]

While each volunteer identified himself by occupation, the number of men employed at the time of enrollment is not known, nor is there documentary evidence of how many were married. Most were evidently single, but Captains Dimmick,

Lippitt, Brackett, Steele, and Marcy were married, as were some of the rank and file. Some wives were taken along with each company as laundresses, and others were put to work as hospital matrons in California. Some entire family groups were taken to California, and there were children aboard each of the three ships in the transport fleet.

All of the men in the regiment were white. Commissioned officers were allowed their own servants, and some of them were black, but they seem to have been the only blacks with the regiment.

The matter of nativity poses a problem as not every unit recorded this information. In the five companies, including Company I, for which records of place of birth do exist, about one-quarter of the men were foreign born. Most came from Ireland and Germany, a number from England and Scotland, and some from France and Switzerland. Of the company captains, only Captain Shannon was not native-born, having been brought to New York from Ballina, Ireland, as a boy of seven. In these five companies the greatest number of foreign-born volunteers were enrolled as replacements on Governors Island.

Walter Murray of Company A accurately described the regiment thus: "There were men of pretty much every class except the most opulent; a large proportion of steady mechanics of all trades, with a smart sprinkling of the b'hoys [rowdies] of New York City, and not a few intemperates and ne'er-do-wells."[5] The professional men and mechanics would later distinguish the regiment in California; the intemperates would keep things lively and the guardhouses full; and the ne'er-do-wells would give the regiment a bad name. The swaggering b'hoys of New York lent a special flavor.

All these men could hardly have had the same personal reasons for going to California with Stevenson's Regiment.

NOTES

1. *New York Herald*, Sept. 6, 1846.
2. Marcy, Washington, to Stevenson, New York City, Sept. 11, 1846, RG 393, NA.
3. Departmental General Orders (hereinafter cited as DGO) No. 45, Monterey, Aug. 12, 1847. RG 94, NA. Mrs. Harris accompanied her not entirely decrepit husband to California and gave birth to a child before reaching Rio de Janeiro. The child, a girl, was named Alta California Harris.
4. Francis J. Lippitt, *Reminiscences* (Providence: Preston and Rounds Co., 1902), 4.
5. Murray, "Narrative," 13.

Chapter Six

Motivation: Providence Plus a Golden Jesus

THE MOTIVES of the volunteers were as complex and varied as their backgrounds were diverse. In writing his *History of California* in the 1880s, Bancroft often used the dictated statements of early California pioneers. He found that former volunteers, looking back, invariably believed—or at least said—that patriotism had been their ruling motive. But Bancroft could not endorse such declarations. He completely discounted a patriotic motive, and oversimplified the motives he did assign to the volunteers. In doing so, he misinterpreted the prevailing spirit in the East in the mid-1840s.

Bancroft believed the individual volunteer's leading motive had been to better his condition in a new country. Many, he thought, were "attracted solely by a love of adventure, and, but for the ice, would as readily have gone to the north pole."[1] Still others were escaping from unsavory records, bad associations, and debts. Bancroft thought no volunteer dreamed of military conflict, but that all regarded themselves as immigrant adventurers bound for a distant land of many charms under the protection of government.

On patriotism, or the lack of it, Bancroft had a kind of evidence. When the war began, response to the call to arms was less in the northeastern states than in the West and South. Much was said and written, but not much action occurred. While the one Steuben company was forming, during the entire month of June, whole regiments had been raised in Missouri and Mississippi. But there was a patriotic response in New York of a special and significant kind not fully understood by Bancroft.

From Camp Polk on Governors Island, Edward Gilbert had sent a dispatch to the Albany *Argus* which was printed August 19. Gilbert was twenty-four years old and to join the regiment had resigned as associate editor of the *Argus*, becoming its correspondent. It was he who convinced John B. Frisbie, an Albany attorney and militia captain, to fill out his company with men willing and wishing to go to California. On reorganization of the company, Frisbie had been elected captain, Gilbert first lieutenant.[2] Gilbert never wrote by halves and had some remarkable things to say about all the volunteers. To a man, they were, first of all, resolved to do their whole duty. Moreover, he continued,

Every man of this expedition feels that he is engaged in an enterprise than which none greater will be found recorded on the historical pages of the nineteenth century. He knows that his country looks upon him as the pioneer in an undertaking which is to make his beloved republic the greatest nation on earth—which is to shower into her lap the profits of half the commerce of the world; and which is to extend the benefits and blessings of education and republicanism over three-fourths of the continent of North America.[3]

There, in 1846, was patriotism. The enterprise was of epic nature, and participation in it was honorable, responsible, and necessary for the future political greatness and economic well-being of the United States. Every volunteer was a moral agent in the enterprise; he would be spreading benefits and blessings as he went among the unenlightened.

"Every man" in the regiment did not feel as Gilbert did, of course. But such expressions of strong intellectual and emotional commitment are not rare in contemporaneous volunteer journals and letters and are frequent in later reminiscences.

Certainly a leading motive for volunteers was the possibility, at least the opportunity, of bettering their fortunes. Since the financial panic of 1837 and the successive crises of 1839 and 1841, the American economy had not recovered. Conditions were depressed and unemployment high. Competition for scarce jobs was further increased by cheap immigrant labor, principally from Ireland. Tens of thousands were leaving Ireland for the United States because of the potato famine. Skilled labor also had troubles. Wages had been cut steadily. Practically all the gains made by the trade unions in the 1830s had been lost. The hard-luck miner of Judge Jones's story "Gambler's Gulch" typifies the volunteer for California. He leaves his humdrum village to improve his financial position in order to marry the girl back home. To better himself, he goes to New York City. To better himself in New York City, he joins the regiment for California.

Some of the volunteers thought that possession of California would bring to the United States the profits of half the commerce of the world, and they fully expected to share in those profits. James Lynch, a private of Company F, had a job when he enrolled in the regiment. In his journal he wrote that he had just finished his apprenticeship as a carpenter, had steady work and the best wages then available. Those wages were not high. Lynch was just twenty-one, single, and ambitious. The much-heralded opportunities of the Far West were attractive. He sailed to California singing a popular song he liked: "Success to California, likewise to Oregon; / And the rooster that crows there must be Uncle Sam!"[4] Mechanics such as Lynch were permitted to take with them the tools of their trade for post-war work.

Joshua S. Vincent, a sergeant in Company I, kept a careful journal. He was twenty-three years old, an employed journeyman printer. He had left Elmira on July 20 with a group

of eleven friends to join Captain Shannon's company in Bath.
He began entries in his journal on September 27, the day
after sailing, with a review of the summer. Looking back to
mid-July, he wrote that it would be "impossible to describe
our extravagant anticipations of the future. In our own minds
each man met with many a wild adventure and hair-breadth
'scape, and performed many a deed of valor on our way from
Elmira."[5] Vincent thought that the men with him were "too
good blood" to back out, but at sailing only five of the eleven
were still enrolled. They had all sacrificed much, he said, to
prepare for their departure and a bright future in California.

Vincent made the most confidential entries in his journal
when he was most bored. On October 29, while his ship, the
Susan Drew, was becalmed for the ninth straight day, he found
everything insufferably tedious, "even anticipations of the
time when we shall return to our homes after a long absence
covered with blushing honors and a great deal richer than
when we started."[6] Vincent sincerely expected to fight, and to
win "blushing honors." (Perhaps it was a family tradition; his
grandfather and great-grandfather had fought in the Revolution.) It is also important to note his intention to return
home after a long and profitable absence. Many of the volunteers expected to emerge rich from their adventure, and on
this they were gambling. But in prospect the adventure was
not without uncertainty, hardship, and risk.

Vincent's superior in Company I, Second Lieutenant
John McHenry Hollingsworth, had joined the company in
New York. He and Sergeant Vincent were the same age.
Maryland-born, Hollingsworth considered himself a farmer.
His great-grandfather, Samuel Chase, had been one of the
signers of the Declaration of Independence. Hollingsworth
expected and hoped to see battle, and he confided a personal
motive to his journal on October 26. (The calm evidently was
conducive to introspection.) He was homesick, but "I must
not let my mind dwell on home, I must go and try to win a
name. If I fall in battle I trust that I shall die like a soldier
with my face to the enemy."[7] The next spring, upon arrival in
California, Hollingsworth heard reports of the progress of

the war on the mainland of Mexico. He and many of his
fellow officers regretted coming with Stevenson "while the
war has been carried on in the enemy's country and we so far
from the scene of strife. . . . We have done nothing and long
for an opportunity of distinguishing or *extinguishing* ourselves."[8] But Hollingsworth was also interested in fortune. He
often thought and talked with his men of ultimately making a
profitable settlement in California.[9]

Not many of the volunteers who kept journals or wrote
letters were specific about their means to fortune, and even
Hollingsworth was sufficiently vague. A general pattern
emerges, however. The men anticipated opportunities in
agriculture, in commerce, and in the employment of skills
and trades needed by the new society that was to flourish.
California's probable mineral wealth had been mentioned in
reports, but at this time was not one of the area's major
attractions. A fortune in California would be won through
work, but not very hard work, in one of the most agreeable
spots on the globe. California's reported eligibility for settlement—and the fact that it was virtually uninhabited—were
strong inducements.

The climate of California, its vastness, and its contrasts
had been featured in reports on that Mexican province from
the 1820s. If the reports were seldom accurate, they were
rarely without some basis, and between 1840 and 1846 a
substantial body of lore had developed. Such idealized accounts were the basis of William Redmond Ryan's motives. A
British subject and an extremely gifted draftsman and paint-
er, Ryan was twenty-three years old. In the preface to a book
he published in London in 1850, he stated that he had been
engaged in sedentary pursuits. A restless spirit, during the
war he "sought relief from the monotony of civilized life, in
a more congenial and adventurous existence amidst the wilds
and mountains of California." There was no patriotism, no
missionary zeal. Quite frankly, Ryan came for the sights and
the climate; he wanted to paint and recover his health. Observant and articulate, he wrote of his impressions of his
fellow volunteers:

There were few amongst us who cared much as to the chances of our revisiting the scenes we were then quitting; for we were, for the most part, thoroughly sick of the life of large cities, and exaggerated to ourselves the delights of a pastoral existence in a new settlement, in which both climate and soil were supposed to render the allotted duties of man more of a pastime than a toil.[10]

Other men besides the sensitive Ryan were in the expedition for their health. Private Charles A. Palmer of Company D, thirty-three years old, was one of the first to enlist in Company D. When he died aboard the *Susan Drew* off Cape Horn on January 7, 1847, Sergeant Vincent wrote, "Mr. Palmer has been a long time sick with consumption . . . his whole object in enlisting as I learn was to take this voyage for his health . . . the weather has proved too severe for him."[11]

These were some of the motives for joining the regiment —patriotism, the search for riches, the flight from poverty, a change of scene, adventure, and the satisfaction of curiosity about a fabled place. In addition, there were some conventional wartime motives that were less admirable—anticipations of booty and rapine. Such unsavory references naturally did not appear in dispatches like those of Edward Gilbert to the *Argus* or in the newspapers supporting the war. Newspapers hostile to the war, however, considered the entire undertaking pillage, and said so. The best evidence of such motives is found in criticism of the regiment.

The fact that Edward W. Clay and Henry R. Robinson took note of the regiment's troubles in New York is persuasive evidence that the regiment was a *cause célebre*. The artist Clay was a brilliant and popular satirist, and Robinson, one of the major eastern lithographers noted for his cartoons and caricatures, put the best—and most salable—of Clay's drawings into stone and lithographed them in his shop in Nassau Street. The subject was almost always topical, reflecting the talk of the day or of the week. While hastily made, the lithographs were superb and are among the best such work of the nineteenth century. Both men had large followings.

The regiment had barely sailed before a Clay-Robinson treatment was on the street and available in the shop. Titled

ONE OF THE CALIFORNIAN BO HOYS TAKING LEAVE OF HIS GAL.

Comic cartoon, 1846, by the brilliant New York topical satirist
Edward W. Clay, drawn on stone and printed by Henry R.
Robinson, the major eastern lithographer noted particularly
for his caricatures. The cartoon is rich in timely regimental detail:
the Irish-immigrant origin of many volunteers (the "bo hoys" or
"b'hoys"), cost of uniforms, suggestions of plunder in "Californy,"
and Colonel Stevenson's difficulties with New York authorities (see
page 73).

"One of the Californian Bo-Hoys Taking Leave of his Gal," this lithograph is filled with detail and the richest satire of many aspects of the regiment. In this dockside scene a volunteer in full dress takes leave of a flamboyantly decked-out woman two heads taller than he. The very young volunteer appears sad, as does the woman, although she is not so young. He is handing her a case, and says:

Good bye Liz! Here's my daggero' type likeness! I'd stand treat but I hain't got the ghost of a red cent left, our uniforms is so very expensive—When I come back from Californy I'll bring you a whole lot of little golden Jesusses and crosses! I will upon the honor of a soldier!

His big girl friend replies, "Well, Jake, as you're goin' away, I've got three shillin' so let's go to George Brown's in Pearl Street and get two stews and a couple of horns!"[12]

References to "little golden Jesusses and crosses," occur repeatedly. Religious figures in precious metal were the treasure to be plundered from the Catholic Mexicans. In Roderick M. Morrison's satiric poem "The Volunteer's Vision," the disappointed volunteer complained to California, "You've got no Golden Jesuses; you've got no pretty women! / And though I have a willing mind, I've got no chance for sinning."[13] Morrison, of course, expected just the opposite.

Although written about the other regiment of New York Volunteers, Colonel Ward Burnett's *High Private* included a list of the inducements reputedly used to secure men to fight in the Mexican War. They were: "roast beef and two dollars a day, plenty of whiskey, golden Jesuses, pretty Mexican gals, safe investments—quick returns, and everything pictured to the fancy."[14]

Such expectations were also referred to in the *Fish Market Reporter*. On December 18, in a mock address, the regimental adjutant spoke of present inconveniences and of prospects. Said he,

You are on the *ocean* . . . you can't go ashore and steal apples and raise Hell in the bean patch. You've got to be peaceable and quiet or our Corporals will give you a pair of wristlets not comfortable—but if you want to keep your hands in, you can practise on raising pies and gin, and the General don't want you to get out of practise cause there's lots of plunder in California.[15]

The frequent mention of such motivation flaws the concept of a benign deliverance, with security and religious freedom guaranteed. Some of the Mexican Catholic churches thus freed would evidently be without their images of worship, and one wonders if the Catholic Irishmen and Germans in the regiment would assist in the sacrilege.

NOTES

1. Bancroft, *History of California*, vol. 5, 504.
2. Frisbie, "Reminiscences," 8-10.
3. Albany *Argus*, Aug. 19, 1846. The *Argus* dispatch was long, most of it devoted to the local Company H. Gilbert took no notice of press or congressional criticism.
4. James Lynch, *With Stevenson to California* (San Francisco: n.p., 1896), 1-2.
5. Vincent, "Log-Book," July 20, 1846.
6. *Ibid.*, Oct. 29, 1846.
7. John McHenry Hollingsworth, *The Journal of Lieutenant John McHenry Hollingsworth of the First New York Volunteers* (San Francisco: California Historical Society, 1923), 1.
8. *Ibid.*, 23.
9. *Ibid.*, 6 and *passim*.
10. William Redmond Ryan, *Personal Adventures in Upper and Lower California, in 1848-9; With the Author's Experience at the Mines*, 2 vols., (London: William Shoberl, 1850), 2-3.
11. Vincent, "Log-Book," Jan. 7, 1847.
12. Harry T. Peters, *California on Stone* (New York: Doubleday, Doran and Company, Inc., 1935). The reproduction of the lithograph appears as Plate 98; the identification is on page 183. For Clay and Robinson see Introductory Essay and *passim*. This is one of the first appearances of the caricature of the urban "b'hoy," who—as "Mose"—was to be so popular in American humor and in the American theater for the next decade. See Constance Rourke: *American Humor* (New York: Harcourt, Brace and Company, Inc., 1931), 116-17.
13. Morrison, "Volunteer's Vision," 4.
14. "A Corporal of the Guard": *High Private, With a Full and Exciting History of the New-York Volunteers, and the Mysteries and Miseries of the Mexican War* (New York: n.p., 1848), 8.
15. Vincent, "Log-Book," Dec. 18, 1846.

Chapter Seven

Departure From New York

C OLONEL STEVENSON showed restraint through July, August, and September. In the face of the steady abuse leveled at him and at the regiment, he issued no challenges, wrote no letters to the newspapers. Som of the criticism may have been unanswerable for being the truth. He could scorn to notice other attacks simply by considering the anti-administration sources. And perhaps he did have peace of mind, secure in the support of the president and the secretary of war.

Certainly Stevenson had very little time to organize the venture and no experience in any comparable undertaking. The entire enterprise was complicated and required integrated effort. While the problems were enormous, they were not beyond his capacity to solve with the aid of carefully selected men. In those first weeks in the White Street Arsenal, and later on Governors Island, the colonel displayed some remarkable administrative ability. With him from the beginning was his son Matthew, twenty-one years old, just graduated from the military academy at West Point. Also from West

Point, where he had been an instructor, came Captain Joseph
L. Folsom, twenty-nine, to serve as assistant quartermaster, to
secure supplies and supervise their loading. Captain William
G. Marcy, twenty-eight, the son of the secretary of war, armed
with a presidential commission in the U.S. Army, was appointed acting assistant quartermaster in charge of
commissary.

A glance at the unexpended commissary stores on one of
the ships, on arrival in San Francisco after six months at sea,
suggests the complex nature of the procurement problems
encountered before the regiment sailed. The day of Stevenson's arrival in San Francisco Bay on the *Perkins*, March 6,
1847, he wrote General Kearny in Monterey informing him
of the force on the ship, food supplies, and ordnance stores
on board. Of antiscorbutics alone, there were 698 barrels of
vinegar, 121 kegs of pickled onions, 14 barrels of "sour
krout," 22 barrels of pickled cabbage. Among unused stores
were over 14 tons of hard bread, 258 barrels of salt pork, 162
bushels of beans, 2 tons of coffee, 4 tons of sugar, 3,845
pounds of soap, 656 pounds of candles. The ordnance stores,
requiring three finely spaced pages to list, included 1,800
muskets, 500 rifles, and 360,000 musket percussion cartridges, percussion caps, quick match, slow match, primers,
fuses. There were 4 six-pound field guns, 2 twelve-pound
howitzers, 4 ten-inch mortars, 20 thirty-two-pound iron guns,
thousands of thirty-two-pound balls and thousands of six and
twelve-pound shells and cannister shot. There were traveling
forges, battery wagons, tools, harness for 300 horses, 600
tents, construction materials—and this was a partial list.[1]

Stevenson's two junior field officers for the regiment
were West Point men, as he had requested. Lieutenant Colonel Henry S. Burton, twenty-eight years old, joined the
regiment from the captaincy of Company F, Third Artillery,
and Major James A. Hardie, twenty-four, from a lieutenancy
in another company of the same regular-army regiment. Both
were effective, able officers who worked well with the colonel
and with company officers and men.

Some changes of company officers occurred on Governors Island, with the increase of second lieutenants in each company to two, on joint orders of the secretary of war and Governor Wright. Lieutenant Matthew Stevenson succeeded to the command of Company G on the resignation of Captain James Dirver. His first election was improperly held, and the returns were contested, but through a subsequent election he was commissioned by Governor Wright. One of the new openings, as a second lieutenant in Company C, was filled by young George Douglas Brewerton, nineteen years old, son of General Henry Brewerton, the superintendent of West Point. Other young officers joined, were elected and commissioned. They were a stable lot; there was very little turnover.

On September 11 Secretary of War Marcy sent Stevenson his operating orders. The object of the regiment was the military occupation of California, in which Stevenson was to cooperate with Commodore Sloat and serve under General Kearny when the latter's Army of the West should arrive in California. Marcy mentioned three points worthy of particular attention—San Francisco, Monterey, and San Diego. Of the three, San Francisco was the most important. "It is important," Marcy wrote, "to have possession of the Bay of San Francisco, and the country in that vicinity. The necessity of having something like a permanent and secure position on the coast of California and probably at this place will not be overlooked."[2]

Marcy directed Stevenson to cultivate the good will of the Californians through liberal and kind treatment. The troops were to be restrained from any acts of license or outrage, and supplies drawn from the country were to be paid for at fair prices. Should there be no vigorous resistance from the Californians, Stevenson's conduct was to be conciliatory.

On September 12 Marcy wrote General Kearny through Fort Leavenworth, advising him that the regiment would sail soon and sending him a copy of Stevenson's orders. Marcy's final orders to Stevenson were written on September 15, suggesting that all three ships put in at Rio de Janeiro for fresh provisions, as their convoy, the sloop-of-war *Preble*, would do.

Before the middle of September, three ships had been chartered and were being loaded. A band consisting of twenty-four men, mostly Germans, had been organized and had carefully rehearsed the "California Grand March," a composition of one of the bandsmen, Frederick C. Grambs. It was "Most Respectfully Dedicated to the Officers of the 7th Regt. N.Y. State Volunteers of the California Expedition."[3] The

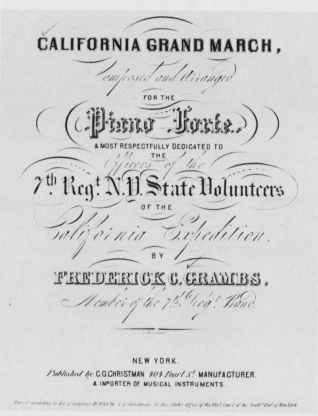

The "California Grand March," sprightly, martial, Germanic schmaltz, was composed by the chief musician of the regimental band and copyrighted in New York on September 26, 1846, the day the regiment sailed for California. (Courtesy Music Division, Library of Congress, Washington, D.C.)

troops were uniformed, more or less, by September 20, having been paid on September 18. The city of New York had presented to the colonel a full set of regimental colors. Three small libraries, the gift of New York publishers and tract societies, were put on board the ships, and every man had his Bible from Dr. McVickar.

Shortly before preparations were completed for embarkation, Colonel Stevenson was faced with legal problems—

HANDWRITTEN LETTER, POLK TO MARCY

President James K. Polk wrote to Secretary of War William S. Marcy from the White House, Washington, D.C., September 14, 1846. Polk expressed his anxiety about the embarkation of the regiment. ["Have you any information from New York since I saw you on Saturday? Has the California Regiment (Stephenson's) gone on board the transports? Have they sailed, and if not who do you know is the cause of their detention?"] Legal proceedings brought by parents of underage recruit replacements threatened to delay departure of the transport fleet. The ships were temporarily detained, not sailing until September 26. (Courtesy of James S. Browne, M.D., Mill Valley, California.)

suits for false imprisonment brought by rejected applicants and suits on the part of parents whose underage sons had lied about their age and had been mustered into the service. Stevenson's reaction seems to have been evasive, he fearing further delay, and preparations for departure were hastened.

On September 24 the men embarked, with baggage that included musical instruments and tool chests. Three companies and a staff physician were assigned to each ship. On the *Thomas H. Perkins* were Companies B, G, and F, commanded by Colonel Stevenson; on the *Loo Choo*, Companies A, C, and K, commanded by Major Hardie; and on the *Susan Drew*, under the command of Lieutenant Colonel Burton, Companies D, H, and I. Company E was divided among the three ships, about twenty men to each.

On September 26 the three transports and the *Preble* were towed through the narrows and sailed for California. The *Commercial Advertiser* took a parting shot:

The Cal. expedition is off at last, shorn somewhat of its numeric force, as it has long been almost wholly of its moral . . . it requires no very abiding or superstitious faith in omens to believe that the issue will be useless and inglorious in strict conformity with the inception and progress.[4]

That writer was mistaken.

NOTES

1. Stevenson, Harbor of San Francisco, to Kearny, Monterey, March 6, 1847, RG 393, NA.
2. Marcy, Washington, to Stevenson, New York City, Sept. 11, 1846, RG 393, NA.
3. Grambs's "California Grand March" had been published early in September by C. G. Christman, 404 Pearl Street, New York, not only a music publisher but a manufacturer and importer of musical instruments.
4. New York *Commercial Advertiser*, Sept. 28, 1846.

San Francisco, 1847

PART TWO

PROGRESS

Chapter Eight

Bound for California

THE THREE TRANSPORTS and the *Preble* sailed out into the Atlantic, straight into a storm. For four days of sober second thoughts, almost every man was seasick. When the gale abated the officers took roll call and ascertained the extent of losses due to last-minute desertion or to men left behind by chance. Some men had been ill on Governors Island or at their homes in New York; others had been at liberty in the city. At sailing, fifty of these men had been left behind. On September 28 they met in the New York City Armory. Among them were one company captain, Nelson Taylor, and Lieutenants Penrose and Vermeule.

After accepting the offer of government rations and quarters while awaiting word from the Department of War, they marched—again—to the Battery for the ferry to their former camp. The *New York Herald* had been caught almost without a cause when the regiment sailed and thus made the most of this opportunity, reporting the meeting in detail and commending the loyal stragglers.[1] These men remained on Governors Island until November 13. They then sailed for California on the tiny storeship *Brutus*, which carried additional provisions for the regiment and for the other United States forces in California.

By the beginning of October, for the first time in well over two months, the regiment no longer received its customary daily space in the New York press.

For most of the volunteers the voyage was memorable, their first time at sea. Many kept regular journals. These form the most interesting if not the most authentic and significant record of the regiment, revealing the nature of the group and the state of mind of the volunteers. Such journals —like any diary—were personal accounts, this being their greatest charm and greatest disadvantage in terms of historical value. Often the diarist wrote only of himself, ignoring events around him, and some journals degenerated into perfunctory daily recitations of weather, latitude and longitude, and the diarist's state of health. Some volunteers were articulate and intelligently observant and produced well-written journals. A little literary skill was often worse than none, however, and the less-pretentious, straight-forward journals are more vivid and often more informative. Among the best are those of Sergeant J. S. Vincent and Lieutenant John McHenry Hollingsworth, both previously cited. While Hollingsworth did write in a self-consciously literary style, that style does not obscure his journal's factual value. Neither journal was later revised, expanded, or embroidered (as many were), and both retain their immediacy.

The transports were sailing ships, dependent on winds and currents, and they followed the usual pre-steamer route to California. This course carried them far out into the Atlantic, almost to the Cape Verde Islands off Africa, then back toward the coast of South America. While each sailed independently, not in sight of the other transports or of the convoy, all arrived at Rio de Janeiro during the last ten days of November.

The two months had been difficult. Sergeant Vincent, who left the best record of the men aboard the *Susan Drew*, described life aboard ship. Eating, reading, and fishing were the most common diversions, followed by the playing of various games, drinking, fighting, and (although he did not mention it) presumably writing in one's journal. Except in the worst weather, once the guard was mounted, evenings were devoted to smoking on deck, singing, and storytelling. Every few days a dance was held, and occasionally there would be a play.[2] Apparently, most men could draw on their own resources for amusement, but as the days and weeks passed, the situation grew increasingly difficult. The ships were small, the largest only seven hundred tons, and they were crowded. With the men so confined, discipline was a problem, not only with a group of late recruits Vincent identified as "the quintessence of rowdyism" but with most of the men.

Within three weeks of sailing mutiny was being discussed on each of the ships, in every case because of punishment thought excessively severe. Mutiny had been mentioned on the *Susan Drew* as early as October 8, just two weeks out of New York, when Private Phillip Kelly was locked in the guardhouse, a small structure on deck, solidly built of planks. After threatening his officers and breaking down the guardhouse door, he was put in irons. Kelly, a popular b'hoy of Company I, was accompanied by his wife and small daughter who were favorites on the ship.[3]

Early in November, on the *Susan Drew*, Captain Naglee ordered his men of Company D to bathe. A few complied but most refused, not caring "to bathe in the tub that some less clean than themselves had been in."[4] A detail of men from Company I was called to enforce the order, and the men were stripped and buckets of water poured over them. Then they were sent to the guardhouse. During the night the guardhouse was demolished. Although the incident is mentioned in every known journal of the men on the *Susan Drew*, Vincent left the most vivid account:

Capt Nagle [sic] is in his glory. . . . At about 4 o'clock in the morning there was such a scene of confusion as is seldom witnessed. Men on

the inside and on the outside were engaged in tearing down the guard house and throwing the pieces overboard some were sitting up in their berths giving orders such as "Clear away the larboard grates" "Take a reef in the door" "bear a hand fore and aft" then some would cry "heave yo-heave ho" "cheerily men" etc. etc. and cheer followed cheer as each piece went over and the whole enlivened by a snatch of "Old Dan Tucker" the chorus of which was
    Get out of the way you old guard house (repeat)
    For you shan't stay on the Susan Drew
And all this time not an officer dared show his head.[5]

Naglee himself entered three pages in his journal on this incident. He said the men not only sang "scurrilous and obscene" songs but also, once the guardhouse was demolished, paraded about carrying a sign which read "Sons of Liberty!"[6] Although he did not say so, Naglee doubtless figured in their songs. After marching around the deck, the prisoners, led by Private Kelly and cheered by all the men, returned insolently to stand where the guardhouse had been, according to Hollingsworth's account. "Mutiny is among us," he added unnecessarily. If the men were to be court-martialed, Hollingsworth hoped he would not be judge advocate and have to do the writing.[7]

Hardly was calm restored than Captain Naglee again invited trouble. For disobedience his young servant was ordered tied and hoisted into the rigging. No one but a lieutenant in Naglee's company would execute the punishment. Said Vincent: "The worthy Capt. and Lieut. heard hints and murmurs from the crowd that they cannot well mistake and will not be very pleasant to reflect upon."[8]

On November 9 Hollingsworth expressed the sentiment at least one other officer shared: "Mutiny again. . . . A vessel is no place for soldiers, it does not suit them [I]t was bad policy to send us by sea. You cannot have any discipline. I think if one were shot it would bring them to their senses."[9] Captain Naglee's sentiments exactly.[10] Naglee and his methods of discipline were not highly regarded by the volunteers. Vincent commented that Naglee "is celebrated for the number of arrests that he makes. . . . He looks upon the men under him only as objects for his amusement and if he had the power I

candidly believe he would slice off their heads and string
them up to the yard arm."[11] Although they once appointed a
duel on board the *Susan Drew*, Captains Naglee and Frisbie
were politely formal, and Captain Frisbie was the most generous in his comments on Naglee. He called him "a very
bright man not a loveable man. . . . I think he would have
done very well if they had given him an independent
command."[12]

On the *Thomas H. Perkins*, with Colonel Stevenson aboard,
fewer violations of rules occurred, but still there was cruel
punishment and some talk of mutiny. Hearing such discussion among the men, after a fractious sergeant had been
triced up by the thumbs and wrists for hours, Captain Folsom
informed Colonel Stevenson. The colonel reportedly told
Folsom that there would be no mutiny. Stevenson made
known the fact that he slept over nine hundred tons of gunpowder and had a train laid from that powder to his berth.
"You can rest assured," he is quoted as telling Folsom, "that
before I will suffer the command of this vessel to pass from
me there will not be a plank left for a soul on board to cling
to; and now, sir, let the mutiny proceed!"[13] On the *Loo Choo*
there were no major incidents but constant minor ones, with
some mutinous talk. Major Hardie, in command, could only
write of the discipline on the ship, "Not Good," and of the
men's military appearance, "Indifferent."[14]

Part of the problem was the two-month confinement and
the excellent weather. The conduct of the men on that part of
the voyage after Rio de Janeiro, around Cape Horn, was
noticeably different. While some were still unruly and others
drunken from supplies they had secured in Brazil, there was
less serious insubordination and no more talk of mutiny.
Officers had learned to work with the men and knew their
limits. In turn, the men responded to reasonable discipline.
In addition, the weather was worse.

The transports had arrived in the harbor of Rio de Janeiro between November 17 and 21. They took on water and
fresh provisions, and waited for fair weather to continue the
voyage. The men were ashore every day and night. While

including long descriptions of the beauty of this land and its women, the diarists and letter writers with very few exceptions commented on the cruelty practiced by the Brazilians toward their Negro slaves. Writing to his brother-in-law in Bath, Captain Shannon revealed some deep-rooted personal feelings that would surface again in California:

Brazil, you must know, is a priest-ridden country. You see it everywhere, and everywhere its effects are seen not indeed what it should be in the piety and good conduct of the people. But in their utter ignorance, supersitition and indolence. And the absence of all energy and enterprise. But it has a far worse feature than this. Slavery dred [sic] and loathsome. And in most dark and revolting features. Here are not the descendents of negroes who were brought perhaps more than a century ago from their land, but the African himself, bearing all the marks of country and tribe as well in the sometimes frightful tatooing perhaps over most of the body, as well as the features. And horrible as the practice is, you almost lose your pity, in the disgust which their appearance excites.[15]

Three years later, in California's first constitutional convention, William Shannon would have an opportunity to do something about slavery.

While in Rio de Janeiro, Captain James Turner of Company B was relieved of his command to return to the United States on a special mission. The regiment was far below regulation strength, and he was to report to the adjutant general in Washington and then enroll recruits in New York. When the three ships left the harbor on November 29, Turner was not the only volunteer who remained ashore. Taking their baggage, twenty-two men deserted.

The *Perkins* did not put into port again until San Francisco. His ship had been the last to arrive in Rio de Janeiro, and Colonel Stevenson was determined to arrive in California before the rest of his command. The *Susan Drew* and *Loo Choo* did make another port, Valparaiso, after a memorable six weeks rounding Cape Horn.

As the *Susan Drew* was blown into the lower latitudes and rough seas, Sergeant Vincent kept his journal and read Byron. On December 28 he read six pages by daylight after ten o'clock at night, with the weather "stormy, boisterous and cold."[16] Two days later the weather was worse, and he entered a splendid description of the effect:

Being at sea at best is very uncomfortable and being at sea—in a heavy rain—is still more uncomfortable; but being at sea—in a heavy rain—a very heavy wind—monstrous high seas—each one looking as though it would swallow the vessel as I would swallow a piece of duff —cold enough to freeze icicles on ones nose—the ship rocking so that all you can do is to get hold of something and *hang on and growl* —is devilish uncomfortable.

That evening he growled, "one squall after another. The difference is about the same as the old indians dinner 'take off succotash and put on succotash.' "[17]

The weather soon improved, and both ships safely reached Valparaiso by January 20, 1847. They were quickly provisioned and on their way by January 23. For most volunteers the stop in Chile was too short. They liked the country, the weather, and the gracious people. Twenty-nine volunteers so much preferred the pleasant certainties of Chile to the uncertainties of California that they deserted.

Once out of Valparaiso, the mood on both ships changed. California was next. (In Valparaiso there was news of Taylor's victories in Mexico but nothing about California.) On January 25 on the *Loo Choo* and two days later on the *Susan Drew*, muskets were broken out and cleaned. Target practice and drills began. So busy were both Vincent and Hollingsworth that they neglected their journals, Vincent's first lapse since New York. When he resumed in four days, he described the changed appearance of the ship. Now it was bustling and lively, with one company or squad or another on deck drilling constantly. As he gave the orders and heard the jingling of the rammers and the click of the locks, Vincent could "almost fancy that we are on the battle field mowing down the enemy by scores."[18] On the *Perkins* drill and target practice had been a daily (except Sunday) procedure since December under the colonel's watchful eye, with the drills often and the dress parades always accompanied by the music of the band.

The *Perkins* entered San Francisco Bay on March 6. Over the village of San Francisco, the American flag was flying. California had been in the hands of the United States for exactly eight months.

NOTES

1. *New York Herald*, Sept. 29, 1846.
2. Vincent, "Log-Book," Sept. 27-Nov. 21, 1846.
3. *Ibid.*, Oct. 9, 1846.
4. Joseph Evans, "Around 'Cape Horn' with Col. Stevenson's Regiment,' " (MS), 3-4.
5. Vincent, "Log-Book," Nov. 3, 1846.
6. Henry M. Naglee, "Diary," (MS), Bancroft Library, University of California, Berkeley, Nov. 3-4, 1846.
7. Hollingsworth, *Journal*, 4.
8. Vincent, "Log-Book," Nov. 8, 1846.
9. Hollingsworth, *Journal*, 6.
10. Naglee, "Diary," Oct.-Dec., 1846, and Jan.-Feb., 1847.
11. Vincent, "Log-Book," Oct. 31, 1846.
12. Frisbie, "Reminiscenses," 33. In correspondence with the family of Captain—ultimately General—Naglee, the author was asked never to give the impression that Naglee was constantly in trouble with everybody (which he was). The family spokesman or family attorney, it was not clear which, thought it acceptable to say that Naglee was "naturally of a controversial nature" and "either much criticized or much admired." I was also told that Naglee had a great many loyal friends throughout his life and was sent his visiting list as proof!
13. Thomas Crosby Lancey in Clark, *The First Regiment of New York Volunteers*, 63-64. The account is probably apocryphal. The amount of gunpowder on board certainly is.
14. Comments of Commanding Officer, Muster Rolls of Companies A, C, and K, Oct. 31, 1846, RG 94, NA.
15. W. E. Shannon, Harbor of Rio de Janeiro, to Bartley Wilkes, Bath, New York, Nov. 25, 1846, letter in possession of Ward Shannon, Bath, New York.
16. Vincent, "Log-Book," Dec. 29, 1846.
17. *Ibid.*, Dec. 30, 1846.
18. *Ibid.*, Feb. 1, 1847.

Chapter Nine

The Best Friends
of California

I N LATE MAY 1846, acting on his standing orders from the secretary of the navy, Commodore Sloat ordered part of his squadron from Mazatlán to California ports. On July 4, the same day that Colonel Stevenson in New York was making public his command, Commodore Sloat's flagship lay in the harbor at Monterey. Three days later he landed a force and raised the American flag. By July 9 this flag was also flying at Yerba Buena (San Francisco) and at Sonoma, and at Sutter's Fort on the Sacramento River two days later.

Sloat's seizure of Monterey was accompanied by a proclamation, which he read at the flag-raising ceremony and posted about the town. In this document, written in both Spanish and English and addressed to the inhabitants of California, Sloat declared that "henceforward California will be a portion of the United States."[1] Despite that statement, the conciliatory tone of the proclamation should have pleased Polk and his cabinet. Sloat declared that he came not as an enemy but rather as the best friend of California. He promised full rights of citizenship, at least the temporary retention by officials of their offices, freedom of worship and the sanctity of church property, the right to import from the United States free of duty, and other blessings. Sloat also assured the Californians of freedom from revolution and from the villainies of the central Mexican government. This was perhaps the most successful point made in the proclamation, as it touched real Californian sensitivities: a general insecurity and long-standing and accumulated grievances against Mexico's neglect.

The condition of California public affairs just before the invasion could not have been more chaotic. Revolution and coups had characterized the 1830s and early 1840s. By 1846 the interior administration of government was completely disorganized. There was no real direction or assistance from the capital in Mexico; there was no military force sufficient or inclined to sustain the constituted authorities; there were no public funds. The government in Mexico provided promises and limitless advice—and orders for vigorous defense against the Americans—but no arms, no supplies, and no money. The Californians probably could not have united against any common foe even if they had had the resources. There were few interest groups in the province, divided ones, and the majority of the small population had no voice in what was supposed to be representative government. Republicanism had failed there.

Of all the internal conflicts, that between northern and southern California was predominant. The political head of government, the constitutional governor, was Don Pío Pico, California-born, with his headquarters in Los Angeles. Also California-born, a northern Californian, was the military head of government, Commandante-General José Castro, whose headquarters were in Monterey. This sectionalism had existed from the initial settlement of Alta California seventy-five years before, but under Pío Pico and José Castro it was aggravated, and the result was turmoil. The officials divided power and then argued about who had authority.

While the Californians indulged in this ruinous if neighborly quarreling, they agreed on the need for defense against the invaders. But their leaders could not provide it, and both fled to the mainland of Mexico as the United States' forces took over. Consul Larkin had told less than the truth about anti-United States sentiment in California in his zeal to urge annexation on Secretary Buchanan and President Polk. But in the more important judgment he had been correct; the Californians could not unite to resist, whatever their will.

This situation and Commodore Sloat's moderation led to a completely peaceful conquest of northern California. Not so in the south. In mid-July Sloat relinquished his command to Commodore Robert F. Stockton who was determined to play a part in the drama and who was no moderate. Stockton sailed down the coast and early in August raised the flag at Santa Barbara, left a small garrison there, and proceeded to San Pedro. On August 13, with a force of sailors and marines, and encountering no resistance, Stockton took the Pueblo de Los Angeles. He too issued and posted a proclamation—an inflammatory, threatening document bitterly abusive of Californian officials and harshly restrictive. He forbade the carrying of arms and, still worse, imposed a curfew. No proclamation for his particular "enemy" could have been less conciliatory or more insulting.[2] As a final gesture before he returned to Monterey, Stockton invoked martial law.

In Monterey late in September Stockton learned the fate of the fifty men he had left at Los Angeles. They had been routed, and southern California was in revolt. Los Angeles was not retaken until January of the next year, and then not until a small force from General Kearny's Army of the West had arrived. By then almost every southern Californian was an active enemy of the United States.

Kearny had taken New Mexico, installed what he called "civil" government, and marched on toward California ahead of schedule. Early in October, still in New Mexico, Kearny met Kit Carson and a small party bearing dispatches from Stockton for the War and Navy Departments and for the president. Kearny learned that California was at peace, having been conquered by the navy, and thereupon he sent back to New Mexico two-thirds of his force, continuing to California with a few more than one hundred dragoons. This remnant of the Army of the West entered eastern California in November and were at Warner's Ranch (in present San Diego County) in early December. On December 6 and 7 Kearny and his men engaged a force of Californians under Andrés Pico, younger brother of the governor, at San Pasqual. The battle was bitter and bloody, by far the worst of the conquest of California. While Kearny retained possession of the field (and thus reported San Pasqual a victory), his men sustained nearly all the casualties—twenty-two killed and a dozen seriously wounded. Reinforced by some sailors and marines, Kearny and his group reached San Diego.

In January the combined naval and land forces, including the battalion of Mormons that had just arrived, put down the revolt. On January 30 Kearny wrote the secretary of war: "The people of California are quiet at this time, but how long they will remain so, is very uncertain." In the same letter he mentioned his plans: "I intend leaving here tomorrow in the Ship Cyane for Monterey & San Francisco to examine those places & the country above here, and decide where to station Col. Stevenson's Regt. of Volunteers, & Capt. Tompkins Compy of Arty (which I hope may shortly arrive here)."[3]

On arrival in Monterey General Kearny found that the artillery company had arrived. Company F, Third Artillery, was Lieutenant Colonel Burton's former company. Made up of new recruits enlisted early in 1846 in Pennsylvania and Maryland (for a regular enlistment of five years), this regular-army company was very well officered. In addition to Captain Christopher Tompkins, there were two first lieutenants, Edward O. C. Ord and William Tecumseh Sherman, and Lieutenant Henry W. Halleck of the Corps of Engineers was attached to the company.

Assigning the company to the Presidio of Monterey, Kearny proceeded to San Francisco where he surveyed military sites and met with the naval officers there. At San Francisco Kearny received the letter from Winfield Scott, general in chief of the army, naming "the senior officer of the land forces"—General Kearny—the governor of California. Scott also designated California the Tenth Military Department of the United States.[4]

Back in Monterey late in February, Kearny made his headquarters in the house of Consul Larkin. On March 1 he and Commodore William B. Shubrick, who was then in command of the Pacific Squadron, jointly issued a circular making Monterey the capital of California and defining their fields of authority. While the navy would patrol the ports, the commanding military officer was "assigned the directions of operations on land—and—administrative functions of government over the People and Territory."[5] In that first week of March, at the end of which the first New York volunteers arrived, stable military government was just beginning in California.

On March 1, 1847, the military forces in California and their approximate strengths were: Companies C and K of the First Dragoons (Kearny's Army of the West), 75 men; the volunteer Mormon Battalion, 340 men; Company F, Third Artillery, 118 men—a total of about 530. The bulk of the force was in the potentially explosive southern area, the dragoons and Mormons holding Los Angeles and San Diego. Naval and marine units nominally held Sonoma and Santa Barbara, and only naval forces were at San Francisco.[6]

San Francisco in March 1847 was a village of some 500 people and seventy-nine buildings—thirty-one frame structures, twenty-six adobes, and twenty-two "shanties." Of the population, some 200 were civilian Mormons who had arrived the summer before, just after California had been taken by the United States. The leader of the Mormons, Samuel Brannan, had expected to colonize California as the land of promise for the Saints then bedeviled in the midwest. Instead, finding on arrival "that damned flag again," as he is quoted as saying, he settled down to await word from Brigham Young. Having a press with him, Brannan founded a newspaper, *The California Star*. On January 30, 1847, the *Star* predicted that at the rate population was growing, having increased 300 in two years, San Francisco was "destined to be the Liverpool or New York of the Pacific."[7]

It was certainly not the New York of the Pacific when the volunteers arrived, but it seemed sufficiently strange. The population was polyglot, mostly whites but including some Indians, Sandwich Islanders, and a few Negroes. A number of the whites were European. Unlike the other population centers, San Francisco was decidedly not a Mexican California town. The village itself, named Yerba Buena until just six weeks before the *Perkins* arrived, was built right at the water's edge. Back toward the entrance to the bay, called by Frémont the Golden Gate, were the few buildings of the old presidio, vacant and in disrepair. They had been unoccupied for two years. A few miles southwest of the village on a creek were the buildings of the former Mission Dolores, also in disrepair but housing some of the Mormon families. Between the village and the mission were nothing but sand dunes.

NOTES

1. John D. Sloat, "To the inhabitants of California," in John and LaRee Caughey, *California Heritage* (Los Angeles: The Ward Ritchie Press, 1962), 160-62.
2. U.S., Congress, House, Ex. Doc. 1, 31st Cong., 1st sess., 31-33.
3. Clarke, *Stephen Watts Kearny*, 271-72.
4. *Ibid.*, 277-78.
5. Marius Duvall, *A Navy Surgeon in California, 1846-47* (San Francisco: John Howell, 1957), opp. p. 92. Reproduction of original circular.
6. Bancroft, *History of California*, vol. 5. The figures on these units are approximately correct. They are derived from information in Chapters XVII, XVIII, XIX.
7. *The California Star*, Jan. 30, 1847. The figures on population and buildings for March are in the *Star* of March 13, Aug. 28, and Sept. 4, 1847. In the last two numbers, Lt. Edward Gilbert, who had been appointed deputy collector of the port, published a census of arrivals by months for 1847 and statistics on building, origin of population, businesses, and commerce and shipping.

Chapter Ten

Deployment

W HEN THE *PERKINS* REACHED San Francisco on March 6, 1847, Colonel Stevenson learned from Captain Dupont of the U.S.S. *Cyane* that General Kearny had arrived in Monterey. As instructed by the secretary of war, Stevenson immediately reported his arrival, the stores he had brought, and the condition of his men. With the exception of a few with slight colds, all men were well and "able to perform any duty you may require of them."[1]

General Kearny received Colonel Stevenson's letter and reports on March 10 and replied two days later. Colonel Stevenson was to remain at San Francisco until the two other transports arrived. His command would then be divided, according to orders enclosed with his letter to Stevenson. Colonel Stevenson and his regimental staff and four companies were to take post temporarily at Monterey. Lieutenant Colonel Burton and three companies were to go to Santa

SAN FRANCISCO, FORMERLY YERBA BUENA, IN 1846-47

Produced in the late 1880s by Bosqui, this lithograph was "authenticated as a faithful and accurate representation of San Francisco as it appeared in March 1847" by Colonel Stevenson, General Mariano G. Vallejo, and George Hyde. To the right of the twenty-gun sloop *Portsmouth* (A, center), appear the regimental transports *Thomas H. Perkins*, *Susan Drew*, and *Loo Choo* (all labeled B); and to the left of the *Portsmouth*, a merchantman, the *Vandalia* (C), and a coasting schooner (D). The structure at the far left, numbered 12, is identified as the first residence of the Russ family. (Courtesy California Historical Society, San Francisco.)

Barbara, while Major Hardie and three companies remained in San Francisco. Each field officer was to keep the medical officer who had accompanied him from New York. In this same set of orders, Captain Tompkins at the Monterey redoubt was directed to keep his battery of light artillery ready for service at the shortest notice.[2] General Kearny was proceeding cautiously.

By early in the day on March 20 neither of the other transports had arrived. Colonel Stevenson again wrote General Kearny, acknowledging receipt of the letter and orders of March 12 and reporting on activities. In the past week Stevenson had landed two companies of men who were engaged in repairing the quarters and storehouses at the presidio, building ovens and kitchens, and repairing the road from the presidio to the beach. While the work was hard, Stevenson reported the men were laboring cheerfully. The mechanics, carpenters, and masons used their own tools since the government-issued tools were on board one of the other ships.[3]

Later that day the *Susan Drew* sailed into San Francisco Bay. Sergeant Vincent was delighted to discover the *Perkins* there and to find the appearance of California so agreeable. He thought the view was one of the finest he had ever seen.[4] For the next week parties constantly went on shore, hunting, exploring the town and surrounding area, and bringing back to the ships curious reports of the things they saw and heard and found—rusty bayonets, copper balls, and strange plants. Some of the little bushes had both red and green leaves, Hollingsworth reported, not connecting that fact with another. "A number of our men have been very much poisoned," he wrote on April 2, "by touching [something]."[5] There was poison oak in the western paradise, and the men would learn to respect it.

On March 22 the colonel ordered a third company to work on the barracks at the presidio and the road to the beach, and sent Lieutenant Colonel Burton to Monterey to report to General Kearny. Before Burton returned, the *Loo Choo* had arrived. "She came into port in gallant style," Vincent wrote. "When she passed our ship we greeted her with 3 times 3 which she returned and the Perkins did the same. As she let go the anchor the Band on the Perkins struck up Hail Columbia and finished with Yankee Doodle. . . . The like I think was never heard in this far distant land before. It seemed to be a general jubilee."[6] Six months to the day after they left New York, the three transports were together in the harbor of San Francisco.

With the arrival of the *Loo Choo*, the volunteers numbered 599. In addition to the 22 desertions at Rio de Janeiro and 29 at Valparaiso, 9 volunteers had died, most of them by drowning. (Unknown to Colonel Stevenson, the *Brutus*, with the 49 stragglers aboard, was approaching California. It arrived in mid-April.)

General Kearny's position in California was greatly strengthened by the presence of these 650 men, more than doubling the force at his command. The area to be controlled was enormous, even excluding the trans-Sierra territory, and the military governor would soon become responsible for Lower California as well. Sonoma, San Francisco, and Santa Barbara were without land forces, and additional troops were needed at Monterey and Los Angeles. The first consideration was control of possible rebel activity by the Californians. Fortifications were needed at San Francisco, Monterey, and Los Angeles, and General Kearny soon learned that he had a serious Indian problem.

Lieutenant Colonel Burton returned to San Francisco from Monterey on March 28 with further orders from General Kearny and with news of the progress of the war in Mexico. The news was all good, if three months old. General Taylor with 25,000 men was supposed to be pursuing Santa Anna toward Mexico City, and General Scott lay before Vera Cruz with 15,000 men. Vincent also reported as fact the untrue rumor that General Castro had been taken prisoner in southern California.[7]

The two busiest people in the entire regiment the last week in March were probably Captains Folsom and Marcy, arranging transportation with the navy and allotting supplies and provisions to the various units about to be sent off. On March 30 deployment began. Lieutenant Colonel Burton with Companies A, B, and F boarded the bark *Moscow* and sailed on March 31 for Santa Barbara. Companies C, H, and K under Major Hardie disembarked from the transports and made camp at the presidio in San Francisco, continuing to work on permanent quarters. On April 2 Colonel Stevenson and the balance of the regiment, Companies D, E, G, and I, embarked on the *Lexington* for Monterey, landing there the next day.

The first activities of the units were similar once the men had made camp. The routine of duty was established; the schedule posted for roll calls, reveille, taps, tattoo, and sick calls; and orders issued for drills, challenges, treatment of townspeople, inspections, and the ordering of guards. Discipline was very strict, and the orders of the field officers were detailed. On the *Moscow* Lieutenant Colonel Burton even specified the procedure for selecting an orderly. "The Guard," he wrote, "will consist of 1 Sergt. 3 Corpls. and 10 Privates, one of these privates (the cleanest at guard mounting) will be selected as the Officer of the Day's Orderly."[8] For officers, almost immediately at all posts, there was duty on courts-martial and boards of survey.

In San Francisco Major Hardie had the services of Companies H and K. On April 1 Company C had been ordered to Sonoma. All the volunteers in San Francisco were busy. The three transports had not yet been completely unloaded, and the *Brutus* had to be unloaded once it arrived. Captain Folsom had rented a storehouse in the village for the stores and ordnance. That storehouse and the town itself required a twenty-four-hour police guard of twenty-seven men, under the command of Lieutenant Edward Gilbert of Company H. Work on the barracks and the road continued, and a detachment of men was erecting sawmills, felling trees, and sawing lumber across the bay in present-day Marin County. On April 18 Hardie informed General Kearny that the *Brutus* had arrived the day before, and he pleaded for forty-six of the men (all except Captain Taylor and Lieutenants Penrose and Vermeule) to be permanently attached there and not sent to their respective companies. Only with this larger detail, Hardie wrote, would he have the minimum necessary for the activities of the post and the guard of the garrison.[9] Kearny had to refuse; the men were needed elsewhere.

The problem was Indians. The hostile Indian frontier was not far away from the settled coastal region, and the Indians of the Napa, Sacramento, and San Joaquin valleys and of the Mojave Desert made regular attacks on outlying settlements, taking lives and stealing horses and cattle. Soldiers were needed in Sonoma and New Helvetia for protection against such raids. Shortly after ordering Company C to Sonoma, General Kearny appointed Don Mariano Guadalupe Vallejo as the United States Indian sub-agent there.[10] The appointment was a good one, since Vallejo was an open friend of the United States, was known to be trusted among the Indians, and was certainly one of the most powerful and influential men in California. Vallejo had founded Sonoma in 1835 and had been director of colonization on the northern frontier. Kearny appointed John A. Sutter Indian sub-agent at New Helvetia on the Sacramento River and ordered Major Hardie to have a detachment of Company C sent to Sutter's Fort.

At the same time Kearny issued another order in Monterey related to control of Indians. With as little delay as possible, a mounted company was to be organized, to consist of forty volunteers from Colonel Stevenson's regiment and thirty-five Californians enrolled for the purpose. Captain Naglee was assigned to the command of the company and was to "take steps to get his command into the saddle on the earliest day."[11] On April 28 Naglee and his mounted company were ordered to move out and make regular patrols along the frontier to protect the persons and property of the inhabitants and to prevent further depredations by the Indians. On April 17 *The California Star* reported these preparations:

A portion of the troops which left here a few days since for Monterey, are destined for service against the Indians in the Tuleres [sic], who have recently been troublesome in their thefts and depredations. Nothing could be more delightful than an excursion through the valley of the San Joaquin, at this season of the year.

Captain Naglee spent all of May and June on this mission, with a loss of three men, two of whom were lost and presumed killed and one drowned. From every post but San Francisco, parties of mounted volunteers launched periodic excursions against the Indians, who were a constant annoyance and general threat.

On Colonel Stevenson's arrival in Monterey, General Kearny assigned him the command of all troops in that area, which amounted to the four volunteer companies, the regular-army company of artillery, and a few dragoons. Throughout April the volunteers worked on fortifications and built barracks into which they moved at the end of the month. Rumors circulated of rebellion in southern California, and on April 28 and May 3 General Kearny ordered Colonel Stevenson and two companies to the Pueblo de Los Angeles. By the order of April 28 Kearny also created a Southern and a Northern Military District. Stevenson would command the former "and use the utmost vigilance in preserving quiet and order therein." Major Hardie would command the Northern Military District "and make such disposition of the troops under his command as shall be most condusive [sic] to the public tranquility and protection from Indian depredations."[12] When the *Lexington* sailed on May 5 with the colonel and Companies E and G, they were accompanied by General Kearny and by Lieutenant Hollingsworth, who had been transferred to Matthew Stevenson's Company G.

Whether or not there was rebellion in southern California (and there was not), Kearny needed these two companies of volunteers in Los Angeles. While the volunteers were enrolled for the war, the Mormon Battalion had been enlisted for twelve months; that period would expire on July 16. Entering Los Angeles on May 10 to a twenty-one-gun salute, General Kearny and Colonel Stevenson reviewed the Mor-

ENCAMPMENT OF COMPANY I, CAMP KEARNY,
MONTEREY, APRIL 1847

Reproduced from a colored drawing in John McHenry
Hollingsworth's manuscript journal. Fanciful in the oriental
treatment of the tents, this drawing is conceivably by Hollings-
worth but is more likely by Sgt. Joshua S. Vincent or Lt. John C.
Bonnycastle. (Courtesy California Historical Society, San
Francisco.)

mon Battalion and set about discovering the situation in
southern California. They found the people receptive, but
rumors were still circulating that General Castro or another
Mexican general, Anastasio Bustamante, might be raising an
army in Sonora to retake California. Colonel Stevenson with
his staff and Captains Taylor and Stevenson and their companies took their posts at Los Angeles where they would
remain until discharge.

Before leaving for Los Angeles Kearny had received a
letter from the secretary of war dealing with Lower California. In his reply, dated April 28, Kearny wrote that, while
these were his first instructions concerning possession of
Lower California, he would send as many of the New York
volunteers as he could spare, one or two companies.[13] Kearny
issued no orders, however, until he arrived back in Monterey
late in May, having judged for himself the condition in southern California. On May 30 he wrote to Colonel Stevenson and
ordered Lieutenant Colonel Burton in Santa Barbara to be
ready to embark two companies on the *Lexington* when it

arrived. In March the navy had taken San José del Cabo, at the tip of the peninsula, Kearny said, and in April, La Paz.[14] Writing these letters was one of General Kearny's last acts in California. Turning the military government over to Colonel Richard B. Mason, who had just arrived in California, General Kearny left Monterey on May 31 to return overland to Missouri.

On July 4 Lieutenant Colonel Burton with Companies A and B sailed for Lower California, arriving at La Paz on July 21 to find the country "quiet." Prematurely and incorrectly, Burton anticipated no further trouble.[15]

By midsummer the volunteers were deployed as they would remain for the rest of the year.

NOTES

1. Stevenson, Aboard U.S. Transport *Thomas H. Perkins*, San Francisco, to Kearny, Monterey, March 6, 1847, RG 393, NA.
2. Kearny: DGO No. 4, Headquarters, Tenth Military Department, Monterey, (hereinafter all orders are from Headquarters, Tenth Military Dpt., Monterey, unless otherwise specified) March 12, 1847, RG 94, NA.
3. Stevenson, Aboard U.S. Transport *Thomas H. Perkins*, San Francisco, to Kearny, Monterey, March 20, 1847, RG 393, NA.
4. Vincent, "Log-Book," March 20, 1847.
5. Hollingsworth, *Journal*, 22-23. Some of the men would never learn to recognize poison oak, however, or to develop immunity to it. They called it the "poison bush," and a year later Captain Dimmick at the presidio was so badly affected that he could hardly see daylight for two weeks. (Kimball Hale Dimmick, "The Diary of Kimball Hale Dimmick," (MS), May 13, 1848, *et.seq.*)
6. Vincent, "Log-Book," March 26, 1847.
7. *Ibid.*, March 29.
8. Lt. Col. H. S. Burton: DGO No. 2, Bark *Moscow*, San Francisco, March 30, 1847, RG 94, NA.
9. J. A. Hardie, San Francisco, to H. S. Turner, Monterey, April 18, 1847, RG 393, NA. Captain Turner was acting assistant adjutant general to Kearny at that point. In a letter written some time later to Capt. F. J. Lippitt in Santa Barbara, Hardie mentioned

progress on the barracks at the presidio. "We have made great improvements in the Presidio since you left," he wrote, "and as our sawmill (across the bay) has succeeded admirably and gives us as much lumber as we want, we shall have ourself [sic] as comfortable quarters as we can devise." (Hardie, San Francisco, to Lippitt, Santa Barbara, n.d.—probably during July, RG 393, NA.

10. Kearny, Monterey, to M. G. Vallejo, April 6, 1847, RG 393, NA.

11. Kearny: DGO No. 8, April 6, 1847, RG 94, NA.

12. Kearny: DGO No. 13, April 28, 1847, RG 94, NA.

13. Clarke, *Stephen Watts Kearny*, 311-12. Part of this letter to Marcy is quoted, with the cited source the Kearny letter-book in the Missouri Historical Society.

14. Kearny, Monterey, to H. S. Burton, Santa Barbara, May 30, 1847, RG 393, NA.

15. Burton, La Paz, Baja California, to W. T. Sherman, Monterey, Aug. 2, 1847, RG 393, NA.

Chapter Eleven

Colonel Mason and the North

I N MAY 1847 COLONEL Richard B. Mason quietly took over as governor of California, without issuing a proclamation or indulging in rhetoric. He was to serve as military governor of the Tenth Military Department for almost two years, until April 1849. Lieutenant William T. Sherman would serve as his assistant adjutant general and Lieutenant Henry W. Halleck as secretary of state. Both Sloat and Kearny (as well as Stockton and Frémont, who had briefly been governors of California) had referred to civil government in their proclamations and orders. Not so Governor Mason. His understanding of California's status was clear and his control firm. California was under military government with supreme power vested in the senior military officer. There was no civil law nor did the Californians have political rights.

When the United States forces occupied California in July 1846, the alcalde was the chief local administrative officer. The office was an efficient instrument of government that had been introduced into Spain's colonies in the six-

teenth century. Legislative and executive but principally judi-
cial duties were combined in this one official appointed by the
governor. The military governors beginning with Sloat found
it expedient to continue the office, and Mason used the alcalde system to great advantage. While some Californians
were retained and appointed as alcaldes, most were Americans and, ultimately, many were ex-volunteers. Their deci-
sions were closely supervised and sometimes reversed by Colonel Mason, who defined the function of the office in a letter
to Alcalde Lilburn W. Boggs in Sonoma in June 1847:

In the present condition of affairs in California, the alcaldes are not
"authorities of California", nor are they Mexican authorities. They
are civil magistrates of California, and are therefore the "authorities
of California" within their respective jurisdictions, subject to removal
from office by the authority of the Governor, and from the circumstances which the country is at present placed, and that must necessarily be so.[1]

Under Colonel Mason the military forces and alcalde-
appointees generally worked very closely together. An exception involving Alcalde Boggs in Sonoma revealed how rapidly
some of the volunteers developed loyalties to a region. Before
General Kearny left for the East he had appointed Boggs, an
ex-governor of Missouri, as alcalde of Sonoma. When the
previous alcalde refused to give up the office or its records,
Colonel Mason wrote to Captain Brackett of Company C on
June 2, 1847, ordering him to seize the records and to install
Boggs as alcalde. According to the *Memoirs* of William T.
Sherman, then a first lieutenant of artillery and Colonel
Mason's acting assistant adjutant general, Captain Brackett
did not carry out the order because of the "delicacy of his
situation." The people of Sonoma were in turmoil over the
incident, and although Brackett had been in the town only
two months, he had started putting down roots. Sherman
wrote that he took care of the problem himself by riding to
Sonoma, kidnapping the previous alcalde by night, and deliv-
ering some unequivocal orders from Mason to Captain
Brackett.[2]

In the early summer of 1847 there was no church in San Francisco. On May 8 the regimental chaplain, Rev. Thaddeus M. Leavenworth, an Episcopalian, urged the organization of a church and the erection of a building.[3] In a week's time a Sunday school was formed and Leavenworth addressed its first meeting, which was conducted by Private John H. Merrill of Company K as superintendent. It met regularly every Sunday forenoon in the office of the alcalde.[4] In the autumn Leavenworth assumed the first of the municipal positions he was to occupy for the next two years. On October 2, by appointment of Governor Mason, he became second (or assistant) alcalde, and a year later was elected first alcalde.

Town lots were available in San Francisco at this time, and a number of the volunteers stationed there bought them. Beach and water lots, which General Kearny had conveyed to the town in March, were auctioned in July 1847, and nearby in the town a nominal price of $12 or $25 would buy a lot of fifty or one hundred *varas* (a vara is somewhat less than a yard). In an appendix to the fifth volume of his *History of California*, Bancroft included a list of all property owners at the end of 1847. By then more than a dozen volunteers had purchased property.

Captain Dimmick in San Francisco and Captain Shannon, in Monterey, both lawyers, continued to practice their profession by appearing as attorneys in cases before the alcaldes— but not for long. Colonel Mason's reaction was swift and his judgment clear. On August 16, 1847, he delivered an order:

All officers, non commissioned officers and privates of the Army, serving in this Department, are strictly forbidden to take part as Attorney, Counsellor or Advocate in any criminal or civil suit, before an Alcalde, or any civil tribunal that is or may be established in this country.[5]

Even without professional work, Captain Dimmick was busy. His Company K and Captain Frisbie's Company H were steadily improving the presidio buildings, roads, and fortifications, and a number of men from each company were required for the Quartermaster's Department. Then there were the ubiquitous reports. One of General Kearny's first orders in California had concerned regimental and company rolls, returns, and musters, to which he enjoined special attention so that the records at Monterey and Washington would be complete. There were detailed monthly returns requiring full explanations of transfers, deaths, desertions, and services of detached units. Every two months a complete company muster roll was required with a written statement citing order numbers for all changes since the last muster. Another monthly report required the identification and explanation of charges for all men arrested and confined. A special form was needed for all deserters. In addition, there were both monthly and quarterly ordnance reports; regular reports on hospital stewards, matrons, and cooks; and acknowledgment of the dozens of orders that originated monthly in Monterey and Los Angeles. Dimmick did not enjoy the paperwork, but like all the officers he was careful about it. (Sherman, in Monterey, would reject reports with the slightest error.)

Dimmick filled letters to his wife with descriptions of his activities and also kept a daily diary, of which only a fragment is known to exist.[7] His diary, however, is an excellent record for the period it covers, his comments spare and pointed. Unlike Major Hardie, Captain Frisbie, and the other officers at the presidio, Dimmick was not social. Invited to parties and balls, he invariably refused. His little spare time was spent hunting, and his evenings reading. On July 18, 1848, he entered in his diary that he had finished *The Confessions of an English Opium Eater*; the next day he "read Warriors of the Genesee by W. H. C. Hosmer"; and the following day his choice was "Charcoal Sketches by Neil." No comments were included. On July 25 his response was "Good"; the night before he had finished *The Vicar of Wakefield*.[8] Dimmick sent most of his salary home to his wife in Norwich with instructions for putting any surplus out at interest. Although not a church-goer, he showed himself a rather narrow Protestant, a point of view he was to change in California. On Good Friday and Easter, April 21 and 23, Dimmick reported with scarcely concealed disapproval that the Catholic population had great doings at the Mission Dolores. On July 30 he noted: "Maj Hardie goes every Sabbath to the Heathen Catholic Church. He is now called by the soldiers the 'pious papist'."[9]

In Monterey Sergeant Vincent was seeing something of the Catholic church at close range for the first time, and his reaction was altogether different from that of Dimmick. Two weeks after Company I arrived in Monterey Vincent reported: "Was present at the Christening of two infants at the Catholic (and only church in the place) Church at which the band of our Reg't was present and played."[10] As a spectator, Vincent regularly went to functions at the church—marriages, christenings, and funerals. In June and July he reported two "singular" ceremonies. The first, on June 3, was Corpus Christi, although he did not identify it as such, and he thought the "performance" and procession "tasty and beautiful in the extreme."[11] On July 11 he reported in detail the celebration of what he amusingly called "St. Rebecca's Day," which was, in fact, the external solemnity of the feast of the Patroness of

Formerly Spanish and later Mexican capital of California, Monterey, after military seizure and occupation by the United States, became headquarters of the Tenth Military Department of the U.S. Army, 1847-1850. This drawing was "taken on the spot" in 1848 by Pvt. William Redmond Ryan of Company D and used to illustrate his two-volume *Personal Adventures in Upper and Lower California in 1848-9*, published in London in 1850.

California, Nuestra Señora del Refugio. Company I was present, invited by "The Padre" to fire a salute. Thus the military and ecclesiastical authorities cooperated, and Vincent was wide-eyed and open-minded at all the novelty. As Vincent penetrated the exotic exterior of life in Monterey and established friendships outside the regiment, he wrote less and less in his journal. Late in November he stopped keeping it altogether.

Company I remained on duty at Monterey until January 1848 when they were ordered to San Diego, leaving only Company D of the regiment in Monterey. Back from their Indian expedition, Company D had spent the late summer of 1847 on unusual duty for Colonel Mason. Captain Naglee had been detailed to settle, by force of arms if necessary, the uncomfortable squatter situation on some of the mission lands. American immigrants were taking up residence on any vacant piece of land and could not seem to understand that much of the land along the coast and in the northern valleys had already been legally granted. The American objection to land possession without land use was evident. Many of the volunteers in their journals commented on the utter neglect of the soil, which seemed to them outrageous and probably immoral; the land was certainly inviting. The alcalde of Monterey, Walter Colton, who also had to deal with this problem of squatters, left an anecdote which perfectly reveals the American attitude:

A woman, from our western border, who had drifted into California over the mountains . . . walked into my office this morning, and rather demanded, than invoked, a decree, that her husband might cut timber on the lands of Senor M———. I asked her if her husband had rented the land. "No." If he had any contract or agreement with the owner. "No." "Why then, my woman, do you claim the right of cutting the timber?" "Right, sir!" she exclaimed; "why, have we not taken the country?" I told her it was true, we had taken the country; but we had not taken the private land titles with it: she seemed to think that was a distinction without a difference.[12]

Company D effectively removed squatters from the lands around the missions at San Jose, Santa Clara, and San Luis

Obispo and then was ordered on another Indian expedition, to the lower San Joaquin Valley and the Sierra. On this tour Captain Naglee himself shot two Indians, for which he was arrested and confined on his return to Monterey in December. Word of Naglee's arrest reached Los Angeles in early January and did not surprise Hollingsworth, who wrote that "his conduct has been disaproved [sic] of by all—in fact his whole course since he has been in California has been marked by cold blooded acts of cruelty—"[13] The captain's action put Colonel Mason in a difficult situation. Naglee did not deny the "executions," as he called them, which he thought justified, and there were no witnesses as the parley with the two Indians and the shootings had taken place just out of sight of the company.[14] Mason held Naglee in arrest until late February 1848, when he was released to conduct his company and a body of new recruits to Lower California.[15] In short order he was in trouble again.

By February 22, 1848, two ships had arrived in Monterey carrying recruits then numbering 187. Captain James Turner, who had returned to New York from Rio de Janeiro, enrolled some two hundred recruits for the regiment in the late spring and early summer of 1847. Once the recruits were assembled on Governors Island, Turner resigned his commission. In late August these men sailed for California in two detachments: one from Philadelphia on the *Isabella*, under the command of Lieutenant Thomas J. Roach; the other from New York on the *Sweden* under Lieutenant Thomas E. Ketchum.

In October 1847 Stevenson had written Lieutenant Sherman to report his receipt of "a private letter from the Secretary of War" informing him that about two hundred recruits had sailed during the summer. Stevenson asked that the companies in Los Angeles "be filled up and the remainder receive their proportion—for the reason that their services are more apt to be required here than elsewhere."[16] At that time Stevenson was right about the needs of the various companies, but the situation had changed by late February 1848. In Lower California Lieutenant Colonel Burton with

Companies A and B had been under attack, had seen considerable action, and needed reinforcing. Thus Mason's disposition of the recruits was 71 to Los Angeles, 114 to Lower California.[17]

On the arrival of these recruits and the fifty men of Captain Naglee's company, Burton took the offensive in Lower California. By the end of April the opposition leaders had been captured and resistance stilled among the Mexicans. On the twelfth of that month, Captain Naglee had distinguished himself again—ordering the execution of a Californian and an Indian prisoner without consulting his superior officer or convening a council of war. On receipt of a report from Burton on Naglee's exercise of authority, Colonel Mason ordered Naglee's arrest and removed him from command. He also ordered Burton to make public in Lower California and the western provinces of Mexico the U.S. Army's official disapproval of Naglee's conduct.[18] When Companies A, B, and D returned to Alta California in mid-October 1848, Captain Naglee was under arrest.

NOTES

1. Theodore Grivas, *Military Governments in California* (Glendale, California: The Arthur H. Clark Company, 1963), 177.
2. William T. Sherman, *Memoirs*, 2 vols., (New York: Charles L. Webster & Company, 1875), vol. 1, 57-58. Brackett later settled in Sonoma, representing that district in the first California State Legislature in 1849-50.
3. *The California Star*, May 8, 1847.
4. *Ibid.*, May 22.
5. Col. R. B. Mason: DGO No. 46, Aug. 16, 1847, RG 94, NA.
7. Dimmick, "Diary," April 16 to Oct. 23, 1848.
8. *Ibid.*, July 18 to 25.
9. *Ibid.*, July 30. Dimmick and his considerably younger— and unmarried—superior, Major Hardie, did not seem to have an amicable relationship. On June 29 Dimmick entered the following: "Maj Jim Hardie . . . ordered government horses for his spanish hores to ride out to see him."
10. Vincent, "Log-Book," April 15, 1847.
11. *Ibid.*, June 3.

12. Walter Colton, *Three Years in California* (New York: A. S. Barnes & Co., 1850), 227-28.

13. Hollingsworth, *Journal*, 39-40.

14. Ryan, *Personal Adventures*, vol. 1, 130-35.

15. Mason: DGO No. 16, Feb. 25, 1848; Orders No. 17, Feb. 28, 1848; RG 94, NA.

16. Stevenson, Los Angeles, to Sherman, Monterey, October 19, 1847, RG 393, NA. The full number for a company had been changed by General Scott's General Orders No. 14 and No. 17 of 1847, authorizing volunteer companies to increase their strength to one hundred privates. Colonel Mason and, in turn, Colonel Stevenson received this information during the forepart of October.

17. Mason: DGO No. 16, Feb. 25, 1848, RG 94, NA. Two musicians were assigned to Company F in Santa Barbara, to account for the total of 187. Colonel Mason had already sent Major Hardie from San Francisco to Oregon to recruit 800 men for the relief of the American forces in Lower California. Hardie returned in late April without having been able to muster a single volunteer. (Bancroft, *History of California*, vol. 7, 446.)

18. Mason: DGO No. 39, June 15, 1848, RG 94, NA.

Chapter Twelve

Fraternity in the South

COLONEL MASON, in his final report to the adjutant general of the army on conditions and military activities in both Californias during 1847 and 1848, commended the volunteers in Lower California who, "under the command of Lieutenant Colonel Burton, routed the enemy, completely dispersed them, and restored peace to the peninsula."

In the same report, but in a different vein, he cited Colonel Stevenson for his service in southern California. From Colonel Mason—the man Sherman called "the very embodiment of the principle of fidelity to the interests of the general government"[1]—such praise was extravagant:

Colonel J. D. Stevenson, since April, 1847, has been in command of the district of country embracing Santa Barbara, Los Angeles, and San Diego, has by energy and good management, maintained most excellent discipline amongst his men, and has preserved harmony amongst the population of that district, which is composed mostly of the native Californians. This required peculiar tact and firmness— qualities possessed by him in a peculiar degree. I will warrant that at no previous time in that district were life and property so secure, the magistrates of the country so effectually supported, and industry so encouraged, as during the past two years. . . . Subalterns and men are entitled to share with their commander the honor due for this creditable state of feeling on the part of a people nominally conquered.[2]

While something of Mason's enthusiasm was doubtless due to his pleasure of being relieved of a vexing command, it was still true that Stevenson had done a creditable job.

In May 1847 Colonel Stevenson had settled down to the administration of the Southern Military District and to the continued administration of his then far-flung regiment. Methodical perhaps best describes his manner of command. If undistinguished except for propriety, his conduct of duties proved the New York critics wrong. The so-called "political adventurer" turned out to be scrupulous to a fault, with copies of *Army Regulations* and *The Rules and Articles of War* always handy. He was second in command in California and cherished the responsibility.

In late May Stevenson ordered work continued on the earthwork fortification being built on the hill overlooking Los Angeles, assigning to this project most of the New York Volunteers, the Mormons, and the available dragoons. The enlistment of the Mormon Battalion would expire in July, and Stevenson secured an agreement that the officers of the battalion would advise him by June 15 if the unit would re-enlist. When the time came, the Mormons decided that they would not. In San Diego Stevenson ultimately secured the re-enlistment of one company but for only six months. Most of the Mormons started for Utah, reducing the forces in southern California by about 250 men.

By July 4 the fort at Los Angeles was completed and was dedicated to one of Kearny's dead at San Pasqual. In one of the daylong ceremonies so dear to the colonel, the Declaration of Independence was read in Spanish and English; the colonel himself gave a speech; and the regimental band played martial and patriotic music. The day ended with a splendid ball given by the officers of the regiment at which the elite of Los Angeles were present, including the wives of Generals Flores, Carrillo, and Andrés Pico.[3]

During the balance of the year and into the next, there was considerable tension, and periodic alarms of Mexican invasion were issued. American control of the area was tightened. It was clearly understood that the United States would never give up California, and the prominent families of Los Angeles accepted the military occupation. Hollingsworth's journal for the last six months of 1847 and the first six months of 1848 is a record of constant social activities, with parties, balls, and fandangos almost every evening. On New Year's Eve Colonel Stevenson gave a ball for selected officers and townspeople which Hollingsworth pronounced "the most elegant affair I have ever seen in California—the supper splendid, the people here had never seen the like before."[4]

The colonel was especially anxious to make a good impression New Year's Eve because of the misconduct of one of his officers a few nights before. The night of December 27 Hollingsworth was at a party, as usual, when he was ordered by Colonel Stevenson to take command of the guard. He described the trouble that ensued:

I went to the guard house and found that the officier [sic] of the guard had been placed under arrest for getting drunk and raising the devil generally—I had been there but a few moments when I heard a great noise in the street and was informed that Lieut V[ermeule] was drunk, and trying to break into a store. I then received orders from the officer of the day to arrest him—I proceeded to do so, found him full of fight, knocked him down and had a general row with him.[5]

Colonel Stevenson requested a general court-martial on December 28, which was ordered by Colonel Mason on January 15 and was held on February 4 in Los Angeles. Second Lieutenant Vermeule was charged with neglect of duty, violation of the forty-fifth article of war (being found "drunk on his guard"), highly unofficerlike conduct, and breach of ar-

rest. While officer of the guard, he had left the guardhouse
and was later found drunk. Ordered to his quarters in arrest,
Vermeule still had a great thirst and made a serious error in
judgment. The specification speaks for itself:

[Second Lieutenant Thomas H. Vermeule] . . . did go to the store of
Mr. Haight known as the sutler's store & behave in an unbecoming
manner by attempting to force open the door of said store & using
highly improper language towards the family of Don Abel Stearns,
the owner & occupant of a part of the house in which said store is viz
Old Don Abel, meaning Mr Stearns I can lick him God damn him,
he is a pimp & his women are pimps too, or words to that effect, &
further did resist the new officer of the day 2nd Lieut
Hollingsworth.[6]

Vermeule pleaded guilty and was sentenced "to be cashiered,"
which sentence was carried out at the end of February after
the findings of the court had been confirmed.[7]

Vermeule had not chosen his man well in thus confront-
ing Abel Stearns, and he must have known it. In all southern
California few men were richer or more influential and none
was more critically important to the success of the occupation
there. Abel Stearns was Massachusetts born, had been naturalized in Mexico in 1828, and had resided in California for
almost twenty years. He had been of great assistance to Consul Larkin and was a foe of Mexico and a friend of the United
States. His "women" were his wife Arcadia and her sister
Isidora, ultra-respectable daughters of Juan Bandini, San
Diego's wealthiest and leading citizen; they were the belles of
Los Angeles. Vermeule would meet Abel Stearns again when
both were delegates to the constitutional convention in Monterey in 1849.

In spite of an occasional unpleasant incident, the conduct
of Stevenson's forces in Los Angeles was generally good. The
court-martial record is not so admirable as that of the Mormons, but better than that of the dragoons. Stevenson took
prompt action against offenders, as rapidly as communication
would permit.

Communication between the capital in Monterey and the
various posts in California was a constant problem from

March to September 1847, as it was efficient only from the north to the south. A ship could reach the port of Los Angeles from Monterey in less than twenty-four hours, but, because of the prevailing currents, the same ship could not return to Monterey in less than two weeks. In August 1847 Colonel Mason completed plans for an express mail service between San Francisco and San Diego. For the next year volunteers carried California's mail, personal as well as official. Six or eight volunteers were detailed as mail riders, and volunteers maintained forage depots and relays of horses in camps about fifty miles apart. Six-day mail service between Monterey and Stevenson's headquarters in Los Angeles was thus provided by way of Carmel Valley, Captain Dana's ranch (present-day Paso Robles), Santa Ynez, Santa Barbara, and San Buenaventura.

Stevenson's duties took him rather regularly to Santa Barbara, where Captain Lippitt had his problems. That Francis Lippitt, the cultivated captain of Company F, and his two "gentlemen" lieutenants should have been permanently posted in Santa Barbara was fitting. A large town of about one thousand inhabitants, of whom no more than a dozen were Americans, Santa Barbara was the seat of the Californian aristocracy. The town was also headquarters for the large and powerful de la Guerra and Carrillo families, whose attitude was one of passive hostility. They had actively opposed the American conquest. Lieutenant Colonel Burton and Captain Lippitt found the doors to the best houses closed to them, including that of Captain José Antonio de la Guerra y Noriega, their Mexican predecessor as commandant of the Santa Barbara presidio.[8]

For Company F there was no such welcome as other companies found in Sonoma and San Francisco, Monterey and Los Angeles. The volunteers were decidedly unwelcome and their presence resented. They, in turn, harbored resentment and were difficult to manage. But well before peace was proclaimed and the men were mustered out in September 1848, Company F and the Santa Barbareños were working closely together.

From his first superficial observation on arrival in Santa Barbara in April 1847, Lieutenant Colonel Burton reported the place very quiet and the inhabitants kindly disposed. The men of his command were quiet and orderly, too, he was happy to report.[9] Both appearances were deceptive, but the disciplinary problems Burton had to handle were minor. Most of them involved nothing more than volunteers galloping their horses or playing ball in the streets or discharging their muskets in disobedience of orders. Undoubtedly, the presence of the lieutenant colonel, able to order a garrison court-martial on the spot, had good effect. The three companies made a sizable and impressive force.

Early in July when Burton sailed for Lower California, however, imminent attack began to be rumored. Captain Lippitt had only sixty-six men and appealed for help, but Colonel Mason could not send reinforcements. Lippitt took measures—doubling the guard, issuing extra ammunition, and keeping the men on the alert. He also arrested and confined a private who, while on patrol, was charged with setting fire to an Indian village on the outskirts of Santa Barbara. Three friends of the man sought his release. When Lippitt refused, they threatened to free the man themselves. Lippitt dispassionately released the prisoner and sent couriers to Colonel Mason and to Colonel Stevenson reporting mutiny. By the time Colonel Mason arrived there was further trouble. Volunteers on patrol were raiding orchards, breaking into buildings, and assaulting Californians on the streets.

Colonel Mason arrived in Santa Barbara on the sloop-of-war *Dale* and on July 30 ordered a general court-martial which met the next day, with Colonel Stevenson as president. The three mutinous privates were found guilty. Two were sentenced to three months' and one to four months' hard labor at the Monterey redoubt, with the loss of all pay for that period. Still in Santa Barbara on August 2, Colonel Mason confirmed the findings and sentences.[10]

On August 1, the day after the general court-martial, the first military commission to be convened in California met to try volunteers charged with offenses against Californians and

Indians. Colonel Mason had read in the *New Orleans Picayune* General Winfield Scott's General Orders No. 20, dated February 19, 1847, at Tampico. These orders created military commissions to try members of the United States forces charged with offenses against inhabitants of occupied territory and to try Mexicans and Indians for offenses against individuals of the American forces. On July 27 Colonel Mason had declared Scott's General Orders to be in full force and effect in California.[11]

Colonel Stevenson was president of this first military commission. Not one of the five men charged with setting fire to the Indian village could be convicted. None would testify against another. In reviewing the findings of the commission, Colonel Mason showed his indignation:

A combined outrage has been committed upon poor, helpless indians by American soldiers, and the facts are concealed by a combined understanding of a body of men, entrusted by their government with carrying the name of freedom and justice to a new country peopled by a race to whom we desire to give laws and morals.[12]

Mason urged the men to reflect upon the severe injury they had done the service and ordered future good conduct. To help ensure that good conduct, Mason had already issued an order allowing Captain Lippitt to organize garrison courts-martial when necessary.

By August 11 more offenses had been committed against the inhabitants of Santa Barbara and two offenses by Californians against individuals of Lippitt's command. In the latter cases Lippitt had sent the volunteer complainants before the alcalde of Santa Barbara, Don Pablo de la Guerra, but received no satisfaction. The alcalde, Lippitt explained, was using Mexican law and "had accordingly allowed the accused to disculpate themselves in part, if not altogether, by their own testimony." The result of all this was clear, Lippitt the attorney wrote:

If the Californians were to be tried for offences against the soldiers by one code, and the soldiers, for offences against the Californians, by another, great injustice would ensue; for a soldier would often be punished when a Californian would escape. This could not but tend to produce and keep up a state of feeling among the troops towards the inhabitants highly important, for the sake of the inhabitants themselves, to be avoided.[13]

The solution Lippitt suggested was to have the garrison courts-martial clothed as military commissions. But Colonel Mason could not grant that power, Sherman wrote in reply. The governor depended on Lippitt's "personal exertions" to reconcile the feelings of animosity existing between the citizens of Santa Barbara and the volunteers.[14]

Lippitt resorted to still stricter discipline and further efforts to establish good relationships with the prominent Californians in the town. In both he was successful, and the mutinous conduct ceased. Offenses commonly committed by the men were seldom more serious than drunkenness and were usually routine offenses, such as trifling on guard or absence from drill. While Lippitt continued to find Don Pablo de la Guerra formidable as alcalde, he continued to send volunteers before him when there were complaints. Lippitt often supplied a Spanish translation of pertinent United States statutes or paragraphs of military law. A mutual respect slowly developed between the two men. By the holidays in December, Lippitt was an invited guest in the de la Guerra house.[15]

Lippitt was still more successful in his relationships after Don Pedro C. Carrillo was appointed collector of the port for Santa Barbara. Educated in Honolulu and Boston, Carrillo was the one pro-American in his family and commanded perfect English. Early in February 1848 Carrillo was appointed first alcalde by Governor Mason. Thereafter, relations were so good that Lippitt began issuing orders reinforcing ordinances passed by the alcalde.[16]

On February 21 Lippitt issued special orders. During the night a band of hostile Indians had appeared and stolen a large number of horses owned by townspeople. The alcalde requested a detachment of men to assist in their capture, and Lippitt immediately detailed Second Lieutenant Huddart and ten men to accompany the alcalde and the mounted Californians.[17] Captain Lippitt even supplied Carrillo, on request, with 150 rounds of musket cartridges for the citizens. Six months before, the alcalde would not have asked, nor would Lippitt have complied.

In writing to Colonel Mason on March 9, Lippitt commended Carrillo for performing his duties in "a fearless and independent manner. . . . His zeal and energy as a Magistrate," Lippitt declared, "would be conspicuous in any of our cities at home."[18]

A critical report on Lippitt's men had undoubtedly reached Colonel Mason, for on the same day, March 9, Lippitt also wrote to de la Guerra and to Carrillo asking for their impressions of the "general behavior and state of discipline for the last three months, so far as you have had the opportunity of judging." The occasion, he explained, was some "misrepresentations having been made to his Excellency Col. R. B. Mason relative to the behavior of the troops at this Post."[19]

De la Guerra's reply, in Spanish, came the same day:

I perceive with regret by your letter of this date that unfavorable reports have been made to His Excellency Col. R. B. Mason respecting the conduct of the company under your command at this post. In answer to your note I state that the deportment as well of the officers as of the troops has been during the last three months unexceptionable with respect to the people in general.

I hope, Sir, that this testimony may serve in part proof to His Excellency Col. R. B. Mason, and to banish from his mind the false idea which vicious reports have caused him to entertain to the discredit of your command.[20]

Carrillo was still more specific. He was surprised that the troops could possibly be held in disrepute; he personally had seen nothing untoward. "In fact," he wrote,

it has been a matter of astonishment to me as well as all others I converse with here, how soldiers placed in the midst of a people of different language, habits, customs, &c. could behave in the exemplary manner which has invariably characterized the Officers and men at this Post, and I feel proud of the opportunity offered to testify to their good conduct, and the cordial and universal good feelings existing between them and the resident citizens of this town.

I will venture to say that the same feeling to the same extent does not exist at any other Post in the country.[21]

Carrillo cited the good conduct of the detachment that had helped him recover the stolen horses and commented on the recent celebration of Washington's Birthday "which was attended by nearly every citizen of the place" without riot, drunkenness, or any unhappy impressions. He concluded:

As the Chief Magistrate of this place, I observe with pleasure the happy influences resulting from such instances as these, which are tending to create a kindred spirit and are cementing stronger and stronger the bonds of friendship, sociability, and proper feeling between Americans and our people. . . . I am sure the sentiments expressed herein coincide with the views of every prominent Citizen.[22]

Of the two letters the more impressive is the simple statement of the formerly reluctant de la Guerra, who had been in Santa Barbara during the turbulent summer of 1847. Carrillo had not, but his comments about the kindred spirit that did exist were correct. James Lynch of Company F summed up the change in attitude in one sentence: "By degrees, the people of Santa Barbara got to like us, and fraternize with us." Fortunately, the volunteers reciprocated. Lynch thought he knew what accounted for the change: "They saw that our occupation of the country meant an end to the eternal discords and revolutions which had been a curse to their fair land."[23]

From April through July all these good feelings were tested by the famous case of the Santa Barbara gun. On the night of April 5 a six-pound cannon belonging to the brig *Elizabeth* disappeared from the beach in Santa Barbara. All efforts of Lippitt and Santa Barbara officials to find it were unsuccessful. On May 21 Colonel Mason imposed a military contribution of $500 on the town to be paid by a capitation of two dollars on every adult male. It was to be collected by Captain Lippitt and Colonel Stevenson between June 25 and July 1, if the gun had not been recovered by that time.[24] Since this military contribution was the first imposed in California,

Lippitt and Stevenson used great care in its collection. While some indignation was expressed, the tax was collected.

In the midst of the excitement over the gun, most of the citizens of Santa Barbara turned out to celebrate the Fourth of July with Colonel Stevenson and Company F. For this occasion Stevenson had prudently ordered the band from Los Angeles.[25] The tension ended on August 7 when Colonel Mason ordered Captain Lippitt to turn over the sum collected in payment for the gun, $500.50, to the alcalde for use as a Santa Barbara municipal fund.[26] The same day Colonel Mason issued a more important document, the proclamation announcing the end of the war and the ratification of the treaty of peace.

A week before, in a simple entry on one of his monthly forms, Captain Lippitt had reported two young privates (one a hatter and one a chainmaker in civilian life) as deserters. With their possessions, but without the many months' pay due them, they had "Gone Northward," Lippitt entered under "Remarks." Now they would be gold seekers. In mid-July news of the immense richness of the mineral region had reached Santa Barbara.

NOTES

1. Sherman, *Memoirs*, vol. 1, 64.
2. Clark, *The First Regiment of New York Volunteers*, 73-74, R. B. Mason, Monterey, to R. Jones, Washington, n.d.
3. J. Gregg Layne, "Annals of Los Angeles," *California Historical Society Quarterly*, XIII (1934), 304-5.
4. Hollingsworth, *Journal*, 38.
5. *Ibid.*, 37-38.
6. Mason: DGO No. 14, Feb. 18, 1848, RG 94, NA.
7. The significance of this incident to the members of the court-martial is seen in the harsh sentences they delivered the same day. A private found intoxicated on guard, who would normally have been sentenced to the loss of a month's pay and allowances, was sentenced "To be confined 30 days in a solitary cell of the Guard House & to be made to walk Post No. 1 from 10 to 12 M & 2 to 4 P.M. each day of the thirty carrying a forty eight lb weight (48 lb) on his back being fed during that time on bread & water & to be con-

fined to hard labor in the Guard House with a 24 lb ball attached to his leg by a chain for 30 days more." A private who refused to button his coat when ordered was confined to the guardhouse for six months at hard labor—with the inevitable twenty-four-pound ball attached.

8. Lippitt, *Reminiscences*, 70.
9. Burton, Santa Barbara, to Turner, Monterey, April 10, 1847, RG 393, NA.
10. Mason: DGO No. 41, Santa Barbara, Aug. 2, 1847, RG 94, NA.
11. Mason: DGO No. 36, July 27, 1847, RG 94, NA.
12. Mason: DGO No. 50, Aug. 21, 1847, RG 94, NA. He also threatened to put the entire company under oath in the event of a repetition and, if necessary, to try the men one by one for perjury.
13. Lippitt, Santa Barbara, to Sherman, Monterey, Aug. 11, 1847, RG 393, NA.
14. Sherman, Monterey, to Lippitt, Santa Barbara, Aug. 24, 1847, RG 393, NA.
15. Lippitt, *Reminiscences*, 72-83. Lippitt had a good background in French and Spanish, both of which he learned from private tutors in Providence. In a chapter on his youth Lippitt wrote that he had learned Spanish grammar and conversation from the Conde de las Casas in a private class of four during his sophomore year at Brown University. He perfected his French in the 1830s while attached to the American Legation in Paris.
16. Lippitt: DGO No. 9, Santa Barbara, Feb. 20, 1848, RG 94, NA.
17. Lippitt: Special Order No. 1, Santa Barbara, Feb. 21, 1848, RG 94, NA.
18. Lippitt, Santa Barbara, to Mason, Monterey, March 9, 1848, RG 393, NA.
19. Lippitt to Don Pablo de la Guerra, Santa Barbara, March 9, 1848, RG 393, NA. The same note was delivered to Don Pedro C. Carrillo. There is no evidence as to what the criticism was, although it may have concerned the men purchasing goods from vessels entering the port. Such trade was moderately permitted but not always strictly controlled.
20. Pablo de la Guerra to Lippitt, Santa Barbara, March 9, 1848, RG 393, NA.
21. Pedro C. Carrillo to Lippitt, Santa Barbara, March 10, 1848, RG 393, NA. Carrillo's letter was in English.
22. *Ibid.*
23. Lynch, *With Stevenson to California*, 20.
24. Mason: DGO No. 36, May 21, 1848, RG 94, NA.
25. Stevenson made splendid use of the regimental band. Ten

days after arrival in Los Angeles, in 1847, Hollingsworth commented generally on the band: "I think it is the best thing we brought
with us. . . . It is a great curiosity here . . . many come to hear it every
evening." (Hollingsworth, *Journal*, 26-27.)

26.   Bancroft, *History of California*, vol. 5, 587. Bancroft secured
a full account of the affair from José Antonio de la Guerra, one of
the five Californians who had stolen the gun. The cannon was discovered ten years later, buried in the sand some distance from
where it had disappeared. In commemoration of the theft and the
assessment, the people of Santa Barbara named two streets—Cañon
Perdido and Quinientos Pesos. The gun also appeared on the first
official seal of the city of Santa Barbara with the legend "Vale
Quinientos Pesos"—"Worth Five Hundred Pesos."

San Francisco, 1850

PART THREE

ISSUE

Chapter Thirteen

Peace and the Golden Lure

NEWS OF THE PEACE negotiations to end the war and confirmation of the rich gold deposits in the foothills of the Sierra Nevada reached San Francisco simultaneously in May 1848. One of the best records of the proximate effect of both is in the diary of Captain Kimball Dimmick at the Presidio of San Francisco. Because he was constantly loaning money at interest to his fellow officers (perhaps to help them settle gambling debts), the captain was most faithful to his diary. Even if he wrote no more than "Nothing worthy of note" or "Same as yesterday," he recorded something daily and was alert to what was happening in San Francisco and in the ranks of the regiment. Dimmick first mentioned gold on May 23. He reported that his men had worked on the fort all day, and then added, "Great excitement about the gold mines on the Sacramento [sic]." On May 25 he mentioned "great excitement" and on May 26 "the greatest excitement."[1]

The first discovery of gold was on January 24, 1848, near Coloma, where some of Sutter's men were constructing a sawmill. During the next few months the word spread slowly. There was considerable skepticism and, on the part of Captain Folsom, a notable mistake. When samples were shown to him in San Francisco, he pronounced the metal mica and reported as much to Colonel Mason.[2] But he, too, became a believer when he accompanied Mason to the gold regions in June and early July. Others took less convincing. Men with large quantities of gold appeared in San Francisco in mid-May; from that time gold talk was in the air. The effect of all this excitement is apparent in Dimmick's entry of May 28: "Last night about 18 men deserted for the purpose of working in the gold mines nine of them from my company."

On May 31, by way of the Sandwich Islands, came news of "the articles of peace made by Mr Trist at Mexico, also the Notice of Death of J Q Adams."[3] These articles of peace were in the *projet* for the Treaty of Guadalupe Hidalgo, signed February 2, 1848, by Nicholas Trist for the United States and by the Mexican commissioners. This treaty, once approved, would end the Mexican war. The news of the imminent end of the war, plus the presence of gold in San Francisco, had the expected effect on many of the volunteers. They were some of the first to fall victim to the malady that came to be known (with good reason) as "gold fever."

There had been some desertion from the regiment in California before the news of gold, but it had been modest considering the pre-California history of the unit. Only twenty-one men had deserted between March 1847 and May 1, 1848, and through 1847 the record of both the regulars and volunteers in California was substantially better than that of the American forces on the mainland of Mexico.[4] Deserters had few places to go, with companies of volunteers garrisoning most California towns, and these men were soon captured or, more often, voluntarily returned to their companies. Punishment was usually some months at hard labor and the loss of pay and allowances for six months or a year. Despite

threats by both General Kearny and Colonel Mason, no deserters in California were executed.

In his 1882 book on Stevenson's Regiment, Francis D.
Clark wrote very favorably of the volunteers' service record
after the gold discovery: "Although the temptation of earning hundreds of dollars per day in the mines instead of the
twenty-three cents received from the Government was almost
irresistible, still, to the honor of the command, few were the
number who deserted, preferring an *Honorable Discharge* and
EMPTY POCKETS to the *golden nuggets* and a *branded name*."[5]
Clark was right that the temptation was almost irresistible,
but, in his efforts to present the regiment in the best light, the
rest of his statement was in error.[6] There were more than a
few deserters.

Gold fever and desertion were greater in those companies closest to the gold region and much less evident in the
companies stationed in southern California. From Captain
Shannon's Company I in San Diego, completely out of the
mainstream, no desertion occurred, and on August 1 Captain
Lippitt reported only two deserters from Company F in Santa
Barbara during 1848.

In Los Angeles, Lieutenant Hollingsworth first reported
the wealth of the gold region on July 18, although the news
had arrived at least a week earlier. He reported that the men
were deserting rapidly (but in fact only six men from the
almost-full Companies E and G deserted between July 1 and
their discharge on September 18). Hollingsworth's entry of
July 18 also mentioned Thomas Vermeule. The night before,
he had been arrested. "We think he has been tampering with
the men," Hollingsworth wrote. "His object has been to injure
the Regiment all he could and raise a party for the gold mines
—these mines will be the ruin of the country."[7] Vermeule was
not charged, but simply urged to leave town, which he did.

By August Hollingsworth was using the common expres-
sion, reporting the "gold fever" raging, and on August 13
had some thoughts himself of leaving for the mines as soon as
he could. The next day he sat on a court-martial trying desert-

ers and reported Colonel Mason "very anxious to have some shot but he would not approve of shooting regulars and he will not get us to shoot volunteers—I for one will not vote for shooting."[8]

Stationed in Sonoma, directly on the favored land route to and from the Mother Lode, Company C felt the effects of the gold discovery most dramatically. On April 30, 1848, Captain Brackett had mustered sixty-three men. On July 30 he could muster but twenty-eight, most of the other thirty-five having deserted in early June. On June 1 Brackett appealed in desperation to Colonel Mason. "The infernal thirst for gold," Brackett complained, "seems to break down every barrier of duty conscience & obligation."[9]

The barriers were breaking down, it was true, from the certain end of the war as well as from the thirst for gold. Slightly amended, the *projet* for the Treaty of Guadalupe Hidalgo was approved by the United States Senate on March 10, and this news was received in California in June. The United States received New Mexico and Upper California— and clear title to the disputed territory between the Nueces and Rio Grande—for the payment of fifteen million dollars and assumption of certain claims against Mexico.

Both Companies H and K at San Francisco were hard hit by desertion, with twenty-one men leaving for the mines between May 24 and 28. On June 6 Captain Frisbie and a party of ten men left San Francisco for the gold regions in pursuit of deserters, on orders of Colonel Mason. Because there were still few people in the area, the search party had considerable success, rounding up both volunteers and regulars from Company F Third Artillery. On July 1 the first of that group of deserters were court-martialed in San Francisco. All were found guilty of desertion in time of war and received punishments equivalent to the sentence given Private Philip Brown of Company C:

To forfeit all pay that is now or may become due him, to receive (49) Forty nine lashes on his bare back well laid on with a raw hide, and to be marked on the left hip with the letter D one inch in length in indelible ink, and at the expiration of his enlistment to have his head shaved and to receive a dishonorable discharge and be drummed out of service.[10]

In approving the sentences of the court-martial, Colonel Mason could not refrain from remarking on their leniency. As examples, he felt the sentences

will not have the restraining influence which the occasion calls for. He [the Colonel Commanding] fears that misplaced kindness may cause hereafter much punishment which would never have been called for, had proper examples been used in the first instances. Court martials can now, if they will, stop desertions, and the Colonel Commanding is determined that no motive or reason shall influence him in shielding a deserter even from the punishment of death, if the Court will have the moral firmness to award such a sentence.[11]

Such sentences did not seem lenient to Captain Dimmick, and there was no chance that he would vote a punishment of death under the circumstances. During most of June and July, one court-martial followed another in San Francisco. Regular floggings may have slowed the rate of desertion, but by then the ranks were already depleted.[12]

On May 30, at Querétaro, Mexico accepted the modification of the Guadalupe Hidalgo treaty, and the war officially ended. By way of Lieutenant Colonel Burton in La Paz, that news reached Monterey on August 6. The next day Colonel Mason issued a proclamation formally announcing the treaty and its terms. From the new order of things he promised for California "a new destiny . . . internal tranquility . . . firm and stable government."[13] On August 8 Colonel Mason issued orders to Colonel Stevenson and Major Hardie, as well as to all post commanders, for the disbanding of the regiment.

First to be mustered out were Companies K and C at the presidio in San Francisco on August 15, followed by Company H on August 25. In late July Colonel Mason had ordered the remnant of Company C in Sonoma to exchange post with the more numerous Company H, a move that Captain Frisbie would not regret. During those two weeks in Sonoma he and his. brother Eleazar, a sergeant in Company

H, regularly enjoyed the company of two of the daughters of General Mariano G. Vallejo and later married them.

The people of Sonoma parted only reluctantly with Captain Brackett and the men of Company C, who had been stationed there for sixteen months. Writing to the *Californian*, an "Old Resident" of Sonoma was most complimentary. He—or she—wrote that much praise was due the members of Company C,

> not only for the military and soldier-like manner in which they have acquited themselves as a corps, but for their gentlemanly and orderly deportment, individually and collectively. We regret to part with them, and cannot let them go without expressing a hope that, when peace shall have been declared, their regiment disbanded, and their country no longer needs their services, they may have fallen sufficiently in love with our healthy climate and our beautiful valley to come back and settle.[14]

Many of the volunteers, after visiting the mines, did return to settle in the Sonoma and Napa valleys, including Captain Brackett.

In San Francisco, Captain Dimmick spent a busy month before leaving for the mines on September 18. Beginning in mid-July Dimmick had observed and noted the immense quantity of goods being sent up the Sacramento River. Once discharged, he lost no time in moving from the presidio into San Francisco, where he engaged in brisk buying and selling. At the same time he began performing legal services, writing deeds and trying suits, many of them for men formerly in his company. He was successful in this profession and very well paid. He also had time for civic responsibilities, on August 29 acting as one of the judges at the election of Dr. T. M. Leavenworth as first alcalde, and on September 16 attending a meeting to consider establishment of a public hospital. On September 19, with a stock of cloth and boots and "15 dozen palm leaf hats" purchased from a Hawaiian trader, Dimmick sailed for Sacramento. A week before, he had performed a symbolic act: he sold his sword and bought a knife. Dimmick was through with the military life.[15]

The four companies in southern California were mustered out in September by Captain Andrew J. Smith of the First Dragoons. Company F in Santa Barbara was discharged on September 8, Companies E and G in Los Angeles on September 18, and Company I in San Diego on September 25.

In Los Angeles Hollingsworth wrote just one line on August 17: "Received the first official news of Peace." With one more entry on August 23—"Commenced making preparations for the Gold mines"[16]—Hollingsworth put aside his journal for six months.

On August 20 Colonel Stevenson acknowledged Colonel Mason's proclamation and orders of August 7 and 8, and began the complicated operation of completing records on the regiment and closing the headquarters of the Southern Military District. By September 18, when Companies E and G were mustered out of the service, Stevenson had not only completed this assignment but had formed a remarkable organization for an assault on California's gold. When Hollingsworth resumed his journal in March 1849, he described Stevenson's group: there were former officers (Captain Taylor and Lieutenants Cutrell, Bonnycastle, Hollingsworth, and Williams), former enlisted men, Californians, and Indians—all with loaded carts, wagons, and pack animals. All were dressed in scarlet shirts bought in Los Angeles, and all, as it turned out, had different ideas of the best route to the mines. Long before reaching Santa Barbara, the group had come apart. Colonel Stevenson went on ahead to Monterey, there to be mustered out on October 26. It was November before he, Bonnycastle, and Hollingsworth were in the mines.

In mid-October the three companies from Lower California arrived in Monterey on the U.S.S. *Ohio*. On October 23 Companies A and B were mustered out, and on October 24 Company D. Company D had arrived under the command of First Lieutenant George Pendleton. The unit's former captain, Naglee, under arrest for the murder of the two prisoners, arrived in Monterey on the U.S. Navy ship *Warren*. For the second time, Naglee's extraordinary luck held. Since the prisoners were killed after the peace treaty had been signed and ratified by the U.S. Senate but before its final acceptance by Mexico, and since Lower California remained part of Mexico by the treaty's terms, Colonel Mason chose to dismiss the charges. He was probably wise to do so. The witnesses—and this time there were many—were quickly heading for the mines.

With mustering out, the military aspect of Polk's experiment with the regiment came to an end. For more than eighteen months the volunteers had provided the largest body of men available to Governors Kearny and Mason to preserve order. They had fought with distinction in Lower California, supplied a measure of control over hostile Indians, and presented a visible reminder to the Californians that the territory was occupied. In addition, they had performed dozens of prosaic and routine duties—building military installations, public buildings, and roads; carrying the mail; and policing the various towns. The experiment had been a success.

NOTES

1. Dimmick, "Diary," May 23-26, 1848.
2. Bancroft, *History of California*, vol. 6, 53.
3. Dimmick, "Diary," May 31, 1848.
4. The secretary of war reported on April 8, 1848, that desertions in Mexico to Dec. 31, 1847, numbered just under 5,000 men, about one-sixteenth of those serving there. (Jay, *Causes and Consequences of the Mexican War*, 283.)
5. Clark, *The First Regiment of New York Volunteers*, 20. Italics and capitals in original.
6. Clark's baseless statement has been accepted by some careful historians and by a number of uncritical ones. From personal experience between May and Oct., 1848, Clark knew nothing of desertion since he was with Company D in Lower California, and he made no effort to present the facts. Clark's partner for five years in a ferry service on the Stanislaus River, James Sirey, was a deserter from Company D before that body of men was sent to Lower California.

7. Hollingsworth, *Journal*, 45.

8. *Ibid.*, 47-48.

9. J. E. Brackett, Sonoma, to Mason, Monterey, June 1, 1848, RG 393, NA.

10. Mason: DGO No. 44, July 19, 1848, RG 94, NA.

11. *Ibid.*

12. For comparison, in Monterey (where no volunteers were serving), the great period of desertion came in July in Company F, Third Artillery. There were no desertions Jan. 1-April 1, 1848; two in April; one in May; none in June; twenty-one in July. (Source of this information is an unsigned, "List and Description of Deserters from the United States Army," undated but probably Aug. 5, 1848, RG 94, NA. The handwriting appears to be that of Lt. W. T. Sherman.) Recruits for Company F arrived in the early autumn on the *Huntress* but deserted as soon as they recovered from scurvy and were able to go to the mines. In September Colonel Mason began to grant furloughs of a month or two to the regular-army soldiers on their promise to return to duty, but the men took advantage of every opportunity to desert. (Bancroft, *History of California*, vol. 5, 520-21.) Bancroft thought more regulars than volunteers deserted since they could not look forward to an early discharge.

13. Richard B. Mason: "Proclamation of Peace," quoted in Bancroft, *History of California*, vol. 5, 591-92. Colonel Mason made known the cession of Upper California, the boundary, and some of the more important terms of the treaty. For one year, residents of California were to have a choice of citizenship. Property rights, including those of the church, were to be respected, and such Mexican land grants as were legitimate under Mexican law before May 13, 1846, were to be recognized.

14. *Californian*, Aug. 5, 1848.

15. Dimmick, "Diary," July-Sept., 1848.

16. Hollingsworth, *Journal*, 48.

Chapter Fourteen

At the Mines

I N THE FALL AND EARLY WINTER of 1848, almost every volunteer was a gold miner. They were everywhere, and in those first months the returns were high in the as-yet-uncrowded diggings. With rudimentary equipment, some men made strikes paying them two and three hundred dollars a day, and others even more. Not all fared so well, for forty- and fifty-dollar days were common. The average return in 1848 has been carefully estimated at approximately an ounce a day per man.[1] Even with gold at a low price, between six and eight dollars an ounce, the return in one day was a much as a volunteer private had been paid in salary for a month.

Most of the volunteers fanned out over the known gold region and into new areas. By the end of the year they were on the Trinity River in the north, the Tuolumne in the south,

"Our encampment this evening was cold and cheerless." A drawing by William Redmond Ryan in his *Personal Adventures* shows the ex-volunteers as argonauts, having partially adopted functional Mexican-California dress. Ryan, formerly private in Company D, spent some months in the "diggings" in 1848 and 1849. "*Serapas* [*sic*]," he wrote, "served the double purpose of beds by night and cloaks by day."

and everywhere in between. There were particular concentrations on the American, the Mokelumne, the Stanislaus, and the Tuolumne rivers. Bad weather and bad luck temporarily forced many men back to the newborn supply centers of Stockton, Sacramento, and Marysville, and to San Francisco and Monterey, but many wintered in the mines.[2]

Winter snows caught Stevenson, Hollingsworth, and Bonnycastle unprepared, encamped on the Mokelumne River. Although they were having reasonably good luck, they hastened to sell their supplies and return to the coast. In less than a month (according to Hollingsworth and to later reports by Stevenson), they had realized about $10,000, primarily by the sale of their goods. Most of the money belonged to Colonel Stevenson.[3] Were it not for the confirmation of Hollingsworth, who was in physical charge of the money for some weeks, the figure of $10,000 might well be dismissed as suspiciously round. In the one printed chapter of his reminiscences, Stevenson relates his experience in the mines: "I went to Mokelumne Hill, founded a town there and was the first alcalde. I resigned, and with $10,000 in gold dust, walked to Sutter's Fort, and thence to Sacramento."[4]

Of the three men, only Hollingsworth returned to the mines. The rest of the winter he spent in Monterey and in the spring set out with his own wagonload of goods for sale—clothing, tools, staple foods. Everything was lost when fire swept his camp in the foothills due east of Stockton. In August he picked up his journal again to enter a short and bitter note. He was resolved to return to Maryland and must do so a poor man. Unknown to Hollingsworth as he wrote, he had been elected a delegate to the convention to frame a constitution for California. When he did return east, it would be to Washington, D.C., as official bearer of that constitution.

If Hollingsworth made no fortune in the mines, he had found loyal and generous friends. One was George G. Belt, formerly a quartermaster sergeant in the regiment. Belt had been discharged on July 1, 1848, in Los Angeles and had gone straight to the mines with supplies. A storekeeper by trade, he soon settled in a promising spot recently named

Stockton. Founded in 1847 by Charles M. Weber, Stockton was the head of navigation from San Francisco on the San Joaquin River. The town was also directly on the land route to the mines from San Francisco by way of the Livermore Pass, and its position as a trade and supply center was thus assured.[5] Belt prospered.

Having heard of Hollingsworth's misfortune, Belt wrote him on July 7, 1849:

> *Dam the difference*, strike a hard blow—& make it up, you can easily do it, providing you dont get *discouraged*. I am at your service, any way that I can assist you will afford me pleasure, you can draw upon me at ten days sight for two or three thousand dollars, if you want it, or any amount of goods. I leave here tomorrow morning for San Francisco, is the reason I say ten days sight, for by that time I will be back from San Francisco. . . . Dont fail to make use of me, either you or any of your partners, so cheer up & laugh at your misfortunes, it can be easily be [sic] made up—[6]

Thus were the good spirits of George Belt, the twenty-three-year-old entrepreneur, well on his way to becoming a very wealthy man. But Hollingsworth was through.

Other volunteers interested in the certainty of business also settled in Stockton. The *Stockton Independent* of May 25, 1875, identified five of the seven earliest settlers as volunteers. They were, in addition to Belt, James Sirey of Company D, William Maxwell and Benjamin Whitehouse of Company B, and former Captain Nelson Taylor of Company E. Belt was elected first alcalde of Stockton in 1849, serving also in 1850, and lived in Stockton until his death in 1869. Nelson Taylor also achieved prominence there. A dentist by profession, Taylor spent a few months in the mines and then settled in Stockton as a trader and absentee owner of a ferry service on the Stanislaus River. He was elected a member of the first state legislature, a trustee of the first state insane asylum, and sheriff of San Joaquin County in 1854. In 1856 he returned to New York to begin the practice of law. He served as a brigadier general of New York Volunteers in the Civil War and represented a New York district in Congress in 1865 and 1866.[7]

Hollingsworth had at least given the gold fields two

chances to make him rich. Not so Colonel Stevenson or John Bonnycastle. Stevenson went directly to San Francisco and there found startling changes and some business opportunities very much to his taste. He perhaps had political ideas and ambitions, too, but his timing and the times were wrong. Bonnycastle, among many others, did not like the climate, the hard work, or the uncertainty of the mines. He went to Monterey and accepted a commission as lieutenant in the regular army, joining those volunteer officers who held regular U.S. Army commissions, every one of whom continued to serve without desertion.

Other volunteers chose to continue military careers. Lieutenant Colonel Burton resumed his rank as captain in the Third Artillery, Major Hardie that of lieutenant in the same regiment, both on duty in Monterey. Captain Marcy, with a U.S. commission from the beginning, remained in the army for a few years, as did Captain Folsom, who continued as assistant quartermaster and served at times as collector of the port in San Francisco. Captain Matthew Stevenson, who pointedly did not accompany his father to the mines, accepted duty with the regular army, and Dr. Robert Murray, who had held the rank of assistant surgeon in the regiment, was offered and accepted that rank in the regular army in Monterey.

The service of these men was decidedly welcome to Colonel Mason and Lieutenant Sherman in their trying circumstances, and, like Sherman, a number of them went on to distinguished military careers. Both Burton and Hardie served as brigadier generals in the Civil War, although neither had further significant California experience after the early 1850s. Because he had bought well-situated town lots in 1847 and had kept them, having their titles confirmed, Hardie became wealthy. The young army officer rose to be the inspector general of the United States Army.[8] Burton left only a fragmentary memoir of his New York Volunteer or California experiences and his official report cannot be located.[9] He had spent most of his duty with the regiment in Lower California and took as wife Doña Amparo Ruiz, a member of one of the prominent Mexican families of the peninsula. Like Burton, other volunteers also married into Californian families, many of them influential.[10]

Captain Marcy, after a visit to the mines with Alcalde Walter Colton of Monterey, served on active duty in Monterey until 1851. He seems then to have filled a number of political or semi-political positions: in 1849 secretary of the constitutional convention, in 1853 engrossing clerk of the California State Senate, and in 1861 a paymaster for the U.S. Navy.[11] Marcy made California his permanent home and died in Alameda in 1896.

Dr. Robert Murray, like Major Hardie, ultimately moved into the top ranks of the U.S. Army hierarchy. In private practice and just twenty-four years old when he joined the regiment as assistant surgeon, Murray was one of the most popular men in the regiment and a committed physician. With him on the *Susan Drew* he brought a substantial medical library and received packs of medical journals by every store-ship. Murray transferred into the regular army as assistant surgeon of Company F, Third Artillery, in Monterey and was in short order promoted to surgeon despite his youth. After duty in the East he served again in California at the Presidio of San Francisco from 1871 to 1874. In 1883 he became the surgeon general of the U.S. Army.[12] Murray was a highly literate person, and his letters to a colleague in Los Angeles (the regular-army assistant surgeon assigned to the dragoons) are considered important to medical historians for the light they throw on mid-nineteenth-century practices in field medicine. He wrote of almost nothing but his patients.

While their service at the time and their accomplishments later were impressive, those volunteers who continued to serve in the regular army were no more than a tiny fraction of the discharged volunteers. In 1848 and 1849 most of the men were involved in the search for gold or in supplying those who were prospecting. While numerous volunteers settled in Stockton, many headed for Sacramento and other supply centers. Captain Shannon chose Coloma, the already legendary place on the north fork of the American River where

James Marshall had picked up the first gold in January 1848. Opening a trading business there that prospered, Shannon also served as alcalde of the Coloma district. Colonel Mason himself had an interest in Coloma, he and Lieutenant Sherman holding shares in a general-merchandise store which returned Colonel Mason $1500 in short order on an investment of $500.[13]

Captain Dimmick set up a business just north of Coloma and spent late September and early October of 1848 selling goods to Indians and "Spaniards." On October 15 he entered an enigmatic note in his diary: "Attended the catholic Service with my Spanish friend on the mountains of the Serra Nuevarda [sic]."[14] California was obviously having its effect on the formerly anti-Catholic Dimmick. For eight days he wrote nothing, leaving no record of his profits or of his personal experience in gold gathering, which he doubtless tried. Then he left the mines and returned to San Francisco, his stock gone and his pockets presumably full. In a few weeks he was settled in San Jose with a law practice; on December 12 he was elected alcalde of San Jose for the ensuing year.

Some of the ex-volunteers, like Kimball Dimmick, spent only a few weeks or months in the diggings. A substantial number remained in the Mother Lode country the rest of their lives, and others spent at least a few years there. Former lieutenants Thomas Ketchum of Company B and George Pendleton of Company D are representative of those volunteers whose interest in remaining in California required them periodically to shift their pursuits. Ketchum, who arrived in California in February 1848 in charge of the recruit detachment on the *Sweden*, served in Lower California with Company B. On discharge late in October, Ketchum and Pendleton, friends from their Lower California service, headed for the southern mines and worked the tributary streams of the Tuolumne River at Woods Diggings and Jamestown Flat in the vicinity of Sonora (present-day Tuolumne County). Sonora was still a small settlement, having just been founded by a third friend, Hiram W. Theall, formerly a lieutenant in

Company D.[15] In mid-1849 Ketchum and Pendleton opened a general store at Jamestown, three miles from Sonora. At first they prospered and then settled down to do a good, steady business supplying the miners of the area with necessities.

The partnership continued until 1853, when Ketchum sold his interest to Pendleton and bought 320 acres of farming land in the San Joaquin Valley near Stockton. To this acreage he added 160 acres of bounty land, a Mexican War service benefit, and raised general produce and cattle. He served as captain of a volunteer company of the Third California Infantry in the Civil War and later served as a brigadier general of the state militia.[16] After the war he returned to the ranch and remained there until 1891. Then he moved into the city of Stockton, where he lived until his death in 1916 at the age of ninety-five.

George Pendleton operated the Jamestown store until 1854, when he sold it and moved to San Diego. There he married Concepción Estudillo and in 1857 became county clerk of San Diego County, holding that office until his death in 1871.

Among other volunteers who spent some years in the area on or near the Tuolumne River were former privates Walter Murray and James O'Sullivan, both of Company A and both printers by trade. In the mines from 1848 until 1852, they accumulated enough gold to purchase from Dr. Lewis Gunn the profitable and important Sonora *Herald*. Dating from July 1850, the *Herald* was the first of all the mining-town newspapers. It was printed on a press brought to California in 1834, the Ramage press used by Don Augustín Zamarano, California's first printer.[17] Murray and O'Sullivan jointly operated the Sonora *Herald* for almost two years.

In late 1853 they sold the journal and went their separate ways. Murray and his wife, Mercedes Espinosa of Sonora, settled in San Luis Obispo, where he entered the dual practice of journalism and the law, having had, by his report, three years of law study in his native England. In 1858 he was

elected assemblyman in the tenth session of the California
State Legislature and served as San Luis Obispo County supervisor, district attorney, and treasurer. He also founded
the San Luis Obispo *Weekly Tribune.* In 1873 Governor New-
ton Booth appointed Murray to a district judgeship for San
Luis Obispo and Santa Barbara counties, a position he held
until his death in 1875.[18]

As Murray moved into increasing spheres of responsibility, and conservatism, his former partner O'Sullivan, for most
of his working life a salaried printer on San Francisco newspapers, chose a radical course. He became a disciple of the
demagogue Denis Kearney, whose slogan was "The Chinese
must go!"; as a member of the Workingmen's Party, O'Sullivan was a delegate to California's second constitutional convention in 1878.

The departure of such men as Murray, O'Sullivan, Ketchum, and Pendleton from the mining area was part of a
greater exodus resulting from the changing circumstances of
the economy. Not only was the fascination over in many cases,
but the early days of picking up loose gold on the ground and
in streambeds were no more. The time was past when one or
two men sluicing could be reasonably assured of a living.
Fewer and fewer great strikes occurred as more and more
people came to the mines. Mining, and specifically gold mining, still employed more Californians than any other single
occupation as late as 1863, but by the mid-1850s elementary
placer and sluice mining by individuals had given way to
large-scale quartz mining involving heavy equipment and the
necessity of considerable capital.[19] It was decidedly unglam-
ourous. The Gold Rush was actually a series of rushes that
continued through the 1850s, however, and there was a large,
floating, prospecting population in which the initial fever
would not be relieved. The Fraser River Rush of 1858 in
British Columbia attracted numbers of Californians, including some volunteers. Other volunteers traveled to the Comstock Lode in Nevada; Hiram Theall left the Sonora area to
follow that lure and stayed in Nevada until his death at White
Pine in 1869.

Many volunteers perished during their search for gold. A large number (impossible to determine with any accuracy) died of disease or drowning, and it is not unreasonable to believe that many of those who left no record after desertion or discharge found their graves in the Sierra snows and rivers. Seventeen volunteers were known to have drowned, and their deaths are so reported in Bancroft's "Pioneer Register." Some volunteers were murdered by Indians or other prospectors. Roderick Morrison, the poet of the parody "Volunteer's Vision," had gone to the mines in the early spring of 1849 and was killed on Carsons Creek by Dr. Henry Freund, former private in Company D. An eyewitness account was left by Levi Stowell in his diary:

Thursday, April 26: . . . Lieut Morrison was shot last Eve by Dr. Friend [*sic*]. Morrison was intoxicated. the trial will be tomorrow. an unfortunate circumstance . . .
Friday, April 27: . . . Voorhies was made Coroner, in the case of Morrison. Mr. Friend was tried to day & acquitted & 30 days given to leave the mines.[20]

Freund had joined the regiment on April 6, 1847, sailed to California with the detachment of recruits on the *Isabella*, and served in Lower California. In 1859 James Lynch (former private in Company I) found Freund's grave in San Luis Obispo County. He had been murdered by Indians two years before.[21]

The "pioneer cemeteries" which dot the Mother Lode country, many of them on flats and hillsides where towns no longer exist, have a share of volunteers among the earliest burials. In a striking number of cases the dead volunteer is identified on tombstone or marker as "of Stevenson's Regiment," his membership already a distinction in the early 1850s, in most cases the greatest or only distinction in a short life.

Of the 836 volunteers, many remained in the gold country through the early 1850s, and at least 80 stayed there for the rest of their lives, leaving a record of some kind, if often no more than an obituary.[22] In many cases, because the volunteer had come to California before the Gold Rush, and because he had been a member of the regiment, he enjoyed a kind of celebrity, particularly if he lived to an advanced age. A fair example is Samuel W. Pearsall, who mined on the Mokelumne River at Big Bar in November 1848 before the settlement of Mokelumne Hill. A native of New York City, Pearsall was a drayman of twenty-six when he joined the regiment on September 14, 1846, not long before its sailing. Private Pearsall served with Company B in Lower California, was discharged with his company in Monterey on October 23, 1848, and went straight to the mines. He remained in the area of Mokelumne Hill thereafter and never married.

Samuel Pearsall's name did not appear in Francis Clark's pamphlets on the regiment in 1871 and 1874, but did in Clark's book of 1882, with an asterisk indicating that the information was from Pearsall himself. There was no information, however, other than his name and address—no offices held, no high military rank, no honors.[23] Pearsall did not subscribe to Clark's book. The only appearance in print of his name other than his obituary was in a biographical volume, a "mugbook," of 1901. Entitled *Representative Citizens of Northern California*, the book presented the standard glossy biography and, as was not uncommonly the case, a hopelessly garbled account of his early years and a glorified version of his later life. The fact that emerged, however, despite the euphemisms employed to disguise it, was that Samuel Pearsall for most of his life had been a handyman. During a number of years mining and prospecting, at times "Mr. Pearsall and his partner secured from sixty-four to sixty-seven ounces of gold daily"—if one were to believe the writer. After that endeavor, he "conducted a saloon." The book commented that this "proved a very profitable venture, bringing him from two to five hundred dollars every twenty-four hours." With a note of candor the article concluded with the fact that the government paid Pearsall twelve dollars a month as a pension, on which he lived "in peace and contentment." He died in Mokelumne Hill during August 1900, a year before the book was published.[24]

NOTES

1. John W. Caughey, *California*, 2nd edition (Englewood Cliffs, New Jersey: Prentice-Hall, Inc., 1953), 244.

2. Both E. Gould Buffum and William Redmond Ryan, who published important books on their experiences in 1850, met many of their former fellows during the winter of 1848-49. Buffum was on the Yuba, Bear, and American rivers, for the most part, and Ryan on the Stanislaus and Mokelumne, although he ranged widely.

3. Hollingsworth, *Journal*, 57-58.

4. *San Francisco Examiner*, Jan. 1, 1892. If Mokelumne Hill had an alcalde in 1848, and if Stevenson held that position, those facts are elsewhere unrecorded.

5. Bancroft estimated the permanent population at one thousand in 1849 and the floating population at twice that. In April 1850 three thousand people stopped there en route to the mines. Bancroft: *History of California*, vol. 6, 466.

6. Hollingsworth, *Journal*, 58.

7. Zoeth S. Eldredge: *The Beginnings of San Francisco*, 2 vols., (San Francisco: Zoeth S. Eldredge, 1912), vol. 2, 555.

8. James Allen Hardie, *Memoir of James Allen Hardie* (Washington, D.C.: privately printed, 1877), 32-47 and *passim*.

9. Although there must have been an official report, it was not published with related papers in House Ex. Doc. No. 17, 31st Congress, 1st sess.

10. Bancroft, "Pioneer Register," *History of California*, vol. 2, 737.

11. *Ibid.*, vol. 6, 675; "Pioneer Register," vol. 4, 729.

12. Viola Lockhart Warren (ed.), "Dr. John S. Griffin's Mail, 1846-53," *California Historical Society Quarterly*, XXXIII, 1954, 253 and *passim*.

13. Sherman, *Memoirs*, vol. 1, 64-65. There was evidently nothing questionable in the conduct of Sherman or Mason, who in fact encouraged his staff to do outside work, driven as they were by inadequate salaries. Commodore Jones, however, was convicted in 1851 of speculating in gold dust with government funds. He was sentenced to suspension from the service for five years and loss of pay for half of that time. Bancroft: *History of California*, vol. 6, 265.

14. Dimmick, "Diary," Oct. 15, 1848.

15. Benjamin Hayes, Scrapbooks, 1850-1874, "California Mining" (13 vols.), vol. 1, 33.

16. Much of this information on "General" Ketchum, as he was known, is from his obituary in the Stockton *Evening Record*, Jan. 26, 1916, and from the introduction by Joseph A. Sullivan to Guy J. Giffen, *California Expedition* (Oakland, California: Biobooks, 1951),

in which the careful research of a Stockton librarian is reported. The information that all who served in the army during the war with Mexico would receive as a service benefit either 160 acres of land on any of the public lands or bounty scrip for $100 (bearing six percent interest), appeared in Colonel Mason's Orders No. 34 of July 20, 1847, RG 94, NA. Mason's source of the information was a common and almost semi-official one, the *New Orleans Picayune* of March 1, 1847.

17. Helen S. Giffen, *California Mining Town Newspapers, 1850-1880* (Van Nuys, California: J. E. Reynolds, 1954), 37.

18. In addition to Murray's own "Narrative of a California Volunteer," described and cited earlier, a sketch of Murray's life prepared by William Beecher Turner, delivered as an address to the Society of California Pioneers on Sept. 15, 1938, is valuable and reasonably accurate source material, insofar as the information can be substantiated. The sketch, preserved in the archives of the society, was prepared partly from the "Narrative" and partly from unspecified and undetermined additional sources. Quite possibly, the source was the Murray family, particularly his numerous children, since it is clear Turner was acquainted with the family.

19. Caughey, *California*, 2nd ed., 257.

20. Marco G. Thorne (ed.), "Bound for the Land of Canaan, Ho! The Diary of Levi Stowell, 1849," *California Historical Society Quarterly*, XXVII, 1948, 160.

21. Lynch, *With Stevenson to California*, iii.

22. The number of former volunteers who stayed in the gold region all their lives is undoubtedly low, but on those eighty men reliable information exists in county histories, newspapers, in Bancroft's "Pioneer Register," or in Clark's book on the regiment. There is no evidence but considerable likelihood that a number of the 354 volunteers on whom no information exists after their discharge or desertion lived inconspicuously in the Mother Lode area.

23. Clark, *The First Regiment of New York Volunteers*, 28.

24. *Representative Citizens of Northern California* (n.p., 1901), 174-75. Pearsall Street in present-day Mokelumne Hill commemorates Pearsall's half century of residence there, as Stevenson Street does his regimental commander.

Chapter Fifteen

Toward Local Control: The San Francisco Guards and Legislative Assembly

THE COMBINATION of the initial excitement about gold in 1848 and the official end of the war created conditions which had not been anticipated either in Washington or California. The Gold Rush of the next year aggravated the situation extremely, and popular groups and movements developed to deal with the disorder. In the critical year from September 1848 to September 1849, former volunteers provided direction and leadership—some levelheaded, some revolutionary—that decidedly eased the transition of California from conquered Mexican province to the thirty-first state of the United States.

The military government was in an unenviable position for that entire year. On August 26, 1848, Lieutenant Sher-

man in Monterey wrote an illuminating unofficial letter to
Colonel Stevenson in Los Angeles. In it Sherman poignantly
described the troubled situation that then existed and correctly anticipated worse to come. The administration, he felt, had
put Colonel Mason "in a tight place that might have been
avoided. . . .

They knew all along that California was not to be given up, that the
population of the country was of a mixed kind calling for the presence of military force to back the civil authorities—that upon the
conclusion of the war the volunteers would of necessity be discharged, and that only two companies of regulars would remain. All
this they knew at Washington and yet they have not provided for it. I
feel sorry that this should be for naturally the people of the country
will laugh at our absurd promises of protection of good laws, the
strong arm, and stable government.[1]

It was certainly true that "they" in Washington did not
plan to give up California, and a great deal had been learned
about the area during 1847. Voluminous reports from the
various military and naval commanders had dispelled most of
the misconceptions previously held by Polk and Marcy. In
view of the fuller knowledge Marcy commanded, his decision
not to send many additional regular troops to California once
peace negotiations were opened, and particularly after the
fall of Mexico City in September 1847, is not altogether
understandable. His failure to do so is still more inexplicable
because of the administration's awareness that ultimate territorial status for any of the lands to be ceded at the end of the
war would be hard won.

No more evidence than the birth and death of the Wilmot Proviso was necessary to recognize that there would at
least be controversy and probably long delay. The sensitive
issue was the extension of slavery, and the proviso, attached
to the Two Million and Three Million appropriation bills in
August 1846 and February 1847, would have excluded slavery from all the territory acquired from Mexico at the end of
the war. While the proviso was not enacted, and the Three
Million Bill was passed only after the proviso was eliminated,
the voting in Congress had been almost strictly sectional.

Northern Democrats and Whigs voted together against the Southern Democrats and Whigs. It was, of course, this sectionally divided Congress that must act to end the war and to provide territorial status for any part of the land acquired by treaty.[2]

Yet Marcy seems to have expected that two companies of regulars would be sufficient in Alta California once peace was declared and the volunteers had assumed their roles as civilian colonists. The unanticipated Gold Rush proved him conclusively wrong.

With the discharge of the volunteers in southern California in September 1848 and the transfer of the remaining dragoons from Los Angeles to Monterey, the towns of San Diego, Los Angeles, and Santa Barbara were without any military force whatsoever. In his August 26 letter to Colonel Stevenson, Lieutenant Sherman admitted that Colonel Mason was disposed to provide protection for southern California but had not the power. "All the women of the lower country may be ravished & men killed," he wrote, "horses stolen & houses burnt & you couldn't get a dozen men to leave the Gold district to go to their aid." September had indeed seen the exodus of volunteers from "the lower country"; there is record of only two volunteers still in southern California in October—Henry S. Carnes and Ira Johnson.

Lieutenant Carnes of Company F remained in Santa Barbara with an appointment from Colonel Mason as collector of the port. His appointment, dated September 3, 1848, presumably paid well; the comparable post in San Francisco on the same date was offered to Edward Gilbert, who declined the position and the $2,000 annual salary. (Edward H. Harrison, formerly quartermaster's clerk in the regiment, accepted the position in San Francisco.)[3] Carnes never went to the mines and spent the rest of his life in and near Santa Barbara, holding a succession of responsible positions. He was elected a member of the state legislature and later, district judge and postmaster of Santa Barbara.[4]

The other volunteer who is known to have been in southern California that October is Private Ira Johnson of Company I. He remained in San Diego and engaged in smuggling, but only briefly. By December he was in Monterey, legitimately earning twelve dollars a day as a builder, and the spring of 1849 saw him in the mines.[5] During late 1850 and for a few years thereafter, volunteers slowly settled in southern California, but only after a certain amount of experience in northern and central California, usually in the mines.

In the last six months of 1848, San Francisco developed into the most important town in California, far outdistancing in population and commerce the traditional Mexican centers of Monterey and Los Angeles. In the preceding two years, San Francisco had shown signs of bidding for importance by its steady if slow growth, but the gold discovery in the north determined its pre-eminence. By the end of 1848 it was a city of some 2,000 people, the population swollen by goldseekers arriving from the Pacific islands, Mexico, and South America, and by those (including many volunteers) who had retreated from the mines to winter on the coast. Goldseekers from the United States began arriving in February, and the population increased to 5,000 in July and a staggering minimum of 20,000 by December 1849. At least 40,000 people arrived by sea in 1849, most of them to pass through San Francisco on their way to the mines.[6]

The discharge of Companies H, K, and C left San Francisco with no military force and no security for persons or property in what was to all intents an American boomtown. The prospects for regular forces to maintain order were not good. Regular-army soldiers were deserting wholesale in Monterey, and, when the navy came into port in San Francisco, the crews deserted. Colonel Mason was well aware of the disorder and confusion in San Francisco, and, in his letter of late August to Colonel Stevenson, Lieutenant Sherman had acknowledged "loud calls for assistance" from San Francisco. But the military governor was powerless.

Even before the discharge of the volunteers, San Francisco was in turmoil. A committee of prominent citizens, including James C. Ward and Quartermaster Clerk Edward H.

Harrison, had petitioned Colonel Mason for the removal of the first and second alcaldes appointed by Mason. In the petition they represented the town as in a "disgraceful state of disorder," with bloody street fights a daily occurrence, the alcaldes defied and publicly insulted on the bench, and both officials "the open associates of the worst characters." The first alcalde at that time was George Hyde; the second was Thaddeus M. Leavenworth, the regimental chaplain and founder of the Sunday School, who had been appointed second alcalde in October 1847. There was strong suspicion that Hyde and Leavenworth had altered town records to suit themselves and granted city lots to their friends. Late in March Colonel Mason replaced Hyde with John Townsend, while Leavenworth continued as second alcalde. Townsend was acceptable to the citizens but, unfortunately, served only until June 1 when he went to the mines. Leavenworth then acted as first alcalde.

The citizens again protested, urging the governor to appoint Edward Gilbert first alcalde. Mason declined to do so for two reasons: Gilbert was still on active duty as a lieutenant in Company H, and Mason had just received the news of the peace treaty from Querétaro. He would not appoint anyone, but on August 7 ordered Alcalde Leavenworth to hold an election. Held on August 29 (with Dimmick as one of the judges), the election resulted in a slight majority and victory for Leavenworth. The same day more than forty citizens protested the election. Mason sustained their objections and ordered another election, which Leavenworth also won.[7]

Out of this disaffection and these conditions grew the San Francisco Guards, an organization important for what it represented and for the men involved. These were men who desired stability, and most of them were former volunteers who had served in the companies garrisoning San Francisco and Sonoma. Kimball Dimmick was not involved, even though he was then in San Francisco, but, like Dimmick, these men had not raced to the mines upon being mustered out. Many of the members later joined the search for gold (which helps to explain why the San Francisco Guards was not an effective organization), but in the forepart of September 1848 they were all in San Francisco.

Responding to a call published in the *Californian* on September 2, a group of citizens met in Portsmouth Square that evening and organized the Guards. Members of this organization would respond when summoned to keep order in the city. As reported in the *Californian* the next week, the meeting was called to order by Thomas J. Roach, formerly lieutenant in Company C, who nominated James C. Ward chairman and Roderick M. Morrison secretary. Ward and Morrison had come to California on the *Loo Choo*, as had most of the volunteers involved in the Guards.

The San Francisco Guards had a militia-company organization, with its commanding officer a captain. Elected "unanimously" was Edward Gilbert. Ward was elected first lieutenant, and several privates from Companies H and K, including Francis Murray and Anthony Durkin, were elected corporals. Some of the officers were not of the regiment; of these, a few were recent arrivals, but more were residents of at least a few years. The first sergeant was W. D. M. Howard, who had come to California in 1839 and was a partner in San Francisco's most important business establishment, the trading firm of Mellus and Howard. Others were men who had been prominent in civil affairs when San Francisco (or Yerba Buena) was but a village.

Of the staff for the Guards, two were volunteers—Dr. William C. Parker elected surgeon, and Edward H. Harrison elected quartermaster. For the internal "civil government of the corps," separate officers were elected. Former lieutenant Theron R. Per Lee of Company C was elected president and Roderick M. Morrison second vice-president. The secretary was Henry Sheldon, part-owner and editor of the *Californian*, then the only newspaper in San Francisco, the *Star* having suspended publication on June 10 when the entire staff went to the mines.

At the first meeting of the San Francisco Guards, Ward, as chairman, appointed a committee to address Colonel

Mason on the loan of arms. The committee members were all former volunteers: Gilbert, Ward himself, Roach, Morrison, and Harrison.[8]

When the committee appealed to Colonel Mason for arms, he refused, although one senses in his reply that he did so reluctantly. In a time of peace, if not quiet, Mason felt he did not have the authority to arm such a body at the expense of the government.[9] Unarmed, and with some of its members drifting off to the mines, the San Francisco Guards came to nothing and played no part in the events of San Francisco in 1849. The group did maintain a kind of ceremonial existence at least through 1850, when a branch organization was formed in Sacramento with James Queen, former sergeant in Company F, elected third lieutenant.

While the formation of the San Francisco Guards was of minor importance, the willingness of that group of ex-volunteers to take affairs in hand was significant. The same impulse led some of them later to form a much more important organization—the San Francisco Legislative Assembly.

Of the ex-volunteers active in the community and political life of San Francisco, the most important was Edward Gilbert. The emergence of Gilbert as a leader was clear by the fall of 1848. He was enormously popular, spoke as eloquently as he wrote, and had written for both San Francisco newspapers as well as continuing to send dispatches to the *New York Herald* and the Albany *Argus*. Probably no one in California was as disinterestedly devoted to the abstract cause of California as Gilbert. He had not changed his opinion written on Governors Island that no greater enterprise than the acquisition of California would "be found recorded on the historical pages of the nineteenth century." The fact of the acquisition had confirmed this opinion.

Declining to run for alcalde and declining also the lucrative position of collector of the port, Gilbert returned to journalism on a full-time basis. In November, when publisher Edward C. Kemble merged the *Star* and the *Californian* into *The California Star and Californian*, Gilbert became editor and seriously began exercising his talents and training at the highest moral level. Early in January 1849 Gilbert, George C. Hubbard (formerly lieutenant of Company K), and Edward C. Kemble brought out a new newspaper, jointly published by all three and with Gilbert as senior editor. The *Alta California* became the spokesman for immediate civil government in California and was the most important newspaper in San Francisco (and thus in California) in the nineteenth century, continuing publication until 1891.

In his peace proclamation of August 7, 1848, Colonel Mason had permitted himself a conjecture about civil government that would trouble him later:

The congress of the United States, to whom alone this power belongs, will soon confer upon the people of this country the constitutional rights of citizens of United States; and no doubt in a few short months we shall have a regularly organized territorial government; indeed, there is every reason to believe that congress has already passed the act, and that a civil government is now on its way to this country, to replace that which has been organized under the rights of conquest. . . . The existing laws of the country will necessarily continue in force till others are made to supply their place.[10]

A considerable note of uncertainty is apparent in Mason's proclamation. He was not at all sure when civil government might come to California.

In a letter to the adjutant general of the United States written on August 19, Mason described what Lieutenant Sherman shortly after called the "tight place" he was in:

For the past two years no civil government has existed here save that controlled by the senior military or naval officer; and no civil officers exist in the country save the alcaldes appointed or confirmed by myself. To throw off upon them or the people at large the civil management and control of the country would most probably lead to endless confusions, if not to absolute anarchy; and yet what right or authority have I to exercise civil control in time of peace in a territory of the United States?

In the absence of any instructions, he concluded, he would continue to exercise control over the appointed alcaldes or future ones elected, to attempt the collection of import duties according to the United States tariff of 1846, and to appoint civilian collectors of the various ports. "I am fully aware," he admitted, "that in taking these steps I have no further authority than that the existing government must necessarily continue until some other is organized to take its place."[11]

During the autumn of 1848, throughout northern California but principally in San Francisco, Colonel Mason's cautious optimism about territorial government did influence the people. They hoped civil government would be proclaimed very soon, and they, too, had serious questions about his authority. Military government was obviously continuing and with it the objectionable feature of uncontrolled alcalde rule. In support of the growing sentiment that no legitimate government existed in California, there was no less an opinion than that of the president of the United States. Polk's special address to Congress of July 6, 1848, urging passage of a bill giving California a territorial government, was printed in part in the *Californian* of September 23 and included a statement on California's status: "The war with Mexico having terminated, the power of the executive to establish or to continue temporary civil governments over these territories, which existed under the laws of nations whilst they were regarded as conquered provinces in our military occupation, has ceased."[12]

Nothing could have been clearer. Nor could there have been higher authority for the position of California which everyone then began calling anomalous. The editor of the *Californian* and secretary of the Guards, Henry Sheldon, editorialized on "civil organization" in late October. He thought that Colonel Mason should take whatever action was necessary to establish a temporary civil government and was not sanguine about prospects of congressional action. He assumed "that months, and perhaps years, will elapse before the national legislature will arrive at a harmonious conclusion upon the basis of a territorial government for California." And he knew why. "The much vexed subject of slavery . . . will prove an insuperable barrier to dispatch," he prophesied.[13]

In early December word arrived that the first session of the Thirtieth Congress had adjourned without providing any sort of government for California. The one bill that was reported out had been killed by debate in the House. Instead of the promised territorial government, there arrived a long, official letter from Secretary of State Buchanan to William Van Voorhies, an agent of the post-office department sent to California to supervise the mails. Through this letter the administration attempted to bolster the position of Colonel Mason, urging patience on the part of the people, and defining the existing government of California in original terms:

The condition of the people of California is anomalous, and will require, on their part, the exercise of great prudence and discretion. . . . The termination of the war left an existing government, a government *de facto*, in full operation; and this will continue, with the presumed consent of the people, until congress shall provide for them a territorial government. The great law of necessity justifies this conclusion. The consent of the people is irresistibly inferred from the fact that no civilized community could possibly desire to abrogate an existing government, when the alternative presented would be to place themselves in a state of anarchy, beyond the protection of all laws. . . . The president urgently advises the people of California to live peaceably and quietly under the existing government. . . . it will endure but for a few months. . . . During this brief period it is better to bear the ills they have than fly to others they know not of.[14]

The reaction to Buchanan's letter was predictable. To those who were troubled by the continuing military government, the promises and advice seemed much less than they had a right to expect. The result was a series of mass meetings in December, January, and February in favor of forming a territorial government.

The influence of Edward Gilbert and other ex-volunteers was prodigious in this movement. Gilbert fanned the flames first in the pages of *The California Star and Californian* and then in the *Alta California*. He took an active part in all the proceedings leading to the constitutional convention of 1849. He was no less active, but behind the scenes with his pen, in the closely related movement to provide responsible muni-

cipal government for San Francisco. The resulting San Fran-
cisco Legislative Assembly, even more than the San Francisco
Guards, was almost exclusively an operation of former New
York Volunteers.

In San Francisco municipal affairs had degenerated seriously in the last three months of 1848. Dr. Leavenworth
continued as alcalde, allegedly kept in office by those he
permitted to buy, or to whom he granted, town lots, the value
of which had skyrocketed with the increased population and
the abundance of gold in circulation. In late December the
town council, its members known popularly as the "land
grabbers," was dismissed by Colonel Mason and an election
for a new council ordered. Of the seven new councilmen
elected, three had been involved in the formation of the San
Francisco Guards and three were volunteers—former lieutenants George C. Hubbard, Thomas J. Roach, and Stephen
C. Harris (the old man described by Sherman as "decrepit,"
who had been discharged in San Francisco in 1847). The
others were former alcalde Townsend, W. D. M. Howard,
R. A. Parker, and John J. Sirrine. The former council was far
from pleased with the results of the election and was able to
have it declared illegal because of insufficient notice. By rally-
ing their forces, the old councilmen were voted back into
office on January 15, 1849.

On January 25 Gilbert reviewed all these dismal developments in the *Alta California*, dismissing the second election as
void. He urged popular action to end the factional dispute
and to provide responsible and representative municipal
government. Gilbert continued with further exhortation on
February 1 and 8, announcing on the latter date a public
meeting to be held at Portsmouth Square on February 12.

At that meeting the San Francisco Legislative Assembly
was born, an organization with broader aims than mere land-
policy reform. According to the preamble to the ordinances
drawn up, the people of San Francisco perceived "the necessity of having some better defined and more permanent civil
regulations for our general security than the vague, unlimited, and irresponsible authority that now exists"—the present

authority being Alcalde Leavenworth backed by Colonel Mason. To achieve these permanent and well-defined regulations, they would legislate everything that "did not conflict with the Constitution of the United States nor the common law thereof."[15]

One of the resolutions of the February 12 meeting called for the resignation of both town councils. They ultimately did resign, and on February 21 an election was held for fifteen assemblymen and three justices of the peace, who were to be empowered to hear all civil and criminal cases in the district. Whereas Leavenworth had been put into office the previous October in an election in which a total of 158 votes were cast, and the second city council in January by a still lighter vote, over 600 people, of a population of 2,000, cast votes for the assemblymen and justices.[16] Gilbert had been persuasive in the columns of the *Alta California*.

Bancroft wrote that the election "brought to the front a very respectable body of men, full of reform projects."[17] Many of those elected were ex-volunteers, two of the three justices of the peace and four of the assemblymen, and in May, when the number of assemblymen was increased by ten, five of the ten elected were volunteers. In addition, and not surprisingly, Gilbert was appointed printer to the assembly, and a former volunteer served as clerk. In all, seven of the ten companies of the regiment were represented in the San Francisco Legislative Assembly, all except Companies D, E, and I.[18]

Attorneys and newspapermen were prominent among the volunteers elected. The one ex-company captain involved was Francis Lippitt, who had gone briefly to the mines and had opened a law office on his return to San Francisco in the fall. The absence of an organized judiciary and the impossibility of securing contracts troubled Lippitt deeply. He had argued forcefully for the organization of the assembly and on March 12 was elected its Speaker.

Former lieutenant Myron Norton of Company C had presided at the organization meeting on February 12, and at the February 21 election he and former lieutenant Theron R. Per Lee of the same company were elected justices of the peace.[19] Both were attorneys. Norton became one of the most active proponents of a constitutional convention and was elected a delegate to the convention from San Francisco. Per Lee had a law practice in San Francisco when the legislative assembly was organized. Later than year he moved to Sacramento, becoming editor of the Sacramento *Placer Times* and, later, part owner of the *Alta California*. He represented the Monterey district in the first session of the California State Legislature.[20]

Four other members of the San Francisco Legislative Assembly had been lieutenants, as had Gilbert. George C. Hubbard of Company K, a printer by trade, was then one of the publishers of the *Alta California* and also served in the first session of the state legislature at the end of the year. Thomas J. Roach, who, like Per Lee, had been active in the San Francisco Guards, had served as deputy collector of the port and became a merchant in San Francisco later in 1849. In 1850 he settled in the far north, at Trinity Bay, and was elected county judge of Klamath County. In 1852 Roach died of drowning.

The other former lieutenants in the assembly, E. Gould Buffum of Company B and George Frank Lemon of Company A, had both served in Lower California under Lieutenant-Colonel Burton, Buffum as collector of the port of La Paz, and Lemon as Burton's adjutant. In La Paz, on December 30, 1847, they were both relieved of duty and ordered in arrest to Mazatlán and from Mazatlán to Monterey.[21] They waited in Mazatlán until late May for transportation and in June arrived in Monterey, where Colonel Mason suspended their arrest "for the present" and ordered them to duty with Colonel Stevenson in Los Angeles.[22] Although both appealed to Colonel Stevenson and Colonel Mason for courts-martial, charges were not brought against them and the trial was never held. They were discharged, honorably, on August 21, 1848, in Los Angeles. In the official records there is no clue as to what may have happened in La Paz, nor is anything revealed in Buffum's remarkable book *Six Months in the Gold Mines* published in 1850. In his book he mentions being ordered to Upper California and arriving at Monterey, and then at Los Angeles, with no suggestion of any difficulty. Hollingsworth also notes their arrival in Los Angeles, and his journal supplies an explanation. "Two officiers [sic] arrived here from Monterey," he wrote on July 6, 1848, "placed under arrest by Col Burton for gambling with soldiers—"[23]

By May, when he was elected to the assembly, Buffum had already been to the mines on the Bear, Yuba, and American rivers. He was then a reporter for the *Alta California* and later in 1849 became its city editor, using his New York experience as printer and reporter for the *New York Herald*, for which he continued as correspondent. His letters to the *Herald* were widely reprinted in newspapers in the East and Middle West and provided some of the soundest advice available for prospective gold seekers.[24] In the fall of 1849, Buffum carefully worked his Upper and Lower California experiences into form, and in May 1850 the publishers Lea and Blanchard in Philadelphia brought out his *Six Months in the Gold Mines; From a Journal of Three Years in Upper and Lower California, 1847-8-9.* The book was an immediate success in a period when guides to California and the mines were glutting the market.[25]

Buffum remained with the *Alta California* until 1851, when he was briefly engaged in the planning of a southern California newspaper, the Los Angeles *Star*, of which he was to be editor. Although he did not become editor, he did contribute fiction to the newspaper, including a short story in the first issue, on May 17, 1851.[26] Instead, Buffum went back to New York and to the *Herald*, but returned to San Francisco in 1853 and was re-engaged on the *Alta California.* In 1855 he was elected to the sixth session of the state legislature as assemblyman from San Francisco. In 1857 he left California for the final time, going to France; and at the time of his death in 1867 he was Paris correspondent to the *Herald.* After an absence of ten years from California, Buffum was well remembered. His newspaper obituaries in San Francisco, Los Angeles, Sacramento, and Virginia City were long. He still had friends in California, many of them "old campaigners in the editorial line, both sides of the Rocky Mountains."[27]

George Frank Lemon was also associated with the *Alta California*, in both its editorial and business departments. He was elected assessor of San Francisco in 1851, and also served as secretary of the Society of California Pioneers for two years. Lemon returned to New York in 1853, but he left San Franciscans with vivid memories of one of the most desperate shooting affrays of local record. In a running argument over a woman, Lemon and Will Hicks Graham kept things lively from July to September 1851 by doing their best to kill each other. They first met in the street in downtown San Francisco, and Lemon wounded Graham. Once recovered, Graham challenged, and the men fought a duel in Benicia in which Lemon was wounded, which presumably settled the issue.[28] Although Lemon made his home in New York, his California experience of six years had been important to him. When the Civil War began, Colonel Edward D. Baker, a noted orator and one of the most prominent members of the California bar, raised a regiment of California Volunteers in Washington and New York. Lemon joined it, commissioned a lieutenant colonel. In 1862 he was killed fighting before Richmond.[29]

The former volunteer officers who served in the San Francisco Legislative Assembly were more active than the former privates, and generally had more distinguished careers, but there were exceptions. Two of the privates later served in the state legislature. Alfred A. Green of Company A was a lawyer practicing in San Francisco in 1849. He was later very much involved with land titles in San Francisco, becoming wealthy and suspect as a consequence, and was a member of the San Francisco Vigilance Committee of 1851. In 1854 he was elected to the fifth session of the legislature, representing San Francisco.[30] Cornelius R. V. Lee of Company F served in the preceding session in 1853, representing Santa Barbara.[31] One wishes that Lee had left an account of himself and his activities that would shed light on his curiously contradictory record. When he joined the regiment, Lee was twenty-four years old and a bookbinder by trade. He was rather steadily in trouble in Santa Barbara with Captain Lippitt (with whom he served in the legislative assembly) and was dishonorably discharged for desertion. In San Francisco he served at the same time as a member of the legislative assembly and as president of the Regulators, who were probably working hand in hand with Alcalde Leavenworth. In spite of these conflicting roles, he was an active member of the assembly, attending meetings regularly.

The three other privates involved in the assembly (Archibald Roane of Companies G and, later, F, Theodore Smith of Company F, and J. Mead Huxley of Company A) had no further recorded public careers. Roane went to the mines later in 1849. Smith and Huxley are lost to record except for the entry in Bancroft's "Pioneer Register" that Huxley served between 1861 and 1865 as an officer in the Civil War and that he returned to California, where he died before 1882.[32]

Through March and April of 1849, San Francisco in effect had two municipal governments, with Alcalde Leavenworth remaining in office and with the legislative assembly enacting operating laws, creating and filling new offices, and abolishing the office of alcalde. On March 22 Myron Norton, as the first justice of the peace (having received the most votes), was named police magistrate to succeed the alcalde. Shortly thereafter John C. Pulis, former sergeant of Company F, was named sheriff to carry out the directions of Norton and the assembly. Pulis was a shoemaker by trade and at thirty-four was older than the great majority of the volunteers. Captain Lippitt had used him on police duty in Santa Barbara and thus knew his man.

In all its acts the legislative assembly assumed that Colonel Mason had no further authority in California, and, while Mason could not officially agree, he adopted a "hands off" policy. For many months Mason had hoped to be relieved of his command. In November 1848, after serving eighteen months as military governor, he had written the adjutant general asking to be reassigned:

The war being over, the soldiers nearly all deserted, and having now been from the states two years, I respectfully request to be ordered home. I feel the less hesitancy in making this request, as it is the second only that I recollect ever to have made, in more than thirty years service, to be relieved from duty upon which I have been placed: the first was asking to be relieved from the recruiting service, in 1832, that I might join my company in the Black Hawk war.[33]

On April 13, 1849, Mason's replacement arrived. Brevet Brigadier General Bennett Riley became governor and commanding general of the Tenth Military Department.

Without Mason's background in California and with a different temperament, General Riley handled the awkward San Francisco situation by conceding first to one side and then to the other. The assembly's charges of maladministration against Leavenworth were persuasive and on May 6 General Riley suspended him. While Leavenworth was under suspension, the assembly directed Sheriff Pulis to seize the records of the alcalde's office and turn them over to the magistrate, Myron Norton. Pulis did so in a dramatic episode of pistol flourishing.[34] When this conduct on the part of the assembly was reported to Riley by Leavenworth in person, the governor reinstated him to the office of alcalde, but the people of San Francisco would now not accept any system of government imposed by military authority.

This attitude was spreading throughout the territory. On April 30 in Sacramento a mass meeting similar to the San Francisco meeting of February 12 was held, and a legislature of eleven members was elected to enact laws for the city and the surrounding district. Henry A. Schoolcraft, former sergeant of Company H, was elected alcalde, to conduct the city's business and to be responsible to the people, not to Monterey.[35]

In late May news arrived that Congress had adjourned on March 3 without providing a territorial government for California. The legislative assembly thereupon took its most important action. Incensed that no civil government had been provided and that the federal revenue laws had been extended over California, on June 4 the assembly called for a convention to form a state constitution. The people would not submit to being taxed not only without representation, but without any government at all that they considered legal. In the "Address to the People of California" the assembly called for the election of twelve delegates from each district of California to meet at San Jose in mid-August, "to form . . . a State Constitution, to be submitted to the people for their ratification or rejection by a direct vote at the polls."[36]

General Riley's reaction to the news from Washington and from San Francisco was swift and—ultimately—gratifying. He capitulated, calling for an August 1 election to choose delegates to a constitutional convention to be held in Monterey on September 1. At the same time local officials were to be elected to serve in the interim. In calling for such a convention, however, Riley made it clear he was not recognizing the legislative assembly. On June 4, he issued another proclamation, addressed "To the people of the district of San Francisco." With a convention in view and an election of local officials scheduled, Riley urged the citizens of San Francisco not to recognize the illegal and unauthorized legislative assembly, which had "usurped powers, which are vested only in the Congress of the United States."[37]

He need not have bothered. On June 5 Alcalde Leavenworth had finally resigned, and, with the prospect of a convention and all local officials being elective, the San Francisco Legislative Assembly formally ceased to be. The meeting of June 4 was its last.

NOTES

1.   Sherman, Monterey, to Stevenson, Los Angeles, August 26, 1848, RG 393, NA.

2.   A concise account of the proviso and Wilmotism, with the voting broken down in party terms, is in Merk, *Manifest Destiny*, 172-76.

3.   Bancroft, *History of California*, vol. 5, 659.

4.   *Ibid.*, vol. 2, 742.

5.   *Ibid.*, vol. 4, 693.

6.   Bancroft: *History of California*, vol. 6, 168. Bancroft's estimates are conservative, carefully arrived at from newspaper figures, Bayard Taylor's *Eldorado* (an especially trustworthy source of statistics), the *Annals of San Francisco*, and other sources.

7.   Frank Soulé, *et al*, *Annals of San Francisco* (New York: D. Appleton and Company, 1855), 201-6; Bancroft, *History of California*, vol. 5, 648-52. Some of the charges against Hyde and Leavenworth

were substantiated, but the initial strength of the feeling toward them probably was due to their serving by military appointment. Later, after Leavenworth had been properly elected, the objections were as much to the power of the office of alcalde as to his conduct of the office.

8. *Californian*, Sept. 9, 1848.

9. Bancroft, *History of California*, vol. 6, 263.

10. *Ibid.*, vol. 5, 611.

11. U.S., Congress, *House Exec. Docs.*, 31st Cong., 1st sess., No. 17, pp. 597-98.

12. *Californian*, Sept. 23, 1848. Polk's entire message appears in Richardson, *Messages and Papers*, vol. 4, 589. Polk's apprehension that the territorial bill would be defeated because of the sectional split on slavery is evident throughout the message, and his skepticism was justified.

13. *Californian*, Oct. 21, 1848.

14. James Buchanan to William Van Voorhies, Oct. 7, 1848, *House Exec. Docs.*, 30th Cong., 2d sess., No. 1, pp. 49-50.

15. *Alta California*, Feb. 15, 1849. Everything to do with the legislative assembly was ultimately collected and published in 1860 by the board of supervisors of the city and county of San Francisco. The volume is *Minutes of the Proceedings of the Legislative Assembly of the District of San Francisco, from March 12th, 1849, to June 4th, 1849 . . .* [with] *Laws Relating to the Powers of Public Officers, and the Administration of Justice* (San Francisco: Published by order of the board of supervisors, 1860).

16. Bancroft, *History of California*, vol. 6, 210; *Minutes of . . . the Legislative Assembly*, 5.

17. Bancroft, *History of California*, vol. 6, 211. He neglected to mention that most of them were Stevenson's men. On the same page, however, in discussing the opportunity for lawlessness because of political discord, he began his discussion of the Hounds, composed of "riffraff of the disbanded regiment of New York Volunteers."

18. Volunteers Myron Norton and Theron R. Per Lee were elected justices of the peace. Assemblymen were E. Gould Buffum, Alfred A. Green, George C. Hubbard, J. M. Huxley, Cornelius R. V. Lee, George F. Lemon, Francis J. Lippitt, Thomas J. Roach, and Theodore Smith. Archibald Roane was appointed clerk. (*Minutes of . . . the Legislative Assembly*, 6-26.)

19. Norton had been commissioned by Gov. John Young of New York to serve under Captain Brackett at Sonoma. Norton was enrolled and mustered in on Governors Island and sailed to California on the *Huntress*, arriving in the fall of 1848. While not carried on Brackett's muster rolls as a result of his late arrival—Company C

had already been mustered out—Norton was on the rolls of the regiment in the adjutant general's office and was honorably discharged.

20. Ralph S. Kuykendall, "The History of Early California Journalism," unpublished doctoral dissertation, University of California, 1918, 146-47.

21. Burton, DGO No. 25, La Paz, Lower California, Dec. 30, 1847, RG 94, NA.

22. Mason, Special Orders No. 19, June 16, 1848, RG 94, NA.

23. Hollingsworth, *Journal*, 43.

24. Many of Buffum's letters to the *Herald* were reprinted by the St. Joseph (Missouri) *Adventure*, the Missouri *Republican*, and the *Weekly Missouri Statesman* in the summer and fall of 1849. Along with letters from other Californians, some of Buffum's letters have been collected, organized according to subject, and printed by Walker D. Wyman as "California Emigrant Letters" in the *California Historical Society Quarterly*, XXIV, 1945, 343-64. Letters of Colonel Stevenson to his son-in-law James H. Brady, which also appeared in the *Herald*, are included.

25. Bancroft recognized Buffum's book as "one of the most important printed contributions to the history of Cal., no less by reason of the scarcity of material concerning the period it covers, 1848-9, than on account of the ability of the author." He found Buffum "careful in his statements . . . an educated man, remarkably free from prejudice, a close observer, and possessing sound judgment." (Bancroft, *History of California*, vol. 6, 98.) Echoes of Buffum are found in four volumes of Bancroft's *History*, and the book has remained one of the principal sources on the Gold Rush and California life in those years.

Although the best, Buffum's book was not the first published by a volunteer. Dr. Felix P. Wierzbicki, a physician of Company F and later of Company H, wrote the first of the guides to the mines, *California As It Is, and As It May Be, or a Guide to the Gold Region* (San Francisco: W. Bartlett, 1849). See Robert E. Cowan, *A Bibliography of the History of California and the Pacific West, 1510-1906* (San Francisco: The Book Club of California, 1914), 248. William Redmond Ryan's *Personal Adventures in Upper and Lower California, in 1848-9; with the Author's Experience at the Mines* is a close second in quality to Buffum and includes twenty-three good drawings. An extremely important book, published in 1852, is often attributed to "a member of Stevenson's Regiment" because of an error of Bancroft (*History of California*, vol. 6, 98.) *Early Recollections of the Mines, and a Description of the Great Tulare Valley* was written by James H. Carson, a sergeant in Company F, Third Artillery.

26. William B. Rice, *The Los Angeles Star, 1851-1864* (Berkeley: University of California Press, 1947), 9-11.

27. *Alta California*, Dec. 29, 1867. The *Alta* obituary ran two full columns and was reprinted almost entire by the *Sacramento Union* and the Virginia City *Territorial Enterprise*.

28. Oscar T. Shuck, *Historical Abstract of San Francisco* (San Francisco: n.p., 1897), vol. 1, 8, 15. While shootings and duels were by no means uncommon, Lemon and Graham were sufficiently prominent and the feud sufficiently dramatic that the newspapers gave considerable space to their differences. The whole affair was revived by the newspapers at the time of Lemon's death.

29. Georgia Willis Read and Ruth Gaines, eds., *Gold Rush: The Journals, Drawings, and Other Papers of J. Goldsborough Bruff*, 2 vols. (New York: Columbia University Press, 1944), vol. 2, 1118.

30. From a journal, Green wrote a narrative of his experiences in the regiment and later in San Francisco. It is one of the less valuable accounts of the regiment, the bulk of it being devoted to a justification of his position in title disputes with the city of San Francisco. Alfred A. Green, "Life and Adventures of a 47-er of California," (MS), Bancroft Library, University of California, Berkeley.

31. Lee was one of the ten members of Company F who returned to Santa Barbara to spend their lives. Lieutenant Carnes, who had never left Santa Barbara for the mines, represented the district in the second session of the legislature in 1851. Their election is impressive for the relationship they had obviously established with the overwhelmingly native Californian population of Santa Barbara. The only other assemblymen from Santa Barbara during the 1850s were native Californians, José María Covarrubias and Pedro C. Carrillo. Pablo de la Guerra represented the district in the state senate.

32. Bancroft: *History of California*, vol. 3, 792.

33. Quoted in Grivas, *Military Governments in California*, 135.

34. Graphic accounts of the seizure of the city records were written by both Buffum and Ryan. Buffum, *Six Months in the Gold Mines*, 117-19; Ryan, *Personal Adventures in Upper and Lower California*, vol. 2, 252-54.

35. *Placer Times*, May 5, 1849.

36. *Alta California*, June 7, 1849. This was by no means the first time the idea of a convention had been raised. Since the previous December, meetings had been held in most northern California cities on similar proposals, i.e., to form first a provisional and then a territorial government. What was now desired was a state constitution. The assembly stressed that "the present state of a great and harrassing political question in the United States must certainly defeat, for several coming sessions, any attempts at an organization of a territorial government for this country by Congress."

37. *Alta California*, June 14, 1849.

Chapter Sixteen

Growing Up with the Country: The Constitutional Convention and Statehood

T HROUGH LATE 1848 and well into 1849, efforts toward municipal reform in San Francisco and the movement for a territorial or state government were closely related. Both activities opposed continuation of military government, and the men involved regularly challenged the authority first of Colonel Mason and then of General Riley. Tracing the activities of former volunteers through the mass meetings, the demonstrations, and the full periods of the committee resolutions, one remembers Stevenson's men marching around the decks of the *Susan Drew* with their signs reading "Sons of Liberty!" The spirit of protest was the same, although the stakes were now higher.

The first of the meetings to discuss the calling of a convention to form a provisional territorial government was held in San Jose on December 11, 1848, almost immediately after the news arrived that the first session of the Thirtieth Congress had failed to enact a territorial bill. The meeting was called by Myron Norton and Kimball H. Dimmick, both of whom were appointed to the resolutions committee.[1] That committee passed resolutions calling for a convention to form a provisional government which would be put into immediate operation and remain in force until Congress should supercede it by a regular territorial organization. A date for the convention was set in January.

The San Jose meeting was reported fully in *The California Star and Californian* of December 16, and the action of the meeting, according to a signed editorial by Edward Gilbert, met with the "unanimous approval" of the people of northern California. Gilbert called for a San Francisco meeting on December 21. On that day and December 23 "two of the largest public meetings ever held in California convened . . . and unanimously declared their concurrence in the course of action recommended by the citizens of San Jose."[2] On the resolutions committee elected at the December 23 meeting were Edward Gilbert, Myron Norton, Henry A. Schoolcraft (not yet off to Sacramento), former captain Henry M. Naglee of Company D, former alcalde George Hyde, B. R. Buckelew, and James Creighton—the first-named four of the seven members were former volunteers.

As in San Jose, the sense of the San Francisco meeting was the necessity for an immediate territorial government, but the date set by the San Jose meeting for a convention was deemed too early. The date was changed to March 5. In addition to the resolutions committee, a corresponding committee was elected, with Gilbert chairman, to contact people in other districts and secure their support. Gilbert threw himself earnestly into this effort. Largely as a result of his persuasive pen and the care he exercised in what was published in his newspapers, similar meetings were held in Sacramento during the first week of January 1849, in Monterey at the end of that month, and in Sonoma on February 5.

To the end of 1848 the people of California had only the conflicting opinions of the president and the secretary of state on California's legal status, and the clear evidence close at hand from Colonel Mason that military government would continue. The administration theory—that until Congress might take action California should patiently bear with the de

facto government existing with their "presumed consent"—
became increasingly intolerable. With careful timing, Edward
Gilbert introduced a new theory on January 11, 1849, in the
second number of the *Alta California*. More precisely, it was a
popular theory, but in this case carrying the prestigious name
of Senator Thomas Hart Benton. The Benton theory of California's legal status and the course Californians should follow
was a seditious one, and it had a tremendous effect on public
opinion in California.

Benton's letter "To the People of California," dated
August 27, 1848, had been printed in the October 13 issue of
the New York *Morning Courier and Enquirer*. While the letter
had been printed in other eastern newspapers and was not
unknown in California, Gilbert had secured it from the New
York newspaper, and through the pages of the *Alta California*
it was given greatest currency. Gilbert reprinted the entire
letter. Benton minced no words. He addressed the "People
of California":

The treaty with Mexico makes you citizens of the United States;
Congress has not yet passed the laws to give you the blessings of
government; and it may be some time before it does so. In the mean-
time, while your condition is anomalous and critical, it calls for the
exercise of the soundest discretion and the most exalted patriotism
on your part. The temporary civil and military government established over you as a right of war is at an end. The edicts promul-
gated by your temporary governors Kearny and Mason (each an
ignoramus) so far as these edicts went to change the law of the land,
are null and void, and were so from the beginning. . . . Having no
lawful government, nor lawful officers, you may get none except by
your own act; you can have none that can have authority over you
except by your own consent. In fact, sanction must be the will of the
majority. I recommend you to meet in convention—provide for a
cheap and simple government—and take care of yourselves until
Congress can provide for you.[3]

Unnecessarily, Benton went on to point out that the people of
Oregon had been successful when they followed his advice
not two years before. These inflammatory sentiments, so
clearly stated, appealed instantly to the majority in California,
as Gilbert could be certain they would.

Gilbert had probably possessed the Benton letter since mid-December but had not published it in the *California Star and Californian* or in the first number of the *Alta California*. In his salutatory in that first number, Gilbert had promised fearless journalism but also moderation and objectivity, with no sensationalism for its own sake. There was immediate reaction to Benton's poor taste in abusing General Kearny and Colonel Mason, and Gilbert printed the criticism in the next number of the newspaper.[4]

After publication of the Benton letter, there was not much question that delegates of the people would "meet in convention" and take care of themselves if Congress did not provide for California. They proceeded with commendable caution, however. On January 24 the corresponding committee in San Francisco, having received a number of requests for postponement of the proposed convention, recommended that the date be changed to May 1 so that the possible action of Congress could be known.

Early in March some of the delegates elected to the convention met in San Francisco. Among them were Edward Gilbert, Myron Norton, and Francis Lippitt from San Francisco; Colonel Stevenson (resident in San Francisco but having been elected in absentia to represent Los Angeles); and former captain John B. Frisbie, elected a delegate from Sonoma. They decided on further postponement and on new elections of delegates from throughout California who would meet in Monterey on the first Monday in August. A still more important decision of this group was to substitute the idea of a state government for the provisional territorial government theretofore considered. The population had grown to such an extent, and the wants of the country were so critical, that they believed only the creation of a state constitution and admission into the Union could resolve California's problems.[5]

When General Riley became military governor of California on April 13, he thus had this body of popular resistance with which to contend, in addition to the related but more localized problems created by the San Francisco Legislative Assembly. The decision to call for an election of delegates to a convention seemed to be Riley's only possible course. The patience of the Californians would not have persisted long after May 28, when news arrived in San Francisco that Congress had adjourned, providing no territorial government but extending the revenue laws over California. Riley's proclamation of June 3 called for an election of delegates to a constitutional convention that would meet in Monterey on September 1. The first reaction to his proclamation was predictable outrage. Those who had been most active in agitating for such a convention denied the governor's right even to *call* the convention, a right they felt was inherent in the people. By June 12, however, wise heads had prevailed, and public meetings in Monterey, San Jose, and, finally, San Francisco had concurred with Riley's recommendations. California settled down, politically, until election day, August 1.[6]

The election proceeded in what Frank Soulé in *The Annals of San Francisco* called "a spirited, though orderly manner," and all the former volunteers who had been candidates for the convention delegations were elected. Not unexpectedly, but impressively, Edward Gilbert received more votes than any other delegate, and Myron Norton received only slightly fewer. Also from San Francisco, Francis J. Lippitt had been elected.[7] Gilbert received 1,512 votes and Norton 1,436 (360 votes more than the next-most-popular candidate, William M. Gwin). Lippitt was elected with 874 votes, about the same number as the merchants W. D. M. Howard (876) and Alfred Ellis (872), both of whom had been active in the San Francisco Guards and the legislative assembly. Gwin, a former congressman from Mississippi, was a frankly ambitious political figure who had arrived in San Francisco not long before the election; he was determined, he later admitted, to become a senator from California.[8]

From the populous San Joaquin district, embracing the favored middle area of the mines, two of the six delegates seated were ex-volunteers, and a strange pair they were—former lieutenants Hollingsworth and Vermeule. To Hollingsworth appearances and honor were all; Vermeule had been cashiered from the regiment in disgrace and later forcibly exiled from Los Angeles. Some odd relationships were to appear and develop as the delegates assembled and met in Monterey.

At the August 1 election, General Riley also had ordered the election of local officials to serve in the interim until state officials could be selected. In Sacramento William Shannon was elected a delegate to the convention and judge of the criminal Court of the First Instance as well.[9] The same occurred in San Jose, where Kimball Dimmick was elected a delegate and judge of the First Instance.

Thus seven of the forty-eight delegates in the convention were former volunteers, all of them officers—Captains Dimmick, Lippitt, and Shannon, and Lieutenants Gilbert, Hollingsworth, Norton, and Vermeule. With the exception of Myron Norton, all were well acquainted from three years before when the fledgling regiment trained on Governors Island. Five of the seven were attorneys, Gilbert a newspaperman, and Hollingsworth—we have only his word—a farmer. Of the entire forty-eight delegates, fourteen were lawyers, and the regiment thus supplied more than a third of the attorneys present at the convention. Their influence was relatively great.

Certain other prominent ex-volunteers influenced the political future of California although they were not delegates or even candidates for the convention. Colonel Stevenson was somewhat active in the preliminary meetings and had once been elected a delegate from Los Angeles to one of the conventions that did not occur. Henry Naglee participated also, as did another former captain, John B. Frisbie. These men were prominent, and at least Naglee and Frisbie might well have been elected, but they were not candidates. In each case, the reason appears to be the same. All were deeply involved in business, to which time-consuming public service must have come second.

A popular practice, almost a sport, among historians of California has been the elaborate tabulation of information on the convention delegates—their ages, nativity, professions and occupations, residences, and length of residence in California. Properly made and interpreted, such a table can be illuminating, but the one produced by Hubert Howe Bancroft resulted in a notable absurdity. In discussing the delegates he wrote:

The heterogeneous personnel of the convention proved a safeguard rather than a drawback; New York being forced to consult Mississippi, Maryland to confer with Vermont, Rhode Island with Kentucky, and all with California. Strangers to each other when they met, in contending for the faith that was in them they had become brothers, and felt like congratulating each other on their mutual achievement.[10]

Bancroft's premise was wrong. While a few of the delegates were strangers to one another, nothing is clearer than the already-established relationships among most of them, in some cases going back well into the Mexican and almost to the Spanish period in California.

In the table Josiah Royce prepared on the delegates, one of the best, only thirteen of the delegates are shown to have been in California for one year or less. The roots of the other thirty-five were decidedly pre-Gold Rush. Six were native Californians and others had become naturalized Mexican citizens, but the majority had arrived between 1840 and 1848 and were included in a group aptly called by Royce "the Americans of the interregnum." These Royce identified as having

in common a lively interest in a permanent and strong government in California; they all had a concern in California that was prior in origin to the gold-discovery and that seemed apt to outlast any immediate good fortunes or reverses that might come to them in consequence of this discovery. They were fearful of the newcoming population, in case it were not soon restrained by fixed laws. And they were indisposed to permit the sectional interests of older states to interfere with the present destiny of California.[11]

Few of the delegates were unknown to Captain Henry W. Halleck, Mason and Riley's secretary of state since 1847, and all the former military men, including Norton, were well known to him. Halleck had been elected a delegate from

Monterey. Shannon, from Sacramento, certainly knew John A. Sutter, and he knew as well the Spanish-born delegate Miguel Pedrorena from the days Company I had been stationed in San Diego. Lippitt's ultimate friendship with Pablo de la Guerra, who had inevitably been elected a delegate from Santa Barbara, has already been discussed. Lippitt was also acquainted with the other Santa Barbara delegate, José María Covarrubias. Hollingsworth knew Los Angeles delegates Abel Stearns and Hugo Reid well (and their wives and Reid's daughter still better). The evidence that Vermeule knew Abel Stearns is as incontrovertible as the appearance of both in Monterey is amusing. Remarkably, nothing seems to have passed between the two during the six weeks they were there.

On September 1, the appointed date, only ten delegates were in Monterey, but the other nine elected Kimball Dimmick chairman pro tempore. When it became clear that no quorum would be present, the convention adjourned until the following Monday. On that day, with a quorum, the convention elected popular Robert Semple of Benicia as president and Captain William G. Marcy as secretary of the convention. Marcy was not a delegate to the convention. For the reporter of the convention, a most important position, J. Ross Browne, a former reporter for the U.S. Senate, was selected. The choice was a good one, but there was, in fact, another strong contender, E. Gould Buffum. On August 14 Buffum had written to Dimmick in San Jose, asking him to use his influence as a delegate and a judge to obtain for Buffum the appointment of clerk of the convention. As qualification, Buffum stated that he was "a ready writer and short hand reporter" and a regular correspondent for the *New York Herald*.[12] No evidence can be found that Dimmick did or did not use his influence. A better clerk or reporter of the convention than Browne would be difficult to imagine, but Buffum's careful dispatches and his 1850 book do prove him qualified.

In the first week the convention settled down to business, with the president appointing a Select Committee on the Constitution and charging it with reporting a plan. Norton and Dimmick were appointed members of the Select Committee. In committee Norton actually framed the first draft of the constitution. On September 8, with Francis Lippitt in the chair and the convention resolved into a Committee of the Whole, the delegates began discussing a proposed bill of rights. William Shannon first asked for recognition and, having secured the floor, moved that the first two sections be two statements from the Virginia Constitution of 1776, with a clause from the Declaration of Independence incorporated:

Section 1. All men are by nature free and independent, and have certain inalienable rights, among which are those of enjoying and defending life and liberty, acquiring, possessing, and protecting property, and pursuing and obtaining safety and happiness.

Section 2. All political power is inherent in the people. Government is instituted for the protection, security, and benefit of the people; and they have the right at all times, to alter or reform the same whenever the public good may require it.

After some discussion—one delegate preferred an alternative statement and another no such statement of rights at all—the sections were adopted, and the constitution-making process was under way.[13] That day nine sections were adopted.

Shannon was to star again on Monday, September 10. When the convention reconvened, the six additional sections reported were adopted. Shannon then secured the floor and moved to insert a sixteenth section, one not reported from the Select Committee. The section he read and moved to adopt was one everyone had been anticipating, although not all were anxious to commit their votes. Shannon read: "Neither slavery nor involuntary servitude, unless for the punishment of crimes, shall ever be tolerated in the State." It was a clear, open, simple statement, on a principle Shannon felt deeply, as his reaction to slavery in Brazil has shown. After a vain attempt to amend Shannon's statement, to forbid, as well, the introduction of free Negroes, the article was passed unanimously.[14]

So it went. There was controversy, intrigue, acrimony, bitter debate and occasionally flaring tempers, and humor, but by and large the convention moved seriously and steadily through its work. Major problems between great interests were compromised, successfully, if seldom easily. In general, the document produced at Monterey was a good one. It endured for thirty years.

While not the noisiest of the delegates, six of the seven former volunteers were consistently effective and active, although they by no means always voted together. The exception was not Vermeule, as one might expect, but John Mc-Henry Hollingsworth. He attended sessions quite faithfully but seldom opened his mouth and always voted with the majority. He seemed altogether out of his element and left no record of those six weeks. At twenty-five, Hollingsworth was the youngest delegate. By his earlier statement, he was terribly distressed by his failure in the mines and was determined to leave California. A statement made by him three years before suggests another possibility. On November 6, 1846, in a pensive moment aboard the *Susan Drew*, just north of the equator, he wrote: "How much I have got to learn . . . it has been part of my life to conceal my ignorance. . . . I never was blest with intellect like any other person."[15]

If Hollingsworth was ill suited to the assignment, others of the former volunteers were extraordinarily well qualified. It would be difficult to describe better theoretical preparation for constitution-making than that of Francis Lippitt. In 1901 Lippitt spoke at the annual banquet of Brown University alumni and included part of this address in his memoirs published the next year. In the speech Lippitt refers to himself as "the graduate" and reports how de Tocqueville, returned from America, had asked at the American Legation in Paris for the address of a bright, educated American to assist him. "The graduate," Lippitt wrote,

had been attached to the Legation, and it was his address that was given. The two labored together for some months; the graduate, sometimes in oral conversations, but chiefly in written memoirs, explaining the mechanism of our political systems, both State and Federal.

De Tocqueville had given him free access to a whole library of volumes he had collected in America, most of them statutes of the different states. But such a wilderness of books was of very little use to him, and what made his task an easy one was the mastery of general principles he had acquired in his senior year at Brown, where he made a thorough study for six months under Professor Goddard of "Rawle on the Constitution."[16]

The political-science training under Professor William G. Goddard is at least one of the sources of the rather conservative republicanism Lippitt displayed in the convention. Only delegate Henry Halleck was as familiar with other state constitutions.

The convention finished its work on October 12. The delegates voted themselves a salary of sixteen dollars a day for their work, celebrated, and the next day signed the constitution. The convention had awarded J. Ross Browne $10,000 for reporting the proceedings and for supplying, as he was obliged to do, 1,000 printed-and-bound copies of the constitution in English and 250 copies in Spanish. This was a tall order; the schedule attached to the constitution called for ratification of the document and an election of state officers on November 13, in just a month. Only one printing plant in California could handle such an order, and it was Edward Gilbert's *Alta California* that printed and bound the volumes. In less than a week the work was done and the constitution was on its way throughout California.[17]

November 13 was a stormy day throughout northern California, and, partly as a consequence of the weather, the voting was light. With the population of California in November 1849 estimated at 107,000, just under 13,000 people voted.[18] The constitution was ratified almost unanimously— over 12,000 votes for and 800 votes against its acceptance. Peter H. Burnett was elected governor, John McDougal lieutenant governor, and Edward Gilbert and George W. Wright California's first two representatives in Congress. No former volunteer had run for governor, but Francis Lippitt had narrowly been defeated for the lieutenant governorship. State senators and assemblymen were also elected. Of the eighteen state senators, two were former volunteers—Thomas Vermeule and Nelson Taylor. Four former volunteers were elected to the assembly—Theron R. Per Lee and James A. Gray from Monterey, former captain John E. Brackett from Sonoma, and Joseph C. Morehead from the San Joaquin.

On December 20 in San Jose, Kimball Dimmick, as judge of the Court of the First Instance, swore in the governor and lieutenant governor, and on the same day Brigadier General Riley issued his final proclamation, relinquishing his office. California's military government was at an end, and its new government—not yet state, not territorial—began to function. Not until September of the next year would California be admitted to the Union.

After the convention in 1849 the seven former-volunteer delegates led lives that were in many ways dissimilar, and several of their lives were tragically short. Of all the volunteers Gilbert had risen to the highest public prominence. In January of 1850, with his fellow congressman-elect George Wright and the two senators-elect, William M. Gwin and John C. Frémont (chosen by the legislature in late December), Gilbert left San Francisco for Washington, D.C. There he worked continuously for California statehood, which was finally secured on September 9, 1850, not at all by his efforts but by the famous compromise plan of Senator Clay. This plan called for admitting California to the Union as a free state while allowing the future territories of New Mexico and Utah to decide for themselves their slave or free status. A few days later Gilbert took his seat in the House of Representatives. He remained in Washington, writing dispatches regularly to the *Alta California*, until early in 1852, when he returned to San Francisco, having been unseated in the previous fall's election.

On Gilbert's return to California, he found that the state capital had been changed to Vallejo, and John Bigler was in the governor's chair. Bigler had been elected by a curious coalition of well-organized land squatters (who were a power in 1851) and Southern sympathizers, as well as by Democrats in general. While himself a Democrat, Gilbert immediately began attacking the state administration and Bigler, putting

himself on the right side of history but on the wrong side of
the governor's partisans. (Bigler's two administrations have
come to be known as among the poorest in nineteenth-
century California politics, and there were some very bad
ones.) One of Gilbert's violent attacks on the governor drew
an abusive letter from State Senator James W. Denver of the
Bigler clique. Gilbert challenged, Denver accepted, and their
duel was fought with pistols at Oak Grove, near Sacramento,
on August 2, 1852. Gilbert died. He was thirty years old.[19]

Gilbert's funeral in San Francisco, befitting such a martyr
and the state's best-known newspaperman and first congressman, was grand. Francis Lippitt and Joseph Folsom were
among the pallbearers. Between the end of the convention in
1849 and his departure for Washington in 1850, Gilbert had
sat for his portrait, by William S. Jewett, and when San Francisco's splendid city hall was built at the end of the decade, the
only painting in the Board of Supervisors', or City Council,
chamber was the portrait of Edward Gilbert.

In March 1872, twenty-five years after the arrival of the
regiment in California, an anniversary banquet was held in
San Francisco, with thirty-nine former volunteers present
and a number of honored guests. Gilbert had not been forgotten. State Senator Philip A. Roach, a pioneer of 1849,
responded to a toast to "The Press":

With your regiment and as one of its number, a member of the press
came to our shore, who established a free, fearless and independent
paper in this city and who was not afraid to speak out boldly. When
it was dangerous to give utterance to his sentiments, he stood up for
the people's rights and by his fearless and brilliant character built up
a paper of influence, talent and ability in this city—the Alta. This
gentleman's name you well know is Edward Gilbert, who laid down
his life for the principles of liberty we now enjoy and for the liberty
of the press.[20]

One of the former volunteers present at that dinner was
Gilbert's captain, John B. Frisbie, rich, esteemed, long married to Epifanía Vallejo—all because a persuasive young zealot
in Albany, in the early summer of 1846, had convinced him
that the future lay in California.

Former captain William Shannon died at the age of twenty-eight. Having been elected judge of the Criminal Court of the First Instance at the August 1, 1849, election, Shannon returned to Coloma after the convention, sold his interest in the general store there, and began the practice of law in Sacramento. Early in November his court in Sacramento was organized, and he served as judge for almost a year. At the general election of October 7, 1850, Shannon was elected to represent the Sacramento district in the California State Senate but died before he could take his seat. Between October 20 and November 12, 1850, a cholera epidemic killed 448 people in the town of Sacramento alone, roughly fifteen percent of the population.[21] Shannon died of the disease on November 3. His name is generally remembered for his introduction of the anti-slavery article but might be remembered as well for his solution of the boundary dispute. There were strong factions in the convention, both for including all of Mexican California to the Rockies, and for drawing the line at the crest of the Sierra. Shannon compromised with an eastern boundary line that, with only slight amendments, was adopted and is today California's eastern boundary.[22]

In addition to Gilbert, two other delegates from the regiment were involved with newspapers. Thomas Vermeule gave up the practice of law and settled in San Jose, where he worked at various times on both newspapers there until his death in 1856.[23] Kimball Dimmick, who had been established in San Jose where he had served as a judge until the fall of 1850, then spent a period in Sacramento at his first calling, printing. In 1851 he returned to Chenango County, New York, and settled his affairs. With his wife he settled permanently in Los Angeles, California, in 1852. Dimmick was elected justice of the peace in 1852, and in July of 1854 founded, as co-publisher, the *Southern Californian*, a newspaper intended to challenge the supremacy of the successful Los Angeles *Star*. His association with the newspaper lasted only a few months, until November 1854, and the newspaper itself but a few months longer.[24] For several years before

1860 Dimmick served as a county judge for Los Angeles County, and in 1861 President Lincoln appointed him United States attorney for the Southern District of California. That same year he died in Los Angeles.[25]

Myron Norton also settled in Los Angeles, where in 1851 he was elected judge of the Superior Court. That same year he served as a major in the California State Militia on an Indian campaign in Los Angeles County, and his superior officer, Major General J. H. Bean, in a letter to Governor McDougal, commended Norton for his bravery.[26] The following year Norton served on the Los Angeles City Council and in 1853 was elected a county judge.

Early that year Norton was involved in an event suggesting that Los Angeles had not altogether changed since the anxious days of 1846 and 1847. In his *Reminiscences of a Ranger* Horace Bell, the acute observer of particularly the seamier side of southern California life, described a number of fancy-dress affairs he attended in Los Angeles in 1852 and 1853: "one of those very elegant and exclusive affairs . . . ended in blood." The scene was the spacious home of Don Abel Stearns, whom Bell identified as "a very wealthy American," and the date was Washington's Birthday 1853. "The ball," Bell wrote, ". . . was a grand and patriotic affair, but very exclusive." About two hundred rowdies, who maintained that an exclusive national celebration was un-American, assembled to break up the Stearns's private party. As the rowdies forced the door,

[one] patriotic exclusive stepped directly to the door and plugged the first gentleman who attempted to enter. Then another, and another, and by this time the affair had assumed all the beautiful proportions of a first-class revolution, and the firing became general. Of the assailants several were shot down, and the assault effectually repulsed; while of the exclusives but one man was wounded, and he the gay and festive Myron Norton. . . . The brilliant Norton received a gentle perforation, that placed him *hors du combat* for some time thereafter. . . . For the next few days the angels were on a war footing . . . [It] took months to cool off the bad blood engendered by that affair of the 22nd of February, 1853, and for some time individual collisions were of frequent occurrence.[27]

In 1855, while a municipal judge, Norton authorized the formation of a Los Angeles City Guard to deal with civic disturbances. Norton remained on the bench in Los Angeles for some years, and was still a judge in 1860.[28] Norton's death is not recorded nor are his activities after 1861. It seems likely that he would have been involved for the Union during the Civil War, and it is possible he lost his life or never returned to California after the war.[29]

A number of former volunteers went east to fight, survived, but continued to live in the East. Francis Lippitt is but one example. Through the 1850s Lippitt practiced law in San Francisco. In June 1861 he was elected colonel of the First Regiment of California Volunteer Infantry, went east to see some action, and in 1865—rather to his surprise—was breveted brigadier general.[30] For the next decade he practiced law in New York City and Providence. In 1875 Lippitt was invited by the attorney general of the United States to join the Department of Justice, where he first prepared cases for presentation before the Supreme Court and then acted as government counsel in the Court of Claims. After five years in the Department of Justice, he resumed the practice of law in Washington, D.C., and finally retired to Annapolis, where he died in 1902 at the age of ninety. Once Lippitt left California in 1861, he never returned. But at the end of his long life, when writing his *Reminiscences* in 1901 and 1902, he considered his participation in California's Constitutional Convention a "satisfaction."[31] Indeed, he had made a major contribution.

Of the seven former-volunteer delegates to the convention, only John McHenry Hollingsworth left California as quickly as he could. He even had his passage provided, since Governor Riley selected him as bearer of the new constitution to the president and of dispatches to the War Department. Nor did Hollingsworth leave California in poverty, as he had despairingly predicted he would. His *per diem* fees for convention duty amounted to almost $600, no California-style fortune, but something nonetheless. He had earned it; attendance must have been extremely painful for him. Henry R.

Wagner, one of the most dogged California historians of the first half of this century, investigated Hollingsworth's later life and found he had first become a collector for the Chesapeake and Ohio Canal. Later he was an officer in the Potomac Light Infantry and briefly served as a major in the First Battalion of District of Columbia Volunteers during the Civil War. Having seen no action, Hollingsworth was mustered out of the battalion on July 23, 1861. There seems to be no record of Hollingsworth for the next eleven years, but in 1872 he finally found his niche. That year he became superintendent of Mount Vernon, where he remained until his retirement in 1885.[32]

The last entry in Hollingsworth's journal, undated, was entitled "Farewell to Monterey and California." From the ring of it, he probably read the piece at one of those gatherings of the California *haut monde* at which he was so popular, perhaps at a farewell party for himself. Much of what he wrote was euphuistic, conventional, and grandiloquent, but one passage has substance:

This [bidding his good Monterey friends good-bye] you may think easy, but hold: have you ever been in peace, in war, in camp, in garrison, in speculation, with the same friends, in sickness and in health, in conditions that required consolation and in conditions where you had had the sweet opportunity of affording condolence? have you been in a country where it grew up with you, when all its hills, vallies [sic], towns, and wealth, and natural beauty changed owners under your eye, and the flag of your country, spreading itself as gracefully as calmly, shed its benign laws over a new people?

Of all the writing by volunteers, there is no more incisive, sweeping, or moving appraisal of their experience than this by Hollingsworth. Then, ever gentlemanly in the presence of ladies ("most virtuous, most worthy, most lovely and fair"), Hollingsworth concluded with the English translation of a traditional Mexican compliment: "May all your daughters be as virtuous as their mothers, and your sons, wise and brave."[33] Hollingsworth had style. The Mount Vernon Ladies' Association must have adored him.

Notes

1. Norton's activities in San Jose, other than agitating, are not known. Dimmick was practicing law, and the day after the meeting was elected alcalde for 1849. The best source of information on the meetings that preceded the convention is in J. Ross Browne, *Report of the Debates in the Convention of California on the Formation of the State Constitution* (Washington, D.C.: printed by J. T. Towers, 1850), referred to hereafter as *Report of the Debates*. The account of these meetings is an appendix entitled "Memorial to the Senate and House of Representatives." Requested by President Taylor in the spring of 1850, to make a stronger case for California's admission to the Union, the "Memorial" is a careful, short review of the events leading to the convention. Edward Gilbert wrote most of this document; as a result, his own role in those events is modestly understated.

2. Browne, "Memorial," *Report of the Debates*, Appendix, p. xvii.

3. New York *Morning Courier and Enquirer*, Oct. 13, 1848; San Francisco *Alta California*, Jan. 11, 1849.

4. *Alta California*, Jan. 18, 1849. Benton's hatred of Kearny, during and after the court-martial of Benton's son-in-law, John Charles Frémont, on charges of mutinous and disobedient conduct —charges brought by Kearny—was sufficient explanation for his calling the general an "ignoramus," but inclusion of Colonel Mason in that category is puzzling. It may simply have been for effect. Gilbert's publication of the statement was probably for effect also and was in equally bad taste.

5. Browne, "Memorial," *Report of the Debates*, Appendix, p. xvii.

6. *Ibid.*, p. xviii.

7. Soulé, *et al*, *The Annals of San Francisco*, 228-29.

8. William M. Gwin, "Memoirs of Hon. William M. Gwin," *California Historical Society Quarterly*, XIX, 1940, 2-3. Gwin succeeded in being elected to the convention by making himself very well known to San Franciscans in less than a month, through a dazzling series of speeches in which he emphasized his experience and his advocacy of nothing less than a state government.

9. In Sacramento James Queen, former sergeant of Company F who had left Santa Barbara for the mines with the company's current records, was elected a supernumerary delegate. He was not seated in the convention. Queen, who was a printer, became a fairly important Sacramento publisher and was active in Republican party circles until his death in San Francisco in 1879.

10. Bancroft, *History of California*, vol. 6, 302-3.

11.   Josiah Royce, *California: From the Conquest in 1846 to the Second Vigilance Committee in San Francisco, A Study of American Character* (New York: Alfred A. Knopf, 1948; originally published in 1886), 205-6. By the term "interregnum" Royce meant particularly the years 1847 and 1848. Royce's table is on page 206.

12.   *Alta California*, Dec. 29, 1867.

13.   Browne, *Report of the Debates*, 33-34.

14.   *Ibid.*, 44.

15.   Hollingsworth, *Journal*, 4-5.

16.   Lippitt, *Reminiscences*, 37. The year appears to have been 1834, when Lippitt would have been 22 or 23 years old. He was born in 1812.

17.   By far the best account of the convention is Browne's *Report of the Debates*, but two secondary sources valuable for their background and interpretation are Cardinal L. Goodwin, *The Establishment of State Government in California, 1846-1850* (New York: The Macmillan Company, 1914) and Woodrow J. Hansen, *The Search for Authority in California* (Oakland, California: Biobooks, 1960).

18.   Bancroft, *History of California*, vol. 6, 305. Of the 107,000, Bancroft estimated 76,000 were Americans; 18,000 foreigners; and 13,000 natives.

19.   *Ibid.*, 687; *Alta California*, Aug. 7, 1852. Denver was rewarded by Bigler in short order. When William Van Voorhies resigned as secretary of state, Bigler appointed Denver to the office on Jan. 11, 1853. Denver was later governor of Kansas, and Denver, Colorado, is named for him.

20.   *Alta California*, March 27, 1872.

21.   Bancroft, *History of California*, vol. 6, 231, 452.

22.   Browne, *Report of the Debates*, 169-73; Hansen, *The Search for Authority*, 137, 169. Little has been written on Shannon. A small pamphlet—Peter T. Conmy: *William Edward Shannon, 1823-1850, Soldier, Lawyer, Statesman* (Oakland, California: 1954)—is valuable in part but not altogether reliable. Conmy neglected most of Shannon's major contributions.

23.   Bancroft, "Pioneer Register," *History of California*, vol. 5, 762.

24.   Rice, *The Los Angeles Star, 1851-1864*, 65-66.

25.   Bancroft, *History of California*, vol. 7, 293; "Pioneer Register," vol. 2, 781.

26.   J. M. Scammell, "Military Units in Southern California, 1853-1862," *California Historical Society Quarterly*, XXIX, 1950, 245.

27.   Horace Bell, *Reminiscences of a Ranger* (Los Angeles: Yarnell, Caystile & Mathes, 1881), 81-82.

28.   Bancroft, *History of California*, vol. 7, 267.

29.   In 1871 when Francis D. Clark produced his first pamphlet on the regiment, he seems to have had evidence, source uncited, that Norton was dead.

30.   Lippitt, *Reminiscences*, 111.

31.   *Ibid.*, 117-20.

32.   Henry R. Wagner, "Introduction: John McHenry Hollingsworth," *The Journal of Lieutenant John McHenry Hollingsworth*, vi-vii.

33.   Hollingsworth, *Journal*, 59-61.

Chapter Seventeen

Outlaws, Hounds, and Filibusters

MOST OF STEVENSON'S MEN were both accustomed and willing to live within the law, and a remarkable number of former volunteers were involved in making the law. But some lived—and as a result some died—outside it.

The first recorded instance involved McKenzie Beverly. Beverly had not come from New York with the regiment but was enrolled by Major Hardie in San Francisco on May 1, 1847, as a private in Captain Dimmick's Company K. He was placed on detached duty in San Jose with the express horses and was almost immediately in trouble. By July he had been sent in arrest to Monterey, where he deserted. He was captured in San Francisco early in November. While awaiting trial for desertion, evidently free to visit the village, he shot and killed Charles Dörnte at George Denike's bakery, which was a saloon as well.[1] Beverly was captured and tried on the charge of murder before a military commission, since a civilian had been involved. Convicted and sentenced to dishonorable discharge and fifteen years solitary confinement, Beverly escaped from the guardhouse at the presidio on the night of January 27, 1848.[2] Colonel Mason offered an impressively large reward—$200—to anyone who would deliver Beverly to Monterey, but he was never caught.[3] Through the following spring rumors were heard that Beverly was in the woods near San Jose, organizing a band of marauders, but while Bancroft in the "Pioneer Register" called him "a desperado at large," there was no further definite evidence of Beverly.[4]

Had Beverly been of a different temperament, and only a little patient, he would have found himself a rich man. Like many other volunteers in the early summer of 1847, Beverly had bought (for $12) a lot in downtown San Francisco, in the block bounded by Montgomery and Kearny streets, between Pine and Bush streets. The other principal lot owners on this block were Robert Semple and volunteers Christian, Adolphus, and Charles Russ. The Russ property was the basis of that family's vast fortune, since the block became one of the most important for downtown San Francisco business. In 1849 lots like that of Beverly (in less desirable blocks) were changing hands at from $30,000 to $50,000. Since Beverly did not fence or build on the property, or get his title to it confirmed, ownership reverted to the city.[5]

Other crimes of violence in Alta California, some of them involving Indians, were committed by or attributed to volunteers. But in Baja California the record was the worst. There, in addition to Captain Naglee's "executions," volunteers committed two murders. On February 22, 1848, at La Paz Private William Sutphen, one of the original members of Captain Steele's Company A, "shot a frenchman to death with his muskett [sic]." Two days later Sutphen broke from the guard, "it being very dark at the time," and was seen no more.[6]

Also in La Paz, sometime during June 1848, Private John Lawson murdered his wife, one of the company laundresses. Lawson was uncommonly old for a volunteer, forty-three, and had come to California as a recruit on the *Isabella*. He had been in Baja California only a month. Apprehended, he was confined on the U.S.S. *Independence* and was returned to Monterey during the late summer. Like Naglee, Lawson was fortunate. Despite Lieutenant Colonel Burton's persistent efforts to have civil charges filed against Lawson, the circumstances led Colonel Mason simply to discharge him dishonorably.[7]

Once the regiment was disbanded, a certain small number of the ex-volunteers turned to crime. William Campbell, of Company K, a twenty-six-year-old blacksmith from Norwich, had deserted from the presidio in San Francisco on October 21, 1847, with a full set of arms. Nothing more was seen of him before the company was mustered out. Also from the presidio in San Francisco, David A. Davis of Company H had deserted on May 26, 1848, in the first great rash of desertions for the gold fields. A twenty-year-old mason, Davis had been one of Captain Frisbie's original men from Albany. On December 17, 1848, near San Jose the two former privates and a companion not of the regiment were captured and charged with highway robbery and attempted murder. When Campbell, Davis, and their companion were taken, they were reportedly in possession of the loot and were identified by witnesses and by their intended victims. Tried before a hastily summoned jury of American townspeople, they were convicted on December 18 and that afternoon were hanged.[8]

On his two long tours through the gold country, E. Gould Buffum saw altogether too much of this kind of popular justice and was one of the first to object to such tribunals. In *Six Months in the Gold Mines* he reported how, just a month after the San Jose executions of Campbell and Davis, he was an unwilling witness at a similar event in Old Dry Diggings, known long thereafter as Hangtown, now as Placerville. Once the crowd had decided to hang the three prisoners, after a thirty-minute trial with little evidence, Buffum acted:

I mounted a stump, and in the name of God, humanity, and the law, protested against such a course of proceeding; but the crowd, by this time excited by frequent and deep potations of liquor from a neighboring groggery, would listen to nothing contrary to their brutal desires, and even threatened to hang me if I did not immediately desist from any further remarks. Somewhat fearful that such might be my fate, and seeing the utter uselessness of further argument with them, I ceased, and prepared to witness the horrible tragedy. . . . This was the first execution I ever witnessed.—God grant that it may be the last![9]

Buffum did not get his wish; later he witnessed two other such executions.

Even the right and righteous Buffum might not have been squeamish about dealing summarily with the murderers of the Reed family at Mission San Miguel in December 1848. The crime was especially bloody and brutal. William Reed, a British sailor, had settled in California in 1837, become a naturalized Mexican citizen, and married María Antonia Vallejo. In 1845 or 1846 he and his wife settled on the lands and in the buildings of the then-secularized Mission San Miguel, near present-day Paso Robles. In November 1848 Reed drove a large herd of sheep to the southern mines and there sold them for high prices, returning to San Miguel with a quantity of gold. In mid-December he and his entire household were murdered. The dead included Reed, his three-year-old son, his wife María Antonia, her unborn child, her brother José Ramon Vallejo, a midwife who had come to attend Mrs. Reed, the midwife's daughter of fifteen and nephew, aged four, an Indian servant and his nephew of five years, and a Negro cook. The *Alta California* reported the murderers had both shot and stabbed their victims and had made a heap of the ten corpses in one of the rooms of the mission.[10]

The crime was quickly discovered and the murderers were overtaken on the coast. One of the five was shot dead by the pursuers and another swam out to sea and was drowned. The three survivors—Joseph P. Lynch, Peter Remer (or Raymond), and Peter Quin—were taken to Santa Barbara, given a fair if fast trial by a temporary court, and sentenced to be hanged. Although there was no reluctance to carry out the sentence, in Mexican Santa Barbara there was some question about the authority of the temporary court, and the findings were presented to Colonel Mason. He answered by immediately sending Lieutenant Edward O. C. Ord, of the Third Artillery, and nine soldiers to Santa Barbara as a firing squad. On December 28 the three prisoners were executed.

One of the murderers was never identified, and three, including Remer and Quin, were believed by Walter Colton, alcalde of Monterey, to have been deserters from the Pacific Squadron. The remaining member of the band, Joseph P. Lynch, was a former volunteer.[11] Like McKenzie Beverly, Lynch had not come from New York with the regiment but joined it in California, in Los Angeles. His name first appears in Captain Matthew Stevenson's muster roll for Company G on December 31, 1847. Lynch had been enrolled as a private by Captain Stevenson and was mustered into the service on December 15. His age was given as twenty-seven, but there was no further background on him. Lynch's conduct in Company G was exemplary. Within two months of his enrollment he was promoted to corporal and served as a noncommissioned officer until honorably discharged with the company in September 1848.[12]

The criminal activities of the aforenamed ex-volunteers are not well known or, if known, the men's relationships with the regiment are not generally mentioned in local and county histories and annals of California crime. Another former New York Volunteer, however, achieved infamy as one of the worst of California's badmen: the famous highwayman of the Santa Barbara area, "Jack Powers." John A. Power, nineteen years old, and his brother Edward, twenty-five, were among the original members of Company G and were mustered in on Governors Island on August 1, 1846. (A third brother, Michael, twenty-two, deserted before the regiment left New York.) On October 1, 1846, Edward Power was appointed third corporal in the company. Upon arrival in San Francisco on April 1, 1847, both brothers were transferred to Captain Lippitt's Company F and thus spent their entire California service in Santa Barbara. While Edward Power was twice promoted and was first corporal when the company was mustered out, the record of neither man was good. They were both familiar with the guardhouse. Their offenses, however, were relatively minor—absence from drill, absence after tattoo, unsoldierlike conduct at drill, and intoxication. Neither was ever court-martialed.[13]

There is no record of either man through 1849, when they were probably in the mines, but Edward Power settled in San Francisco, where he died in 1850. That same year John Power, then twenty-three, turned up in Los Angeles as a gambler and the leader of a gang of heavily armed, generally undesirable types. Late in 1850 a vigilance committee made him unwelcome in Los Angeles.[14] Between 1851 and 1856, as Jack Powers, and most of the time with a price on his head, Power and his gang made the area between San Luis Obispo and Santa Barbara one of the most dangerous in the West. For most of that time the identity of the leader of the highwaymen was a well-kept secret, but it is clear that in 1852 and 1853 the headquarters of the group was the Rancho Arroyo Burro north of Santa Barbara. Power and his men were evicted from the ranch as squatters in April of 1853. Several members of the gang died in the small battle that ensued, and some of the men of Sheriff W. W. Twist's posse were also killed.[15] Since Power was not known as a highwayman, the sheriff thus lost an opportunity. Early in 1857 the band was dispersed, and Power with several of his men fled to Mexico. Three years later, in Sonora, he is said to have been killed in a knife fight with one of his associates.[16] As a final bizarre touch, one can also read, if not necessarily believe, that both Power and his adversary died in the fight, and the Mexicans left their bodies in the street to be devoured by hogs.[17]

The activities of these and other criminals or of later filibusters, however, did not cause the greatest damage to the reputation of the New York Volunteers. The blemished name of the regiment resulted from the celebrated affair of the Hounds and, more particularly, from the treatment of the affair by Frank Soulé in *The Annals of San Francisco* and by Bancroft in his *Popular Tribunals*.[18] While it is true that an

organization known as the Hounds (or Regulators) did exist
in San Francisco from late 1848 until July 1849, and true also
that some former volunteers were involved, little contemporary comment can be found. Almost nothing was written of
them in journals and letters, and the *Alta California*, certainly
alert to civic problems, did not recognize their existence until
late June, and then only in passing. Nor did the legislative
assembly and its justices of the peace deal with the Hounds as
a group. The conclusion is irresistible that the myth of the
Hounds sprang full-blown from the head of the journalist
Frank Soulé, simply because the people of San Francisco rose
against the Hounds in that city's first case of popular justice.

The group apparently originated in late 1848 and was
made up of former volunteers, convicts from Australia (the
"Sydney Ducks"), and probably men from many quarters who
had decided to winter in San Francisco before returning to
the mines. Their leader, Samuel Roberts, was a former volunteer. He was a carpenter by trade and at the age of twenty had
joined Company E as a private in New York. His record of
conduct in the company had been good until mustering out;
he had been confined briefly on two occasions for absence
without leave.

While almost totally dependent on Soulé's account in the
Annals, Bancroft did admit in *Popular Tribunals* that criminal
intent had not been part of the original purpose of the
Hounds. The association began, he reported, as a loose organization for the mutual assistance of young, single men.[19] For
a while in 1849 its headquarters was a large tent on one of the
corners of Kearny and Commercial streets, the tent known as
Tammany Hall, with which name the New York connection is
clear. The Hounds were given to parading the streets on
Sundays, in a drunken kind of disorderly military formation.

That there was a violent element in the Hounds is certain. In the late spring of 1849, as the Peruvian and Chilean
populations grew, in a segregated area of bars and brothels
on the eastern slope of Telegraph Hill, cases of extortion,
arson, and assault increased alarmingly in San Francisco.

After a week of work a Sunday-night visit to the Chilean prostitutes was routine, and such nights often ended in fights and general mayhem. On one June night a "Hound" was fatally wounded in a fight, and the violence escalated. On Sunday night, July 15, the Hounds attacked "Little Chile" in force, burning tents, clubbing and shooting victims, and plundering the area.

This raid roused the townspeople, and on July 16 Alcalde Leavenworth called a public meeting in Portsmouth Square. W. D. M. Howard presided. Those present formed themselves into four companies of one hundred men (each under a captain, of which Francis Lippitt was one), to police the city and apprehend the Hounds. That same afternoon, according to Bancroft, seventeen of the Hounds, including their leader, Samuel Roberts, were arrested and confined on the *Warren* lying in the harbor.

On Tuesday, July 17, at another mass meeting, a grand jury of twenty-four citizens was selected, and William M. Gwin, a recent arrival in California, and James C. Ward were elected associate justices to "assist" Alcalde Leavenworth in presiding at the trial of the Hounds. Four counsels for the people were appointed, including Francis Lippitt, to prosecute the Hounds, and two attorneys, one of them Myron Norton, were deputed to defend the accused men. The next day the trial began, the Hounds charged with conspiracy, riot, robbery, and assault with intent to kill. Roberts was found guilty on all counts, and eight of the men (only one of them anywhere identified, as a "Saunders") were found guilty on one or more counts. All were sentenced to imprisonment and large fines. There being no prisons, the sentences were not carried into effect.[20]

Hubert Howe Bancroft was so enamoured of popular tribunals that he dealt at length with the case of the Hounds, even though disappointed in the verdict of the people's court. He would have preferred the Hounds to have exterminated all the South Americans and then been hanged. "Society," he wrote, "would have been the gainer."[21] To make his point, he did not scruple to generalize about the regiment in a way most remarkable, considering his treatment throughout his *History of California.* In one of those volumes he concluded that

there can be no doubt that the standard of character and ability was much higher than in most volunteer regiments of this or any other period. An extraordinary number, both of officers and men, reached in their western home and elsewhere enviable positions in military and political life: as lawyers, judges, and merchants; as men of wealth and local influence. And a majority of the rest may point with pride to their humbler record as respectable law-abiding citizens.[22]

In *Popular Tribunals* he thought otherwise:

That delectable troop, the regiment of New York volunteers, was made up to a great extent of the riffraff of eastern cities. Of no value at home, they were brought hither at public expense to fight Mexicans, or Californians; which being found unnecessary shortly after their arrival the company was disbanded. Having no occupation, and averse to labor, naturally many of them fell back on their old pastime of pilfering.[23]

Students and writers of California history are thus well advised to read *all* of Bancroft.

One of the closest students of the period, Josiah Royce, more accurately assessed the Hounds' incident: "a typical illustration of the short and easy methods of the early golden days, but . . . otherwise comparatively insignificant."[24] It should be noted, however, that former volunteers were thus arrayed on both sides of the law—Thaddeus Leavenworth, James C. Ward, Francis Lippitt, and Myron Norton one side, and Samuel Roberts, at least, on the other.

As a result of the Hounds affair, Governor Riley was forced to take action to provide a measure of protection for San Franciscans. In July he authorized a military company to be called the First California Guard. A combination artillery-infantry company, it was commanded by a former volunteer, Captain Henry M. Naglee, then a prominent banker. One of the two first lieutenants was the ubiquitous Myron Norton. This militia body was armed with muskets but was evidently more ceremonial than effective. It was, however, the initial legal militia organization in California and continued its existence under state law.[25]

Through a militia law enacted by the first legislature, California was partitioned into four militia divisions. Former captain John E. Brackett was elected major general and commanding officer of the Second Division. Former sergeant major Alexander C. McDonald was elected brigadier general in one of the brigades of Brackett's division. At the same time, Theron R. Per Lee was elected adjutant general, and Joseph C. Morehead quartermaster general.[26] Like the First California Guard, the California militia was seldom called upon to perform military duty, except for minor Indian campaigns. In both forces, however, Stevenson's men held positions of authority and responsibility. Unfortunately, such responsibility was not justified in every case. In April 1851 Quartermaster General Morehead absconded with several hundred muskets to arm an expedition he led into Sonora and Lower California. Stevenson's Regiment thus contributed California's first filibuster.[27]

Joseph C. Morehead had been one of the two youngest commissioned officers in the regiment. He was just eighteen when elected a second lieutenant in Captain Naglee's Company D. He served under Naglee on Indian campaigns and in Lower California. In November 1849, at the age of twenty-one, Morehead was elected to represent the district of San Joaquin in the California State Assembly. Shortly after he became quartermaster general of the state militia, he led an expedition to the Colorado River against the Yuma Indians. He seems to have had a gift for leadership and perhaps had developed a taste for glory at the side of his former captain, Henry Naglee.

In the spring of 1851 Morehead organized three separate bands of filibusters. One marched overland from Los Angeles into Sonora; another landed at La Paz in June; and Morehead led the third, which sailed to Mazatlán. The prospects for a revolution having worsened, and with the Mexican authorities alerted, all three parts of the expeditionary force disbanded.[28] There was, significantly, none of the elevated theoretical underpinning for Morehead's expedition that there had been for Stevenson's to California. The spirit was different. Glory for the United States and regeneration of the Mexicans were not involved. The freebooting motives actually involved were pure adventure, possible landed power, and loot.

Other volunteers probably joined William Walker in 1853 on his ill-fated filibustering expedition from San Francisco to Baja California, which encountered massive hostility at La Paz. Eight former volunteers are known to have accompanied him to Nicaragua in 1855. That expedition was a kind of success, with Walker becoming president of the republic for a time. He was executed in Honduras in 1860 but had survived longer than most of his sixty men. Of the eight former volunteers on the Nicaraguan expedition, one died on the *Vesta* in 1855, en route to Central America, and five of the remaining seven died in Nicaragua in 1856.[29] The two former volunteers who survived their filibustering experience with Walker were Private John A. Bartlett of Company E, who never returned to California, and Private Henry Uhrbrook of Company G, who did return to California, to live inconspicuously and to die in Santa Clara in 1875.[30]

William Roach, a former sergeant in Stevenson's regiment, led the life of most dramatic contrast on both sides of the law.[31] For fourteen years, between 1853 and 1866, he figured in a vicious Monterey County vendetta and met a violent death. An Irish immigrant of 1830, Roach had joined Captain Naglee's Company D as a private on September 14, 1846, on Governors Island. Serving first in Monterey and then in Lower California, Roach was steadily promoted and was the company's first sergeant when mustered out in September 1848. One of his promotions, from corporal to fourth sergeant, was for gallant conduct on Indian campaigns in the San Joaquin Valley, on the recommendation of Captain Naglee.[32]

Roach settled in Monterey and when the county was formed in 1849 was elected county sheriff. He was, reportedly, political boss of the county. In 1852 a wealthy Californian landowner in the county, José María Sánchez, was accidentally drowned. In mid-1853 Roach succeeded in getting himself appointed guardian of the Sánchez estate, valued at $300,000. He resigned as sheriff, having insured that another former volunteer, Aaron Lyons, would replace him.[33] In a few months Roach was accused by one of his bondsmen, Lewis F. Belcher, of stealing from the estate gold valued at $85,000. The feud began. After some time in jail and more in court, Roach was released and in the early 1860s bought a ranch near Watsonville in Santa Cruz County. When drinking, he is said to have liked to talk about his past exploits and associations—a habit that brought warnings from his friends, who were not proud of the part they had played in the drama.

Roach was killed as he was returning from a late drinking bout in Watsonville, where he had gone to vote in a county election. Guy J. Giffen wrote that Roach was drowned, and perhaps he was—*after* he was thrown into a remote well, strangled and with his head "bashed in with a huge rock."[34] When the feud ended with the death of Roach in 1866, a total of fourteen men had been killed, including Belcher. The Sánchez gold was never recovered.

NOTES

1. *California Star*, Nov. 20, 1847.

2. The confirmation of Beverly's conviction and sentence is in Colonel Mason's DGO No. 8, Jan. 18, 1848, RG 94, NA. Private Henry Woolard of Company K, who was presumably guarding Beverly, was court-martialed in April for aiding Beverly and for concealing the escape from the officer of the guard. Woolard pleaded not guilty and was acquitted.

3. Mason, Special Orders No. 8, March 8, 1848, RG 94, NA.

4. Bancroft, "Pioneer Register," *History of California*, vol. 2, 719. Bancroft did not identify Beverly as a sometime member of the regiment.

5. Bancroft, *History of California*, vol. 5, 676.

6. Captain Seymour Steele, "Report of arrests and sentences . . . for the Month of February, 1848," Company A, Los Angeles, California, RG 94, NA. In Steele's muster-out roll for his company, of Oct. 24, 1848, Sutphen is listed as a deserter while under arrest.

7. Burton, Monterey, to Mason, Nov. 30, 1848, RG 393, NA; Lt. Henry C. Matsell, "Muster-Out Roll," Company B, Oct. 23, 1848, RG 94, NA. Bancroft identified Lawson no further than as a member of Company B, adding that he died in Monterey in 1849. (Bancroft, "Pioneer Register," *History of California*, vol. 4, 709.)

8. Frederic Hall, *History of San Jose* (San Francisco: A. L. Bancroft and Company, 1871), 232.

9. Buffum, *Six Months in the Gold Mines*, 84-85.

10. *Alta California*, Jan. 25, 1849.

11. Colton, *Three Years in California*, 391-92. Colton may have known what he wrote but may also have been reproducing current talk and reports about the case. The *Alta California* of Jan. 25, 1849, said three of the five were thought to have been sailors who had deserted. In discussing the murders, Bancroft did not identify Lynch as a former volunteer but did so in the "Pioneer Register" (*History of California*, vol. 5, 639-40; vol. 7, 450; "Pioneer Register," vol. 4, 720-21.) Guy J. Giffen in his *California Regiment* (page 67), while correctly identifying Lynch as one of the murderers, wrote that three of the other four, not named, were also former volunteers. The basis for his statement is unknown, as no Quin (or Quinn) or Remer (or Raymond) appears on the rolls.

12. Capt. Matthew R. Stevenson, "Muster-Roll," Company G, Feb. 29, 1848; "Muster-Out Roll," Company G, Sept. 18, 1848, RG 94, NA.

13. Capt. Francis J. Lippitt, "List of Men Tried by Court Martial or Confined in the Guard House," Company F, Sept., Nov. 1847; Feb., March, May, June 1848, Santa Barbara, California, RG 94, NA.

14. Edward McGowan, *McGowan vs California Vigilantes* (Oakland, California: Biobooks, 1946), 45 and *passim*.

15. *Alta California*, May 7, 1853; June 8, 1853.

16. Bancroft, "Pioneer Register," *History of California*, vol. 4, 783.

17. Giffen, *California Expedition*, 84.

18. A survey of exactly how the Hounds, Soulé, and Bancroft produced an odd image of the regiment is in the introduction to the Bibliographical Essay for this study.

19. Bancroft, *Popular Tribunals*, 2 vols. (San Francsico: The History Company, 1887), vol. 1, 78-79. The extensive citations so valuable in Bancroft's seven-volume history of California are entirely

lacking in *Popular Tribunals*. There is clear intrinsic evidence, however, of Bancroft's major dependence on Soulé. The versions are in some ways distinct, although there is no clue to Bancroft's other sources.

20. In reporting the trial and convictions, the *Alta California* of July 26 named Samuel Roberts as the leader of the Hounds but did not identify him further. In addition to this account, the affair is discussed in detail in Soulé's *The Annals of San Francisco*, 227-28, 553-61, and in Bancroft's *Popular Tribunals*, vol. 1, 78-102.

21. Bancroft, *Popular Tribunals*, vol. 1, 101.

22. Bancroft, *History of California*, vol. 5, 505.

23. Bancroft, *Popular Tribunals*, vol. 1, 78.

24. Royce, *California*, 321.

25. Bancroft, *History of California*, vol. 7, 454-55.

26. *Ibid.*, 455-56.

27. *Ibid.*, 459.

28. John C. Caughey, *California*, 301, 321; Bancroft, *History of California*, vol. 6, 583-84.

29. Former sergeant Charles Richardson (Company B) died aboard the *Vesta*. The other five were former privates James Linton (Company E), William G. Tait (Company A), and Peter G. Veeder (Company H), former lieutenant John S. Norris, (Company K) and former acting lieutenant Charles G. Scott (Company B). Bancroft, "Pioneer Register," *History of California*, vol. 4, 714, 755; vol. 5, 694, 714, 742, 761.

30. Bancroft, "Pioneer Register," *History of California*, vol. 2, 712; vol. 5, 753.

31. Paul P. Parker, "The Roach-Belcher Feud," *California Historical Society Quarterly*, XXIX, 1950, 19-28; Bancroft, *History of California*, vol. 7, 206. Bancroft did not identify Roach as a former member of the regiment. Parker quite accurately traced his record in the regiment.

32. Col. J. D. Stevenson, Special Order No. 35, Headquarters, Southern Military District, Los Angeles, California, Oct. 14, 1847, RG 94, NA.

33. Lyons had also been a member of Company D, from Aug. 1, 1846, then being fourth corporal. When mustered out, he was third sergeant.

34. Giffen simply says of Roach: "A resident of Monterey County and for a time sheriff of the county; drowned at Watsonville, September 3, 1866." (*California Expedition*, 86.) An account of Roach's death and the discovery of his body, with a short account of the feud, is in the Watsonville (California) *Pajaro Times*, Sept. 8, 1866. A detailed account, with careful citation, is in Parker's "The Roach-Belcher Feud."

Chapter Eighteen

Businessmen and "Pioneers"

S AN FRANCISCO'S BUSINESS COMMUNITY developed in the blocks around the plaza known as Portsmouth Square. In 1849 and 1850 a number of former-volunteers-turned-businessmen had stores, offices, and warehouses there.[1] In August 1849, on Washington Street, Edward Gilbert's *Alta California* printing office faced the square. Next door was Palmer, Cook & Co., later taken over by Henry M. Naglee, and next door to Palmer, Cook, was the land office of Colonel Stevenson and Dr. W. C. Parker. Across the square in the Laffan Building, Myron Norton had his law office. A block away, on Montgomery Street between Washington and Clay, was Naglee & Sinton, one of San Francisco's first banks. In the same block was Frisbie & Co., a mercantile brokerage, in which Captain Frisbie and his brother Eleazar were partners. On Montgomery between Pine and Bush, the Russ family, jewelers and silversmiths by trade, had opened a jewelry store. On Webb Street, no more than a lane and almost on the water, Palmer B. Hewlett, former lieutenant in Company I, had built and operated a boarding and rooming house. On California Street just below Kearny Street was the U.S. Army quartermaster's office, with Captain Folsom still in charge. Central (or Long) Wharf was then being extended far out into the bay, and Captain Folsom, in his private capacity, was a partner in the company that subscribed $120,000 for the construction. Edward H. Harrison and James C. Ward were also partners. Stevenson's men, and the colonel himself, were very much a part of San Francisco business.

Of the family groups within the regiment, the Russ family was most numerous. Father Christian Russ, forty-five years old, and his son Adolphus, twenty, had enlisted as privates in Company C, and younger sons Augustus and Charles were musicians attached to Company F. With Mrs. Russ and younger children, there may have been twelve of the Russ family with the regiment. They bought property with a careful eye to the future and held it. Their jewelry business prospered, and on other property they had acquired on Harrison Street they opened an amusement park, Russ Gardens. On their prime Montgomery Street property, acquired in 1847, the family built the Russ House, for many years one of the city's leading hotels. In the 1920s the Russ Building was erected on the site where the Russ House had stood for so long. It was San Francisco's tallest and largest office building for over three decades and it is still one of the best-known business structures in the city.

A close-knit German family, the Russ family was never socially prominent, but always exceedingly rich. Charles Russ took to the mining life and until 1858 made many mining tours including the Fraser River Rush. Adolphus Russ represented San Francisco in the California State Legislature in 1867, and one of the younger children, Henry, was in later years a prominent San Francisco supervisor. Of them all, Adolphus Russ showed the greatest civic responsibility. He was also devoted to the regiment, always attending regimental reunions. He was faithful to his former commander, regularly appearing at the birthday party for Colonel Stevenson given by the Society of California Pioneers on January 1. He and his brother Charles were pallbearers at Colonel Stevenson's funeral in 1894.[2]

Everything the Russ family touched seemed to make them wealthier, including their amusement park in the Mission district. Other volunteers also ventured successfully into the entertainment field. In 1850 Alfred A. Green, formerly of Company B, built San Francisco's first racetrack, also in the Mission district.[3] Henry M. Naglee was for some years owner of the American Theater, one of San Francisco's largest and best. In fact, Stevenson's men are credited with giving the first plays in California, other than the traditional Mexican *pastorelas*, while still in service in Sonoma, Santa Barbara, Monterey, and Los Angeles.[4]

The most spectacular success in a number of business enterprises was achieved by Captains Folsom and Naglee. Through 1847 and 1848 Folsom became the owner of dozens of San Francisco city lots, evidently putting all the money he had and could raise into such property. By 1849, still in the army, he was an exceedingly wealthy man simply from rents alone, and he invested in many of the important developments in the city. In late 1849 Folsom left California briefly and returned in 1850 with a prize—title to the California estate of William A. Leidesdorff. Leidesdorff had come to California in 1841 as a ship captain, bought property in Yerba Buena, and had become a prominent and successful trader. In 1844 he was naturalized a Mexican citizen and that same year was granted the eight-square-league Rancho del Rio de los Americanos in the Sacramento Valley between Sutter's Fort and the foothills of the Sierra. Leidesdorff died in May 1848. W. D. M. Howard was first appointed administrator of Leidesdorff's estate, for which he and others were claimants and which by 1849 had immense value. Of all those interested, Folsom showed the greatest ingenuity. Leidesdorff had died without family in California, and Folsom's trip "East" was in fact a trip to the Danish West Indies. There he sought out Leidesdorff's mother and other heirs and bought from them—Bancroft says "for a song"—their entire interest in the estate.[5] His title to Leidesdorff's San Francisco property was adjudged valid, as later was his claim to the Rio de los Americanos ranch. Folsom thereby became one of the wealthiest men in California.

Folsom did not live long, however, to enjoy the fortune resulting from his shrewdness. In July 1855 he died at his country estate near Mission San Jose, at the age of thirty-eight. A travelling correspondent for the *Alta California*, writing nostalgically of San Francisco in 1848, mentioned a number of former volunteers but became lyrical in describing "the gallant, the talented, the noble-hearted and much lamented gentleman soldier, Captain J. L. Folsom!"[6] Many people did not share his opinion, however, and for the ultimate good of Folsom's reputation it is probably as well he died young. On some of the eight square leagues he owned in the Sacramento Valley—almost six hundred square miles—the town of Folsom and Folsom State Prison now stand, as well as vast Folsom Lake. One of San Francisco's principal streets bears his name.[7]

Another San Francisco street, just two blocks long, in an outlying lower-middle-class subdivision built in the 1920s, is Naglee Street—San Francisco's memorial to Captain Henry M. Naglee. In January 1849 Naglee, with a partner not of the regiment, Richard H. Sinton, opened their banking business, an exchange and deposit office, in Kearny Street facing Portsmouth Square. When the rented building burned, the business was transferred to a lot Naglee owned at the corner of Montgomery and Merchant streets. Sinton soon withdrew and the business (then H. M. Naglee & Co.) was closed by a run on September 7, 1850.[8] Naglee then turned, very profitably, to dealing in real estate. The next year, on the Montgomery and Merchant site, he built the three-story Naglee Building, San Francisco's first fireproof structure. He later claimed title to the 35,000 acre Rancho el Pescadero on the San Joaquin River, which title the Land Commission confirmed, and in 1852 bought a small ranch of 150 acres near San Jose.[9] Naglee began to develop both properties but also continued in business in San Francisco. In 1852 Adams and Company failed; it was the major express and banking firm in

California, with branches in almost every town and mining camp. Naglee was ultimately named receiver and brought suit against the previous receiver, Alfred A. Cohen, for irregularities. The supreme court decided in favor of Naglee, for $269,000. The assets of Adams and Company had been deposited with Palmer, Cook & Co., which could not produce them. When that bank failed, the entire economy of San Francisco and California was affected, and faith in credit and banks was shaken for years.[10]

Naglee was particularly interested in viticulture, and his original San Jose property was planted to vineyards and orchards. On additional property purchased in that area, he raised imported shorthorn cattle. In mid-1859 Naglee went east to visit relatives and spent most of the year 1860 in Europe, returning to San Francisco early in 1861. Later that year, with a commission as a lieutenant colonel in the Sixteenth Regiment of the regular army, he again went east to fight for the Union. In February 1862 he resigned that commission to become a brigadier general of Volunteers in General Hooker's Division and spent much of 1862 and 1863 in the field, in a number of battles. He left the army early in 1864. In 1865 he married Marie Antoinette Ringgold, the daughter of soldier-poet George Ringgold. (Francis Lippitt had also bid for her hand.) For the next twenty years in California, until his death in 1886, Naglee developed his properties, introduced the first flood-control measures in the San Joaquin Valley, and as a profitable hobby at San Jose produced and distributed one of California's best brandies—"General Naglee's."[11]

There is no recorded instance of Henry Naglee ever having smiled, so it is not likely that he was amused in 1867 when Mary L. Schell published her one and only book. Entitled *The Love Life of Brig. Gen. Henry M. Naglee*, the volume contained eighty-one letters written by Naglee to Miss Schell between 1858 and 1864.[12] In the introduction to the book, Miss Schell made it clear, as Naglee did in his letters, that the two had had an understanding. He paid her bills, and she thought he was to marry her. He did say so, but he married

Miss Ringgold instead. Miss Schell sued for breach of promise, but, she wrote, on the advice of friends she withdrew the prosecution, "her delicate and refined nature dreading to pass the ordeal of a public trial." She thereupon resolved to publish the letters to vindicate her cause, that not offending her nature. She did apologize, however, not for publishing the letters, but for the letters themselves: "viewed with the most good-natured eye, and bearing in mind the fact that heroes are not always remarkable for their intellect, we must admit that they are by no means of a classic style of literature."[13] In his letters Naglee salutes her variously as "My Chere, Chere Petite," "My Dear Little Sweetheart," and "My Dearest, Darlingest, Sweetest Baby." The letters themselves are sufficiently repetitious and tiresome, although very indiscreet. Writing to her from Washington, D.C., on December 1, 1859, he enclosed a drawing of himself, nude, doing his daily gymnastics in his bathtub, the drawing detailed to his unmistakable moustaches. Not to be accused of weakening her case, Miss Schell had the drawing reproduced in the book.[14] Bromidic as he was, the general should have remembered "a woman scorned."

In the end as in the beginning, however, Naglee disdained nearly everyone. He summed up his point of view in an illuminating paragraph in one of the letters, one especially full of tender advice. From Marseilles, on April 30, 1860, he instructed Miss Schell

to take everything coolly, and to smile at the great want of good sense and folly of the big world. You will learn that the world is made of a little sense and an ocean of poor simple things, who have barely sense enough to put food in their mouths after it is placed before them. You will learn that it is the duty of every one to take care of himself first.[15]

Naglee followed his own advice. His difficulties in the Union Army, as he described them late in 1863, appear to be clear cases of disobedience of orders and insubordination. He thought himself, however, "the mark of the especial spite of the War Department." He believed General Hooker was jealous of him because "I was becoming too well liked; too much influence." Then Naglee interpreted the problem:

The nigger is the constant thought of the Administration, and complaint was made that I required the negroes to be out of the street by nine o'clock, and that I put two regiments of colored troops to work, and returned two white regiments. I hardly think any policy or punishment they may adopt will make me prefer a negro to a white man. . . . But what, in the name of heaven, can you expect from Lincoln, Stanton, Halleck and Hooker?[16]

Miss Schell discovered what she could expect from Naglee and, as a result, produced a book that is unique in the literature of the men of Stevenson's Regiment. But because of Miss Schell's admitted interest and lack of objectivity, she should not have the last word on Henry Naglee. His former comrade-in-arms Captain Frisbie best described him in 1884: "Negley [sic] was a very bright man not a loveable man."[17]

John B. Frisbie wrote his reminiscences of the regiment and of more than thirty years' residence in California while living in Mexico City. Frisbie's opinion of Naglee may have been colored by the fact that Naglee had not only made but preserved his fortune. Frisbie had not. With his ability and with the prodigious Vallejo properties and useful name behind him (because of his marriage), Frisbie became successful in a variety of pursuits. He was bank president, later a railroad director and officer, rancher, general entrepreneur. In 1860 he sent the first shipload of California wheat to Europe, inaugurating that commerce which became a mainstay of California's economy. He served in the California State Legislature in 1867 and was undoubtedly the leading citizen of the city of Vallejo in Solano County. In the *History of Solano County* published in San Francisco in 1879, not by subscription, Frisbie's biography to that date required three pages, and a full-page lithograph was included as well.[18]

In 1879 John Frisbie went broke. Three years earlier, when the Central Pacific Railroad leased and took control of the California Pacific Railroad, of which Frisbie was vice-president, he held 18,000 shares of California Pacific stock, capitalized at one thousand dollars a share.[19] In 1879, except for some Mexican mining property of undetermined value, he was penniless, through a general collapse that felled many like him. He, his wife, and some of their children moved to Mexico. There he lived through the decade of the 1880s, exploiting his property, and returned to California about 1890, well off and possibly rich. He died in San Francisco in 1909.

In 1850 most of these men from the regiment were involved in the formation of the Society of California Pioneers—before California was even a state. Other volunteers were also involved, as were a number of men not of the regiment. Considering that California was but four years out of Mexican hands, and only two of those years by treaty, the date is remarkably early for the inception of such an organization. The explanation surely lies in the fact of the Gold Rush which brought so many "newcomers" and such rapid and dramatic change.

The first assembly of "old residents" or "pioneers" occurred in August 1850 in connection with the public observance of the death of President Taylor. A call was issued by W. D. M. Howard, Samuel Brannan, and James C. L. Wadsworth who had been a sutler's clerk in the regiment, asking all old residents to unite and march together in the procession. The response was so great that further action was suggested. The following announcement appeared in several San Francisco morning papers on August 30:

The early pioneers of California are requested to call at the Iron Warehouse of Howard & Mellus, on Montgomery Street, on Saturday evening, 31st of August, at 7 o'clock. It is expected all old pioneers and residents of three years and upwards will attend. The object of the meeting will be announced.[20]

By late September 1850 a constitution and bylaws for the Society of California Pioneers had been drawn up and published, and officers elected. W. D. M. Howard was president, and there were three vice-presidents—Jacob Snyder, Samuel Brannan, and George Frank Lemon. Captain Folsom was recording secretary and James C. L. Wadsworth his assistant. Three of the officers were thus from the regiment, and volunteers Adolphus Russ, Colonel Jonathan Stevenson, Patrick Lynch, J. Mead Huxley, William Huefner, Henry Naglee, Francis Lippitt, and John and Eleazar Frisbie were among the charter members. Membership was limited to those who could prove three years' residence in California, and the purpose of the society was defined in the first article of its constitution:

To cultivate the social virtues of its members, to collect and preserve information connected with the early settlement and conquest of the country, and to perpetuate the memory of those whose sagacity, enterprise, and love of independence, induced them to settle in the wilderness and become the germ of a new State.[21]

In the great public celebration of California's admission to the Union, October 29, 1850, the Pioneer Society took a prominent place in the long procession, right behind the native Californians, who followed the grand marshal of the parade, Colonel Stevenson. Captain Frisbie delivered the first oration to the society at its meeting of January 1, 1851, and the society was conspicuous in the funeral procession of Edward Gilbert in August 1852. In 1853 the constitution of the society was revised offering membership to any male who resided in California before January 1, 1850. In the same year the society began the collection, from members and from any source, of documents on California history from earliest times to statehood.[22] All that collection, including the record of what it contained, burned in the San Francisco fire of April 1906. The collection doubtless included records of the regiment and of volunteer activities.

NOTES

1. Because of erratic numbering, frequent fires and changing ownership, the first San Francisco city directory, Charles P. Kimball's *The San Francisco City Directory, September 1, 1850* (San Francisco: Journal of Commerce Press, 1850), is most inaccurate. However, by using it carefully, with advertisements and news stories in the *Alta California* and a partial listing of business firms prepared by Bancroft, a reasonably accurate reconstruction of business houses at any given date in 1849 and 1850 can be made. Those sources and others specified have been used in this chapter.

2. *San Francisco Chronicle*, Jan. 2, 1890; San Francisco *Call*, Feb. 19, 1894.

3. *Alta California*, March 25, Sept. 15, 1851.

4. *San Jose Pioneer*, May 4, 1878. Although there is no record of such performances in 1847, the likelihood is very great that the volunteers did give plays that year. They had entertained with plays on the ships coming to California. Vincent mentions a performance of *Bombastes Furioso* on the *Susan Drew* on New Year's Eve 1846 (Vincent, "Log-Book," Jan. 1, 1847). Hollingsworth reported the opening of a theater on July 4, 1848, in Los Angeles. He added: "We shall have some fine acting—I often wile away an evening at it—" (Hollingsworth, *Journal*, 43).

5. Bancroft, *History of California*, vol. 3, 742.

6. *Alta California*, April 30, 1866.

7. In addition to Folsom, other important San Francisco streets are named for Stevenson, Harrison, and Leavenworth.

8. Eldredge, *The Beginnings of San Francisco*, vol. 2, 553-54.

9. Bancroft, *History of California*, vol. 4, 672; vol. 6, 745.

10. "History of San Francisco—1856," *San Francisco City Directory, for the Year Commencing October, 1856* (San Francisco: Harris, Bogardus, and Labatt, 1857), xxxvii; *Correspondence Between Henry M. Naglee, Receiver, Palmer, Cook & Co., and Edward Stanly* (San Francisco: Whitton, Towne & Co., 1856), 3-18 and *passim*.

11. California Department of Public Works, "Field Notes," Book No. 92. (A description of the reclamation measures undertaken by Naglee on the Pescadero ranch in 1876-1877.) Naglee's viticulture is reported in detail and the product with appreciation by John Codman in *The Round Trip* (New York: G. P. Putnam's Sons, 1879), 106-8.

12. Mary L. Schell, *The Love Life of Brig. Gen. Henry M. Naglee, Consisting of a correspondence on Love, War and Politics* (San Francisco: n.p., 1867).

13. *Ibid.*, vi.

14. *Ibid.*, 54.

15. *Ibid.*, 73.

16. *Ibid.*, 158-59.

17. Frisbie, "Reminiscences," 33.

18. *History of Solano County* (San Francisco: Wood, Alley & Co., 1879), 44-48. Frisbie's is the longest biography in the book.

19. Bancroft, *History of California*, vol. 7, 585.

20. *San Francisco Herald*, San Francisco *Pacific News*, Aug. 30, 1850.

21. *San Francisco Herald*, Sept. 27, 1850.

22. *The Calaveras Enterprise*, San Andreas, California, June 14, June 21, 1967.

Chapter Nineteen

Colonel Stevenson

T HERE WAS ALWAYS something larger than life about Colonel Jonathan D. Stevenson. Once mustered out of the service and back from the mines, he quickly developed into a good example of a well-known type, the professional veteran. With his ramrod-straight back and the semi-military dress he affected the rest of his life, Stevenson seemed the "Old Warrior" himself. Not quite eccentric enough to be a character, he was, rather, a familiar figure as he lived on in San Francisco for almost fifty years.

Early in 1850 Stevenson sat for his portrait by William S. Jewett who recorded the sittings in his letters, adding "this is a great place for heroes of the Mexican War."[1] So it was. Stevenson was a joiner, a great talker, and a born grand marshal for every manner of parade and procession. If not leading the parade, he would lead a delegation from one or another of the patriotic and fraternal groups he had helped organize

—the Pioneer Society, the Masonic Veterans Association, the Associated Veterans of the Mexican War, or the Society of the Survivors of Stevenson's Regiment.

As the decades progressed Stevenson was identified in the newspapers as distinguished, respected, esteemed, revered, venerable (when in his nineties), and usually as too well known to need identification. He was a favorite of newspapermen who could count on him for interesting if not notably accurate copy. They called him "The Old Soldier," "a grand old pioneer," "a pioneer among pioneers," and often "The Child of the Century," since he had been born January 1, 1800. Stevenson obliged with martial recollections and with formulas for growing old gracefully. (He avoided excesses, occasionally took a whisky punch, and had an electricity treatment every day.) The newspapermen, in turn, generously refrained from mentioning the great mistake of Stevenson's life—his failure at city building.[2]

In January 1849, just back from the mines, Stevenson had gone into partnership with Dr. W. C. Parker, one of the regiment's two assistant surgeons. Their business was real estate. Stevenson had gold from his ventures in the Mother Lode country, and Dr. Parker owned a great number of building lots in San Francisco. He had bought some of the lots in 1847 and secured more in September 1848 when thirty-six very valuable beach and water lots were granted "on petition" to him and a W. S. Clark.[3] The "land grabbers" were then running San Francisco, and Parker and Alcalde Leavenworth were friends. Almost certainly there was irregularity in the transaction.

In February Stevenson and Parker, while keeping their agency in San Francisco, bought the ten-thousand-acre Rancho Los Medanos from José Antonio and José Miguel Mesa.[4] The ranch was sixty-five miles from San Francisco on Suisun Bay where the Sacramento and San Joaquin rivers enter the bay. There they planned a city. They had seen San Francisco rise from practically nothing, and Stockton and Sacramento from less, and they reasoned, quite incorrectly, that their site was natural for development. Many paper towns and cities

COLONEL JONATHAN DRAKE STEVENSON.

"The Old Soldier" and "Pioneer Among Pioneers," was still firm-jawed and vigorous at age eighty-six and served actively as court commissioner of the San Francisco Superior Court. The photograph was taken eight years before his death in 1894. (Courtesy of The Society of California Pioneers, San Francisco.)

were similarly laid out in California the same year but none with greater pretensions than Stevenson and Parker's city of New York of the Pacific. They hired Lieutenants W. T. Sherman and R. P. Hammond to survey and plot the city and to make the soundings of Suisun Bay. In his *Memoirs* Sherman recalled the undertaking and the fee each man received— $500 and ten or fifteen building lots in the new city.[5]

On May 17, 1849, Stevenson and Parker launched their city with a notice to the public in the *Alta California*. It was a long announcement, stressing the deep-water location near the mouths of the two rivers, the fine climate, and the unlimited possibilities for expansion. The possibilities of this second New York sounded almost as good as those of the original, and better than those of San Francisco. To help promote the city and do the necessary clerical work, Stevenson hired Stephen C. Massett, just arrived with a letter of introduction. Massett left a record of their first meeting. As Massett reported the conversation, Stevenson told him,

"You are just the young man for me. You, of course, understand drawing deeds, mortgages, &c.; in fact, the general routine of a lawyer's office. You've been in a good school, and I think we can get along very well together. I have just purchased a tract of land—am going to build a new city—a second New York, sir! I call it, sir, 'New York of the Pacific,' sir. I'll make you Alcalde, sir! Notary Public, sir! Mayor of the City, sir! Come and breakfast with me, sir, to-morrow . . . At six o'clock, sir—always rise with the lark—nothing like getting up early, sir—business man, sir. Go to bed early—keep steady—don't drink, and your fortune's made in no time!"[6]

Massett took the job, which paid well, and found that the rush for lots in the embryonic city was great:

It was something in this style:—Man, just from the mines, comes in, and wants to invest his surplus "gold-dust."
"Got any good lots, Col.?" Col. S——— rises, and with a long stick points to the map, offering a few remarks like these to the astonished and bewildered purchaser.
"You see, sir, these lots are what we call water lots, sir. I couldn't part with these under $1000 a lot, as from their position—*this being the head of navigation*, sir—that is a fixed fact, sir—they will command shortly a very high figure. Now these on F. street I have reserved for

the 'public schools.' I am determined to have an institution of this
kind properly cared for—and next to this, sir, I have placed these
lots on A. M. and A. [sic] for the 'Court House,' 'City Hall,' and the
'Hall of Records and Mayor's or Alcalde's office,' " (pointing to me,
and remarking that I had just arrived from New York to take charge
of this highly responsible, lucrative, and dignified position!)

The excited miner, with visions of prospective wealth, in the
rapid and astounding advance of real estate in this golden land,
pulls out his buckskin bag, and away rattles the gold into the Chinese
scales; he takes *two lots*, pays his $500 (they are $250 apiece). I make
out the "deeds," record them immediately, in fact do everything that
in such cases is usually done, made, and provided.

The man leaves his gold-dust, and takes his deed—neither one
nor the other to be heard of afterwards.[7]

It was not only the unknowledgeable and unsuspecting
that purchased lots in New York of the Pacific. Dr. John S.
Griffin, who had come to California with Kearny, bought
one, as did Dr. Victor Fourgeaud, a resident of San Francisco
since 1847.[8] Others were convinced, too. E. Gould Buffum
thought New York of the Pacific would unquestionably flourish, although he did not buy a lot. He devoted two pages in
his book to the development, calling it "beautifully laid out,
with large reserves for churches, a university, and other public edifices," and he thought the great Pacific railroad, when
built, would undoubtedly terminate there.[9] In June 1849 the
former consul of France in San Francisco, J. A. Moerenhout,
reported to the French minister of foreign affairs in Paris
that New York of the Pacific was one of the five most promising settlements between San Francisco and the mines. His
letter of June 16 read in part:

Land values all over the country have increased a thousand per cent.
At Yerba Buena lots somewhat near the shore or toward the center
of town bring four to ten dollars the square foot. At Benicia lots sell
for three thousand dollars, and it is the same with all the new settlements that are now being formed on the Sacramento and San Joaquin under the names of Sacramento City, Sutterville, New York
and Stockton.[10]

Six months after he began selling lots in New York of the
Pacific, Colonel Stevenson did the expected, petitioning that

the state capital be located there. At that time the city did not seem to be populated, and he and Dr. Parker made the same proposal again in May 1850. But when the legislature voted to move the capital from San Jose, New York of the Pacific got only one vote.[11] New York of the Pacific grew steadily until it consisted of three houses and a landing barge, and before the end of 1850 was an acknowledged failure. The introduction of fast, shallow-draft river steamers made a stop there unnecessary. Not until the early years of this century was the area developed at all. Stevenson never quite recovered from the collapse of his new city and in all his talking about himself to newspaper people, he never spoke of it.[12]

By the autumn of 1850 most of Stevenson's operations were back in San Francisco. In October he and Parker privately extended Sacramento Street eight hundred feet into the bay, along Howison's Wharf, and built new offices there. Their partnership continued into 1852, and their friendship was lifelong.[13] In June 1851, when Colonel Stevenson married an Australian divorcée, Mary Elizabeth Carnegie, Dr. Parker was best man.[14] The Stevensons resided first on the eastern slope of Nob Hill and later moved to a house Stevenson built at 2109 Van Ness Avenue. Dr. Parker was still a family friend in 1894 when he helped Mrs. Stevenson secure her widow's pension.

In 1852 Colonel Stevenson applied for bounty land, and a warrant was issued to him in January 1853. By that time he had begun practice as an attorney-at-law, with small qualification it would appear, even when none was legally necessary. He specialized in representing former naval and military personnel with claims against the state and federal governments. Stevenson advertised widely in California newspapers in 1853 and 1854. The following advertisement appeared in *The Illustrated San Diego Herald* on October 1, 1853:

Claims to Seamen for Extra pay, Fremont Battalion, Mormon Battalion, and New York Volunteer claims.
J. D. Stevenson & Co., Parson's Buildings, north side Clay st. between Montgomery and Sansome sts.

Purchase or prepare applications for pay, mileage, land warrants, and all other claims of the Fremont Battalion, Mormon Battalion, New York Volunteers, Moorhead and Bean's Expedition and claims of Seamen for extra pay in the Naval and Revenue Service on the Pacific during the War with Mexico, and since 1850.

By concentrating on business and taking little part in public affairs during 1849 and 1850, Colonel Stevenson had lost any opportunity he might have had for political activity. By the time New York of the Pacific had failed, California politics were in the hands of able younger men, many of them from his regiment. Not until the Grant administrations did Stevenson receive a political appointment.[15] In 1872 he was named United States shipping commissioner at San Francisco, a post created by the Shipping Act of June 7 of that year. In the beginning Colonel Stevenson seems to have accomplished something as shipping commissioner. In his published report to the San Francisco Chamber of Commerce in 1873, he included letters commending him for reducing the extortionate charges made by boardinghouse keepers for the engagement of seamen, and a resolution from the masters of twenty ships and the consul of Great Britain, who found "Col. Stevenson . . . entirely the master of the situation he holds."[16] Through the Hayes, Garfield, and Arthur administrations he held the position until in 1885 he was "turned-out," as he put it.

Stevenson then became commissioner of the San Francisco Superior Court, either a poorly paid or unpaid position, and by 1890 was entirely dependent on his veteran's pension of eight dollars a month. In 1893, when he applied for an increase in pension, he testified that he had no income from any other source and that his house and lot—worth $17,000, if they could be sold—were mortgaged for $12,000. "The moneys borrowed on these mortgages," he wrote, "have been and are being used for living expenses." His application was rejected. Colonel Stevenson died on February 14, 1894. His funeral was Masonic,[17] and there were full military honors at his burial in Laurel Hill Cemetery.

Jonathan Stevenson had lived in California forty-seven years, exactly half his life. If a somewhat absurd figure, he had maintained a certain dignity. In the poverty of his last years he never drew on the available relief fund of the Society of California Pioneers, nor did he ever intimate in his newspaper interviews that his life had been a disappointment. The greatest event in that life had been the command of the First Regiment of New York Volunteers. He had performed that duty well and was proud of it. There were both better men and worse in the regiment he had brought to California almost fifty years before.

NOTES

1. Elliot Evans, ed., "Some Letters of William S. Jewett, California Artist," *California Historical Society Quarterly*, XXIII, 1944, 160, 163.

2. Representative articles on Colonel Stevenson appear in the following: *Alta California*, Oct. 9, 1859; *Frank Leslie's Illustrated Newspaper*, March 10, 1866; *Alta California*, March 27, 1872; *San Francisco Call*, Oct. 25, 1888; *San Francisco Chronicle*, Jan. 2, 1890; *San Francisco Examiner*, Jan. 2, 1892. The *San Francisco Examiner*, Jan. 1, 1892, on Stevenson's ninety-second birthday, carried a chapter of his reminiscences entitled "Born With the Century." All San Francisco and most California newspapers, as well as many in New York, carried a long obituary and other stories on Stevenson just after his death in Feb. 1894.

3. Bancroft, *History of California*, vol. 5, 654.

4. Other volunteers were also fortunate in securing large tracts of land in 1849 and 1850; Captains Naglee and Folsom have already been mentioned in this regard. Three former volunteers, Captain Brackett, George N. Cornwell (Company H), and Martin F. Gormley (Company F) had their titles confirmed in a large part of the twenty-league Soulajule grant in Marin County; and Leavenworth became the owner of the Rancho Agua Caliente in the Sonoma Valley. (Bancroft, *History of California*, vol. 3, 711; vol. 4, 674.)

5. Sherman, *Memoirs*, vol. 1, 73-74. Sherman remembered that he had received the permission of the commanding general to undertake the work for pay, and that he had sold enough of the lots to make another $500. He had "let the balance go."

6. Stephen C. Massett, *Drifting About* (New York: Carleton, 1863), 113. Massett was generally very deft at delineating character in the various sketches in his book, and his caricature of Colonel Stevenson is probably close to the mark. The conversational style is remarkably similar in the written account of Stevenson's confrontation with Captain Folsom on the *Susan Drew* in 1846 concerning the proposed mutiny. Much of the same style appears in quotations from Stevenson in newspaper interviews. While working for Stevenson, Massett gave the first professional theatrical performance in San Francisco.

7. *Ibid.*, 115.

8. Ernest A. Wiltsee, "The City of New York of the Pacific," *California Historical Society Quarterly*, XII, 1933, 24-34. This carefully researched article traces the history of the Los Medanos property to the early 1930s. The site of New York of the Pacific is now the city of Pittsburg.

9. Buffum, *Six Months in the Gold Mines*, 150-51.

10. A. P. Nasatir, ed., "The French Consulate in California, 1843-56," *California Historical Society Quarterly*, XIII, 1934, 367. Moerenhout had been the consul of France in San Francisco between 1846 and 1848.

11. Wiltsee, "New York of the Pacific," 30-31.

12. Long after, Stevenson did once write of the venture in *Memorial and Petition of Col. J. D. Stevenson of California* (San Francisco: J. R. Brodie & Co., 1886), but mentioned New York of the Pacific in the briefest way. In this memorial to Congress Stevenson asked reimbursement for some $2,600 he claimed he had expended (and probably had) in the sounding and charting of Suisun Bay. The claim was still pending when he died in 1894 and, in a codicil to his will, was made part of his estate. (*San Francisco Call*, March 16, 1894.)

13. When the two men went their separate ways in business, Dr. Parker continued in the real estate business, then became a stock broker, but never practiced medicine. He lived in San Francisco until 1876, then in Oakland, and died in Santa Cruz in 1896.

14. An almost complete record of Colonel Stevenson's activities from 1851, and the one used here, is his veteran's pension file in the National Archives. He, and later his widow, had many dealings with the Bureau of Pensions of the Interior Department in Washington, D.C. For documentation this was fortunate since San Francisco municipal and court records were largely destroyed in the fire of 1906.

15. It may or may not have been a coincidence that when Stevenson was appointed, a former volunteer was representing California in Congress. (See Chapter Twenty.)

16.   *Report of J. D. Stevenson, U.S. Shipping Commissioner, to the Chamber of Commerce, at San Francisco, Cal.* (San Francisco: Woman's Publishing Company, 1873), 9.

17.   In July 1849 Colonel Stevenson had helped organize the Masonic Lodge in California. On October 4 a notice over his name appeared in the *Alta California* calling for subscriptions to a joint stock company to erect a Lodge building. He was chosen the first grand master of the Master Masons.

Chapter Twenty

The Issue

THE TOTAL NUMBER of men involved, including those who came to California with the First Regiment of New York Volunteers, those who arrived later to serve in the unit, and those who were enrolled in California, was 841.[1] In March 1847, 599 arrived on the *Susan Drew*, *Thomas H. Perkins*, and *Loo Choo*; 49 on the *Brutus* in April 1847; 187 on the *Isabella* and *Sweden* in February 1848; 1 on the *Huntress* in October 1848; and 5 were enrolled by various means in Upper and Lower California.

Reliable information exists on the later lives of 487 volunteers, or fifty-eight percent of the total number. They left clear if often hidden records of their lives and deaths in California or elsewhere by holding office, joining associations, owning property, paying poll or property taxes, appearing in censuses, and applying for bounty land or pension; by writing or by being written about; by responding to Francis D. Clark's questionnaires between 1870 and 1890 with information that is verifiable; or by being identified in necrologies of California undertakers, organizations, or local communities.

Of those 487 men, the great majority—388—remained to live and die in California, eighty of them in the many counties comprising the gold region. The balance—99 men— left California permanently, most of them by the mid-1850s but some not until the Civil War and others still later.

On 354 former volunteers no reliable information exists. The whereabouts of all these men (and of a great many on whom there actually are good records) were unknown to Francis Clark and Bancroft. Names of about one hundred appear in post-1848 documents and lists, but in those cases there appear no means to distinguish the person as a former volunteer from another of the same name. The population of California grew so rapidly after 1848 that duplication of names was common.

Some of those 354 applied for bounty land from addresses in California and elsewhere, and were issued warrants, which they apparently sold, there being no further record of them. Not one of them applied for pension under the Mexican War Survivors' Act of January 29, 1887, which made eligible for pension Mexican War service personnel who had reached their sixty-second birthdays. Almost all surviving volunteers were qualified in the year of the act or the year following and all by 1892. It is likely, although not certain, that these 354 men were dead by 1887. It is still more likely, if equally uncertain, that many of them met their deaths in California's mining country in the early years of the Gold Rush. Epidemics, dysentery, exposure, and accident took an extraordinarily heavy toll of life in those years.

Of special interest are Companies F and I, since their formation and composition are discussed in detail earlier in this account. Both companies remained relatively stable during their California service, with little desertion and a minimum of transfer. (Neither company received any of the recruits of 1848, who were assigned to Companies A, B, D, E, and G.)

When mustered out in Santa Barbara early in September 1848, Company F numbered fifty-eight men. Eleven of them left no further record. Ten others, having spent at least some time in California, permanently left the state for Mexico, Hawaii, Cuba, Nevada, Missouri, Pennsylvania, and New York. The remaining thirty-seven, two-thirds of the company, spent the rest of their lives in California. Six of them stayed in the gold country and ten remained in and near Santa Barbara where the company had been stationed. Three settled in Sacramento, four in Stockton, and fourteen elsewhere in California, most of them in San Francisco.

Of the sixty-six men with whom Captain Shannon had sailed from New York, forty-seven remained when Company I was mustered out in San Diego on September 25, 1848. Five had died of disease or had been killed by Indians; three had been discharged; two had deserted in Rio de Janeiro, five in Valparaiso, and two while the company was stationed in Monterey; and three had been transferred to other companies of the regiment. Of the forty-seven at mustering out, eight left no further records, but two-thirds of the company, thirty-one men, remained in California. Eleven of them lived in the gold region, principally in the southern mines of Calaveras and Tuolumne counties. Two were killed by Indians in 1848 and 1849 and another was later slain by the California bandit Tiburcio Vásquez. Those who survived the mining experience settled in San Francisco, Sacramento, Sonoma, San Diego, and Monterey. Of the eight who left California, one went to Minnesota, two to Oregon, one to Nevada. One lived in California many years until, almost in old age, he was attracted by the Oklahoma land rush. Of the entire company, only three returned to New York. Two returned to Bath, the only two of the twenty-six remaining from the original company formed there.

One man from Company I settled briefly in New York City in the mid-1850s. He was former orderly sergeant Joshua S. Vincent whose "Log-Book" has been cited extensively in Parts One and Two of this narrative. Vincent's Mexican War pension file indicates that he was in Stockton in August 1849, where he received written proof of his discharge from former lieutenant William H. Smith of Company I whom he encountered there. Two years later he was in San Francisco, and on

August 15, 1851, applied to the commissioner of pensions for bounty land. A warrant was issued in October and sent to him in San Francisco, but there is no record of his having taken possession of the land. In 1856 Vincent was in New York City painting frescoes in public buildings. Two years later, he had become an itinerant printer, having resumed his original trade. He worked on the Milwaukee *Sentinel*; the Jackson, Mississippi, *Mississippian*; the St. Louis *Republic*; and the Carbondale, Illinois, *New Era*, which he founded. He did not fight in the Civil War. About 1870 he settled in the Ozark Mountains of southern Missouri and there, at Linn Creek, he established the *Reveille* in 1879. The newspaper remained in the hands of Vincent's heirs until 1935. Vincent married for the fourth time in 1890 and died at Linn Creek on April 14, 1891.

Vincent had applied for pension on March 2, 1887, on a printed application form he had received from Francis D. Clark, 38 Cortlandt Street, New York City, which named Clark the applicant's "true and lawful attorney to prosecute this claim." Thus we know that Clark utilized his extensive file on the volunteers and made his historical hobby pay.

Back in 1848, on Governors Island, Dr. McVickar had accurately foreseen that the volunteers would "find alike their dwellings and the their graves in a far distant land." But that New York newspaperman was mistaken who in 1846 postulated that Stevenson's Regiment was useless and predicted that the issue of such a California expedition would be inglorious. President Polk and Secretary Marcy had not requested or required glorious results. They asked only for an effective military organization that would perform a civilian colonial function when the need for armed force had passed.

Stevenson's Regiment did provide the bulk of all the soldiers in both Californias for eighteen months, satisfying two demanding military governors. Apprehensive of insurrection and ill equipped to deal with it, General Kearny had greeted the regiment's arrival in 1847 with relief. Only with reluctance did Colonel Mason see the volunteers leave the service in 1848. As a regular-army officer, he must have remarked with chagrin, as Lieutenant Sherman did, that the desertion rate among volunteers, while high, was still lower than that of the regulars.

The circumstances of the volunteers coming to California as and when they did had important consequences. The men's ties to the East were not strong; their motives for volunteering, while widely varied and not all high-minded, were powerful; and they were in the West, many of them settled, when one of the great world movements of the nineteenth century began in California. If most had been provincial when they left New York, by 1849 they no longer were.

The real issue of Polk's experiment came with the volunteers' solid contributions toward social order and political stability in 1848, 1849, and 1850. Their contributions in those spheres by no means stopped after that time. In the state senate and assembly, almost without interruption, former volunteers were prominent for thirty-five years. Between 1849 and 1885 in all but nine scattered years at least one former volunteer, and usually more than one, served in the California State Legislature. From the regiment came one of California's first congressmen. Another, serving two terms between 1871 and 1875, had not been an officer but a private in Company A. He was Sherman O. Houghton, who also served as mayor of San Jose and married, in turn, Mary Donner and, after her death, her cousin Eliza Donner, both survivors of the Donner Party tragedy.

While the officers of the regiment tended to leave more complete records of themselves than did enlisted men such as Houghton, their public service over the years was no greater. Twelve of the twenty volunteers who ultimately served in the California State Legislature had been enlisted men in the regiment. The regimental officers of 1846-1848 warranted and held higher rank during the Civil War than did former enlisted men. But there, too, there were exceptions. Former sergeant William H. Christian, of Captain Dimmick's Company K, served throughout the Civil War as a brigadier general.

Those volunteers with a pronounced sense of mission, among whom Edward Gilbert was foremost, had an unusual opportunity to exercise it in California. They soon made their way into public life, law, and journalism and made their marks. Those anxious to pursue wealth, as almost all appeared to be in late 1848, had an uncommonly good chance to find it. That appearance was as deceptive among the ex-volunteers as among the forty-niners, however. The great adventure and excitement of seeking gold was undoubtedly their controlling passion. Those who really wanted a fortune straightaway went into business.

Since the volunteers had not been carefully selected for "varied pursuits," as Marcy had specified and Stevenson had hoped, the almost immediate growth of large cities in California was providential. Most volunteers followed urban trades. As new incentives were created, volunteers were there —everywhere—in countless occupations. In describing his fellow volunteers on Governors Island, Walter Murray had called them "men of pretty much every class except the most opulent." In California, after the first year or two of Gold Rush society, volunteers were again in every class, decidedly including the most opulent.

From the criminals cited (and in the interest of accuracy all known have been included), it is clear that the number of former volunteers who lived outside the law was not small, nor were their crimes particularly modest. But the total figure is probably smaller than those critics of the regiment back in New York and Washington would have predicted in July and August of 1846. Those opponents of the venture would have been surprised at the number of volunteers who served, enforced, and interpreted the law in California, and at the number who made that law.

Most volunteers were not villains and most did not become millionaires, army generals, or even politicians. The majority of Stevenson's men led ordinary, productive lives in a state of the United States their regiment had helped to make.

NOTES

1.   While this figure differs from those of regimental historian
Francis D. Clark and of Hubert Howe Bancroft, it is confirmed by
the complete muster-out rolls of the ten companies (August 15,
August 25, Sept. 8, Sept. 18, Sept. 25, Oct. 23, Oct. 24, 1848), by the
muster-out roll of the field and staff (Sept. 18 and Oct. 26, 1848),
and by the later discharges of Lts. Myron Norton and Jeremiah
Sherwood, RG 94, NA. (Sherwood had been on detached duty with
the Dragoons when Company G was mustered out and was put on
indefinite furlough. He was not formally discharged until 1873,
having waived all claim to back pay.)

Bibliographical Essay

The self-appointed historian of Stevenson's Regiment was Francis D. Clark, a private in Company D. Nineteen years old when he was mustered in during May 1847, Clark was a recruit replacement in the detachment that sailed to California on the *Isabella*, arriving in February 1848. Mustered out in October 1848, Clark went to the mines, studied law, and served the three years after 1852 as justice of the peace in San Joaquin County. In 1855 he returned to New York. He served during the Civil War as a major and later as military secretary of the Department of North Carolina.

Back in New York City before 1870, Clark began compiling information on Stevenson's Regiment. In 1871 and 1874 he had printed for distribution two rolls of the survivors, the first a single sheet, the second a twenty-page pamphlet. Finally, after "over one thousand written communications" and "some fifteen hundred printed circulars and postal cards addressed to comrades," Clark published his ninety-four-page book, *The First Regiment of New York Volunteers* (New York: George S. Evans & Co., 1882). Most of Clark's book, which is invaluable, is devoted to lists by companies of all known survivors in April 1882 and those known to have died. The balance of the book is of adulatory, though often most informative, communications. Clark was reasonably careful but for some reason worked with incomplete musters, evidently those of June 1848, it appears from my research. Using muster-out rolls would have saved Clark from many errors. In August 1883 Clark did a final twenty-page pamphlet, correcting errors in and making additions to his book of the previous year, and left a manuscript, "List of the Regiment in 1897," now in the Library of The Society of California Pioneers in San Francisco.

Hubert Howe Bancroft used Clark's book and other sources in preparing entries for volunteers in his "Pioneer Register," printed as an appendix in Volumes II-V of the seven-volume *History of California* (San Francisco: Vols. I-IV, A. L. Bancroft & Company; Vols. V-VII, The History Company, 1884-1890). Bancroft used some information from Clark's book in his discussion of the regiment but as well used military records, contemporary California newspapers, and journals and statements of volunteers procured by his staff. Bancroft also used incomplete musters.

Anyone working in California history must regularly refer to Bancroft. The last three volumes of his undigested history are exceedingly rich in information on the regiment, richer by far than Bancroft knew. He and his research-and-writing assistants were devoted to great detail. They included endless lists of pre-1849 property owners, political and civic leaders, and individuals in local annals throughout California. In such lists, Stevenson's men very often appear, unidentified as former volunteers. Both Clark and Bancroft proved most valuable for clues to profitable further research in local and county records. Neither, however, is objective or ultimately reliable.

The influence of each is clearly traceable in what has been written about the regiment. The worst of both Clark and Bancroft, the errors of each and some additional errors, appear in Guy J. Giffen: *California Expedition* (Oakland: Biobooks, 1951), a carelessly prepared volume produced for the centennial of California statehood, fortunately in a quite limited edition. It amounts to an alphabetical listing of volunteers from Clark's lists and Bancroft's "Pioneer Register" and is mainly characterized by misspelling. It is safe to say that nothing of significance has been written about Stevenson's Regiment since Bancroft. Nevertheless, interest in and perhaps perplexity about the regiment have persisted, with the publication in this decade of a reprinting of Clark's *Stevenson's Regiment in California* and James Lynch's *With Stevenson to California* in one volume, *The New York Volunteers in California* (Glorieta, New Mexico: Rio Grande Press, Inc., 1970). In that volume Professor David E. Livingston-Little provides a provocative introduction, alluding to his correct suspicion that the nature, activities, and influence of the regiment have been underestimated. He reiterated that suspicion, with some evidence, in an article published in JOURNAL *of the* WEST in April, 1972, entitled "U.S. Military Forces in California," an article included in a collection of Mexican War articles from JOURNAL *of the* WEST edited by Odie B. Faulk and Joseph A. Stout, Jr., *The Mexican War: Changing Interpretations* (Chicago: The Swallow Press Inc., 1973).

One of Bancroft's prejudices is conspicuous in his writing on the regiment. He thoroughly approved of extra-legal means of achieving and maintaining social order and found vigilance committees and lynch law quite salutary in their effect. So interested was he in such practices that he devoted two volumes of his *Works* to *Popular Tribunals* (San Francisco: The History Company, 1887). Untroubled, he could coolly describe community after community taking direct action until the quiet oaks were "tasselled with the carcasses of the wicked." The moral effect was extreme—extremely good, in his opinion.

Unhappily for the reputation of Stevenson's Regiment, some of the discharged volunteers provoked a popular tribunal in San Francisco in 1849. The misdeeds of the Hounds were described in foul detail by the premier yellow journalist of San Francisco, Frank Soulé, in his *The Annals of San Francisco* (New York: D. Appleton & Company, 1855). Using the sensational *Annals* and documentary sources on the citizens' group that crushed the Hounds, Bancroft, the presumably dispassionate historian, condemned the former volunteers in the Hounds. Though admiring the worthy citizens inordinately, he failed to identify as Stevenson's Regiment men the former volunteers among those citizens—the "court"-appointed defense attorney, the prosecuting attorney, the very judge before whom the culprits were tried. And there were others. This convenient selection, or perhaps simple oversight growing out of the historiographic method of Bancroft and his collaborators, has had a prolonged effect on the reputation of the regiment.

Before Bancroft, John S. Hittell published one of the centennial sketches of cities and states prepared at the suggestion of the U.S. government. In *A History of the City of San Francisco and Incidentally of the State of California* (San Francisco: A. L. Bancroft & Company, 1878), he concluded, after writing a few paragraphs about the arrival and nature of the regiment, that "Stevenson's men as a class became permanent, many of them worthy, and some of them prominent, citizens of California." (Page 112)

After Bancroft, Zoeth S. Eldredge published *The Beginnings of San Francisco*, 2 volumes (San Francisco: Zoeth S. Eldredge, publisher, 1912). Although his information was unattributed, he drew heavily on Bancroft and concluded: "Though their record in California was not altogether enviable, and some of their number ended their careers on the gallows, the muster roll of the regiment contains the names of a large number of men of standing who attained positions of wealth and influence." (Vol. II, p. 553)

California historians for most of this century have been content to equivocate, like Eldredge, or, in the absence of a monograph, to dismiss the regiment. A look at a few of the most widely adopted textbooks on California history is warranted, and startling.

Andrew F. Rolle, in the first edition of his *California, A History* (New York: Thomas Y. Crowell Company, 1963), devoted a nineteen-page chapter to the "American Conquest" —Frémont, Kearny, the naval forces, and one paragraph to Stevenson's Regiment and the Mormon Battalion, "lesser American commands." Of the regiment Rolle wrote:

On the sixth of March another unit, consisting of 250 members of Colonel Jonathan D. Stevenson's regiment of New York volunteers, arrived in San Francisco. Within a few months their discharge was also completed and many of those men were absorbed into the California population. By March, 1848, nearly all volunteers were discharged from active service. (Page 204)

Almost everything in the three sentences is misinformation. The strength of the regiment is minimized by the author's mention only of the force on the first of six ships that carried the volunteers to California. There is no allusion to service or battle in Lower California. The volunteers were discharged in eighteen, not "a few" months, and the first of them not until August 1848. In context, one gets the decided impression that this was a "lesser command" precisely because General Kearny had arrived and the fighting was over.

In his discussion of the 1849 constitutional convention, Rolle identified the secretary as "William G. Marcy, formerly captain of Stevenson's volunteer regiment," but did not mention the seven former volunteers who were delegates.

Rolle devoted a full page to the importance of the San Francisco Legislative Assembly, which championed a temporary civilian government because Congress had failed to provide a territorial government. He did not identify the leaders, who were members of the regiment. But Rolle did identify the Hounds as "partly composed of remnants of Stevenson's Volunteers." (Page 241) The regiment fared no better, although no worse, in the second edition of Professor Rolle's book published in 1969.

In Professor John W. Caughey's *California*, subtitled "A Remarkable State's Life History," (Englewood Cliffs, N.J.: Prentice-Hall, 1970), the third edition of a remarkably fine survey of California history, the single mention of the regiment is a reference to Lieutenant-Colonel Burton and the volunteers in combat in La Paz, Baja California. While there is no credit to the regiment for either its part in the conquest or the successful occupation, or the former volunteers' presence and influence in the constitutional convention, neither is there any association of former volunteers with the Hounds.

Professor Walton Bean in his first-rate *California: An Interpretive History* (New York: McGraw-Hill, 1968), while neglecting to mention the regiment in his seven-page section on "The Mexican War" or in an eighteen-page chapter on "The American Conquest," did acknowledge former volunteers prominently in his discussion of "The Provisional Government Movement" and just as prominently, shortly thereafter, as having contributed to the Hounds. In the second edition of Professor Bean's survey, published in 1973, there was no change.

Thus the reputation of the regiment; thus the influence of Bancroft.

For this account of the First Regiment of New York Volunteers the chief sources were the regimental records from the Office of the Adjutant General of the United States and the Department of War, now in the National Archives (Record Groups 94 and 393), and records of the regiment in Record Group 92, Orders of the Quartermaster General of the United States, also in the National Archives, as are pension records from the Veterans Administration. Other sources of major value were miscellaneous orders and correspondence in the Office of the Adjutant General of the State of New York; diaries, letters, and books of individual volunteers; New York and California newspapers; municipal and county records; dozens of local and county histories; historical journals; and numerous secondary and specialized studies. With some exceptions, sources treated critically in the text or in footnotes are not discussed at length here, if they are included at all.

Bibliographies

While the writer consulted a number of special bibliographies, the three most general have been the most helpful. Both editions of Robert E. Cowan's *A Bibliography of the History of California and the Pacific West* were used. The first (San Francisco: The Book Club of San Francisco, 1914) contains just under one thousand fully annotated items; the second, 3 volumes (San Francisco: John Henry Nash, 1933), almost five thousand items less fully described. Still more valuable was

California Local History; A Bibliography and Union List of Library Holdings (Stanford: Stanford University Press, 1970), the second edition, revised and enlarged and edited by Margaret Miller Rocq. Oscar O. Winther's *The Trans-Mississippi West, A Guide to Its Periodical Literature, 1811-1938* (Bloomington: University of Indiana Press, 1942) and his supplementary *A Classified Bibliography of the Periodical Literature of the Trans-Mississippi West (1957-67)* (Bloomington: University of Indiana Press, 1970) was continuously helpful.

General and Special Histories

Two histories of westward expansion were particularly helpful in preparation for this study. All of Frederick Jackson Turner's *The United States, 1830-1850* (New York: Henry Holt and Company, 1935), subtitled "The Nation and Its Sections," was valuable and necessary for an understanding of the last few years of the period in the West, but Chapter XII on the Polk administration was especially important. Chapters 23-25 of Robert E. Riegel's *America Moves West*, revised edition, (New York: Henry Holt and Company, 1947) on the attraction of Mexico, Manifest Destiny, and the Mexican War itself were the most important parts of that significant book.

Reading all of both volumes of Justin H. Smith's *The War with Mexico*, 2 volumes (New York: The Macmillan Company, 1919), as one frankly must, was a necessary exercise in patience before moving on to studies of the war published earlier and later. Of the latter, Charles L. Dufour's *The Mexican War* (New York: Hawthorn Books, Inc., 1968) was illuminating although virtually silent on the California aspects of the war.

Of the fourteen earliest histories and reviews of the Mexican War, all published by 1850 and all consulted for this study, the two most important were entries in a competition sponsored by the American Peace Society of Boston. The prize-winning volume was Abiel Abbott Livermore's *The War With Mexico Reviewed* (Boston: The American Peace Society, 1850). Because Livermore laid bare the nature of the war and the elaborate official pretexts for it, the book was extremely valuable, granting the author's completely prejudiced point of view against the war and his exaggeration of the slavery issue in the genesis of the war. Chapter XX on "The True Destiny of the United States" is an especially profound statement of anti-expansionist sentiment. A runner-up in the competition, a poorer book but at the same time a much more inclusive one, was William Jay's *A Review of the Causes and Consequences of the Mexican War* (Boston: Benjamin B. Mussey & Co., 1849) which significantly was already into a fourth printing in the year of its publication. Whereas Livermore substantially ignored California, Jay devoted two chapters to the "Seizure and Surrender of Monterey in California, by Commodore Jones" and to the "Conquest of California."

Because both books were begun before the conclusion of the war, they can profitably be read and considered in the light of Frederick Merk's *Manifest Destiny and Mission in American History* (New York: Alfred A. Knopf, 1963), a penetrating interpretation of the forces that attended the extension of American sovereignty to the Pacific coast. Chapters I through VII were particularly valuable for an understanding of the 1840s and early 1850s, and Chapters VIII and X for the demise of continentalism. For the present study, Chapter VI on "Sectional and Party Attitudes" was most helpful; almost everything consulted for this study supported Professor Merk's conclusions.

While it contains little on California, Alfred Hoyt Bill's *Rehearsal for Conflict: The War with Mexico, 1846-48* (New York: Alfred A. Knopf, 1947) is a suggestive study, aptly titled, of those men in the Mexican War who figured in both Union and Confederate armies in the Civil War. It is especially evocative of the spirit of the period, only slightly less so than Bernard DeVoto's *The Year of Decision: 1846* (Boston: Little, Brown and Company, 1943), which concentrates on overland routes to the West and on the war in mainland Mexico into the early months of 1847, with especially valuable insights into the lives and personalities of both the major and minor political and military figures involved.

Polk, The Diary of a President, 1845-1849 (New York: Longmans, Green & Co., 1929), edited by Allan Nevins— covering the Mexican War, the acquisition of Texas and Oregon, and the conquest of California—was used in this study, although the first three volumes of Polk's *Diary*, 4 volumes (Chicago: A. C. McClurg & co., 1910), edited by Milo M. Quaife, were also used. Volumes III and IV of *Compilation of the Messages and Papers of the Presidents, 1789-1897*, 10 volumes (53 Cong., 2d sess., H. Misc. Doc., No. 210, pts. 1-10, Washington, D.C., 1907), edited by James D. Richardson, were used as sources of Polk's messages to Congress. One of the most telling biographies of James K. Polk and one which details his California policy is E. I. McCormac's *James K. Polk, A Political Biography* (Berkeley: University of California Press, 1922). If somewhat at variance with the view of that policy that emerges from this study of Stevenson's Regiment, the McCormac book was still a most important one. Another view of Polk's California policy, one that cannot be ignored, is presented by Richard T. Stenberg in "Polk and Frémont, 1845-1846," in the *Pacific Historical Review*, Vol. VII (April 1938), pp. 211-227. Important aspects of James Buchanan's relationship with Polk and his conduct as secretary of state are developed by Philip S. Klein in *President James Buchanan, A Biography* (University Park: Pennsylvania State University Press, 1962), especially in Chapters XIII and XIV, "Politics Under Polk" and "Conquering a Continent." Extremely valuable information was found throughout the seventeen articles from JOURNAL *of the* WEST collected and edited by Odie B. Faulk and Joseph A. Stout, Jr., and published under the title *The Mexican War: Changing Interpretations* (Chicago: The Swallow Press Inc., 1973).

The figure of Secretary of War Marcy emerges clearly in a biography of General Kearny. Dwight L. Clarke's *Stephen Watts Kearny, Soldier of the West* (Norman: University of Oklahoma Press, 1961) is a friendly biography of the brigadier general and probably does some injustice to Frémont while devoting some two hundred pages, Chapters IX through XVIII, to the Army of the West and Kearny's conduct in New

Mexico and California. The Kearny-Frémont controversy did not directly affect Stevenson's Regiment, fortunately, and has only been touched upon in this study of the regiment.

General and Special California Histories

Of general histories of California, in addition to Bancroft and the Rolle, Caughey, and Bean texts mentioned earlier in this bibliographical section, a number of other California histories were used. More readable than Bancroft but far less rich in documentary detail is Theodore H. Hittell's *History of California*, 4 volumes (San Francisco: N. J. Stone & Company, 1885-1897). Its greatest strength, however, lies exactly in the period of Stevenson's Regiment and the first years of statehood, covered in Volume II. A one-volume survey, employing different emphasis and also extremely valuable, is a combined and revised edition of Robert Glass Cleland's *From Wilderness to Empire* and *California in Our Time* (New York: Alfred A. Knopf, 1959), edited by Glenn S. Dumke.

Among other secondary works, one of the most helpful was the 1948 edition of Josiah Royce's *California, From the Conquest in 1846 To The Second Vigilance Committee in San Francisco* (New York: Alfred A. Knopf, 1948). This edition of Royce's study, subtitled "A Study of American Character," has a particularly illuminating introduction by Robert Glass Cleland, analyzing Royce's relationship with Henry L. Oak, first assistant to Hubert Howe Bancroft and author of many of "Bancroft's" *Works*, and with John C. and Jessie Benton Frémont. Royce's special interest in social conditions in California in the decade following the occupation resulted in a book of uncommon interest, one most unpopular in California when first published in 1886.

While repetitious and difficult to use because of poor editing, the best study of military government in California is Theodore Grivas's *Military Government in California, 1846-1850* (Glendale, California: The Arthur H. Clark Company, 1963). While Grivas's conclusions do not always seem to follow from his evidence, the book does make sense of the often-confusing affairs under Governors Kearny, Mason, and.Riley. A much more ambitious study and one too little known, Woodrow J. Hansen's *The Search for Authority in California* (Oakland: Biobooks, 1960), describes governments in California from the Mexican Revolution to statehood for California and is carefully and very well written.

Federal and State Public Records, Printed and Manuscript

For this study of Stevenson's Regiment the most important source of information to the date the companies were mustered out was the great body of primary material in the National Archives in Washington, D.C., comprising records of the Office of the Adjutant General of the United States and of the War Department, principally Record Groups 94 and 393 and Record Group 92, Orders of the Quartermaster General of the United States. Veterans Administration records were also most valuable. Because of loss in transit en route to Washington, and for other reasons, the adjutant general's records on the regiment and those of the War Department are not complete. They are, however, reasonably complete, remarkably so perhaps. Documents and official correspondence relating to the formation of the regiment and some records throughout the existence of the regiment are carefully preserved and organized by the New York State Division of Archives and History in Albany. Of them, the archives of the adjutant general of the State of New York and copies of official correspondence with Governor Silas Wright were most important. The California State Archives in Sacramento hold some documentary material relating to the regiment and to the men in it. In the California State Archives is an important manuscript, "Journal of the Convention of California" (of 1849), important to use for any study of the constitutional convention and particularly important to use with J. Ross Browne's *Report of the Debates in the Convention of California on the Formation of the State Constitution* (Washington, D.C.: John T. Towers, 1850).

Of printed federal public records the most valuable was the *Congressional Globe* for both sessions of the Twenty-ninth, Thirtieth, and Thirty-first Congresses. For the period 1846-

1850, *House Executive Documents*, *House Miscellaneous Documents*, *Senate Executive Documents*, and *Senate Miscellaneous Documents* are also rich in material on California, and, as cited, in material on the regiment. Of these Congressional records other than the *Congressional Globe*, the single most important volume was *House Executive Document* No. 17 of the first session of the Thirty-first Congress. This important one-thousand-page volume contains much official correspondence and many documents relating to California for the years 1847-1849.

Books and Manuscripts of Volunteers

Of printed books by volunteers those of Felix P. Wierzbicki, E. Gould Buffum, and William Redmond Ryan have been discussed at ample length in the text and the notes to Chapter Fifteen. Francis J. Lippitt's *Reminiscences* (Providence, R.I.: Preston & Rounds Co., 1902) is without question one of the most interesting books written by a former volunteer, who also was one of the most interesting and able men participating in the experiment. James A. Hardie's *Memoir of James Allen Hardie* (Washington, D.C.: privately printed, 1877), written while he was inspector general of the United States Army, and James Lynch's *With Stevenson to California* (San Francisco: privately printed, 1896) are mostly interesting from the distinct points of view of the field officer and the private, neither of them especially perceptive or literate (at least in these two books) and both books are inferior to many personal memoirs and accounts of the regiment that remain in manuscript. *The Journal of Lieutenant John McHenry Hollingsworth of the First New York Volunteers* (San Francisco: California Historical Society, 1923) was extremely helpful and the society has been generous in permitting me to quote extensively from it, but a more careful editing of the journal from the original manuscript in the Library of the California Historical Society is warranted. The California Historical Society has also permitted my extensive use of Joshua S. Vincent's manuscript "Log-Book." Although he served only briefly with the regiment in California, George D. Brewerton devoted some pages to the regiment in his *Overland With Kit Carson, a Narrative of the Old Spanish Trail in '48* (New York: Coward-McCann, Inc., 1930), which first appeared in part in *Harper's New Monthly Magazine* in August 1853.

At least three former volunteers prepared reminiscences for Hubert Howe Bancroft at his request. In manuscript or typescript they are in the Bancroft Library of the University of California, Berkeley, which has graciously consented to my use and quotation from them. They are John B. Frisbie's "Reminiscences"; Alfred A. Green's "Life and Adventures of a '47'er of California"; and the Hon. Walter Murray's "Narrative of a California Volunteer." Also in the Bancroft Library is Captain Albert B. Brackett's "A Sketch of the First Regiment of New York Volunteers in the Mexican War; commonly called Stevenson's California Regiment," which was dependent on a journal or narrative of Captain John E. Brackett. The Bancroft Library also contains the important manuscript collections of Henry M. Naglee; Joseph Evans' "Around 'Cape Horn' with Col. Stevenson's Regiment"; and Lieutenant Colonel Henry Burton's private "Diary" and, in the same copybook, part of his "Letter-Book."

In the Huntington Library, San Marino, California, with whose permission I have used excerpts, are the fragmentary but fascinating "Diary of Kimball Hale Dimmick," Dimmick letters, and a number of letters of Captain Joseph Folsom in the Leidesdorff papers. Other Folsom papers and letters are in the W. D. M. Howard papers in the Library of the California Historical Society in San Francisco. A significant collection of Colonel Stevenson's letters is in the Robert Ernest Cowan Collection in the library of the University of California, Los Angeles, which has permitted my study and use of them, and some of Stevenson's "Letter-Books" are in the Library of the New-York Historical Society, which has generously assented to their use. All the known letters of Captain William E. Shannon are in the California State Library, Sacramento, or in the possession of Ward Shannon of Bath, New York.

Scholarly Journals

For much of the time since 1922 the *California Historical Society Quarterly* has been the leading journal of state and local history in California, and in its pages have appeared many hundreds of documents, letters, diaries, and other primary material as well as interpretive articles often of a very high order. Contributed by professional historians and dedicated amateurs in about equal measure, these scholarly editions and articles were used extensively in this study, as cited throughout. The names of volunteers appeared with extraordinary frequency in the first forty volumes of the *Quarterly*, to which an *Index* was published in 1966, and in the succeeding fourteen volumes, to which an *Index* appeared in 1977. Files of most other journals were also studied—the *Pacific Historical Review*, the *Huntington Library Quarterly*, the JOURNAL *of the* WEST, the *Quarterly* of both The Society of California Pioneers and of the Historical Society of Southern California, and others distinguished and useful but too numerous to mention here.

Newspapers

Newspapers have been cited often herein and were a rich source of information. Since the regiment was controversial during its first few months in New York, in the summer of 1846, it received much space in the newspapers, primarily editorial comment. Most favorable to the regiment and its announced purposes was the *New York Herald*. In defending the regiment the *Herald* devoted more space to it than any other newspaper. (For this reason, clearly, Francis D. Clark quoted only from the *Herald* in his history of the regiment.) Also favorable to the regiment were the New York *Sun* and, usually, the *New York Evening Post*, which, like the *Herald*, must be used with prudence. Distortion was also evident in those New York newspapers inimical to the regiment, chief among them Horace Greeley's *New York Tribune*, the New York *Journal of Commerce*, and the New York *Courier and Enquirer*. The controversial nature of the regiment's purposes brought points of view violently to the surface. Outside New York City but in New York State, especially in Albany and Norwich, the editorial opinion was similar to that presented in *The Steuben Farmers' Advocate* of Bath, New York, it appears from the studies conducted and from the use of *Niles' Weekly Register*.

Because volunteers were involved in reporting as well as in making news in California, the files of *The California Star*, the *Californian*, *The California Star and Californian*, and the *Alta California* were all extremely valuable. Outside San Francisco, the *Placer Times* of Sacramento was most useful.

Index

Adams and Company, 214-15
Adams, John Quincy, 132; attempted purchase of Calif., 17; and Mexican War, 37
Albany Argus, 27, 60, 161
Alcalde rule, 105-6
Alta California: history of, to 1840, 9-12; Disturnell map of, 10; extent of, 11; population in 1840, 11-12
Alta California. See San Francisco *Alta California*
American Peace Society, 4
Annals of San Francisco (Soulé), 202-3, 243-44
Ashmun, George, 37-38

Baker, Edward D., 169
Bancroft, George, 21
Bancroft, Hubert Howe: on constitutional convention delegates, 183; on Hounds affair, 202-3, 243; *History of California*, 242-43
Band, regimental, 72, 85, 97; in Los Angeles, 117; in Santa Barbara, 125
Bartlett, John A., 207
Bath, New York, 27
Bath (New York) *Steuben Farmers' Advocate*, 27-29, 45

Bell, Horace, 191
Belt, George G., 143-44
Benton, Thomas Hart, 179-80
Beverly, McKenzie, 197-98
Boggs, Lilburn W., 106
Bonnycastle, John C., 137, 143, 145
Brackett, Albert B., 253
Bracket, John E., 41, 56, 134, 136; in Sonoma, 106; elected assemblyman, 188; in Calif. militia, 206; narrative of, 253
Brannan, Samuel, 218-19
Brewerton, George D., 71
Brown, Philip, 134
Browne, J. Ross, 184, 187
Brutus (storeship), 80, 97
Buchanan, James, 16, 164
Buckelew, B. R., 178
Buffum, E. Gould, 167, 227; *Six Months in the Gold Mines*, 168, 174 n.24; letters of, 174 n.24; and Constitutional Convention, 184; on popular justice, 199-200
Burnett, Peter, 187
Burnett, Ward, 48 n.10, 66
Burton, Henry S., 98, 115, 135; joins regiment, 70; in Lower California, 102, 111-12; in Civil War, 145; diary of, 253

Bustamente, Anastasio, 101

California As It Is (Wierzbicki), 174 n.25
California Expedition (Giffen), 242
"California Grand March": cover illustrated, 72
Campbell, William, 199
Carnes, Henry S., 157
Carrillo, Pedro C., 122; commends volunteers, 123-24
Castro, José, 88, 101
Clark, Francis D., 133, 236; *First Regiment of New York Volunteers*, 241; regimental historian, 241-42
Company A (Capt. Seymour G. Steele commanding): sails on *Loo Choo*, 74; arrival in San Francisco, 96-97; to Santa Barbara, 98; to Lower California, 102; action in Lower California, 111-12; mustered out, 137
Company B (Capt. James Turner, Lt. Henry C. Matsell commanding); sails on *Thomas H. Perkins*, 74; arrival in San Francisco, 86; to Santa Barbara, 98; to Lower California, 102; action in Lower California, 111-12; mustered out, 137
Company C (Capt. John E. Brackett commanding): sails on *Loo Choo*, 74; arrival in San Francisco, 96-97; assigned to Presidio of San Francisco, 98; ordered to Sonoma; 98; detachment of, to Sutter's Fort, 99; desertion from, 134; returns to Presidio of San Francisco, 135; mustered out, 135; commended in *Californian*, 136
Company D (Capt. Henry M. Naglee commanding): sails on *Susan Drew*, 74; arrival in San Fran-

cisco, 96; to Monterey, 98; ordered to remove squatters, 110; on Indian duty, 110-11; to Lower California, 111; mustered out, 137
Company E (Capt. Nelson Taylor commanding): sails on *Loo Choo*, *Susan Drew*, and *Thomas H. Perkins*, 74; arrival in San Francisco 86, 96-97; to Monterey, 98; assigned to Los Angeles, 101; mustered out, 137
Company F (Capt. Francis J. Lippitt commanding): 234-35; organization of, 43; occupational profile of 52-53; sails on *Thomas H. Perkins*, 74; arrival in San Francisco, 86; to Santa Barbara, 98; reception in Santa Barbara, 119; mutinous conduct, 120-22; commended by de la Guerra, Carrillo, 123-24; desertion from, 125; 133; mustered out, 137
Company G (Capt. James Dirver, Capt. Matthew Stevenson commanding): sails on *Thomas H. Perkins*, 74; arrival in San Francisco, 86; to Monterey, 98; to Los Angeles, 101; mustered out, 137
Company H (Capt. John B. Frisbie commanding): conditions of acceptance, 40; organization of, 46; sails on *Susan Drew*, 74; arrival in San Francisco, 96; at Presidio of San Francisco, 98, 107; ordered to Sonoma, 135; mustered out, 135
Company I (Capt. William E. Shannon commanding); 235; organization of, 27-29; assignment, 29; conditions of acceptance, 40; organizational problems of, 44-46; occupational profile of, 53-54; sails on *Susan Drew*, 74;

arrival in San Francisco, 96; to Monterey, 98; Monterey encampment of, illustrated, 100; ordered to San Diego, 110; desertion record, 133; mustered out, 137

Company K (Capt. Kimball H. Dimmick commanding): conditions of acceptance, 40; organization of, 46; sails on *Loo Choo*, 74; at Presidio of San Francisco, 98, 107; mustered out, 135

Constitutional Convention (1849), 177-93; call for, 171-72; Benton urges, 179; election of delegates to, 181-84; proceedings of, 184-87; constitution signed, ratified, 187

Constitutional Convention (1878-1879), 149

Covarrubias, José Maria, 184

Creighton, James, 178

Criminal activity: in San Francisco, 197-98, 202-5; in Lower California, 198-99; near San Jose, 199; at Mission San Miguel, 200-1; near Santa Barbara, 201-2

Cutrell, William E., 137

Dale (U.S.S.), 32

Dana, Richard Henry, 7

Davis, David A., 199

de la Guerra, Pablo, 121-23, 184

Democracy in America (de Tocqueville), 55

Departure from New York, caricatured, 65

Desertion, 134-35, 139 n.12; in New York, 42-47; in Rio de Janeiro, 84; in Valparaiso, 85; from Company F, Santa Barbara, 125; from Presidio of San Francisco, punishment for, 132

de Tocqueville, Alexis, 55, 186-87

Dimmick, Kimball H., 40, 55, 135-36; reproved by Mason, 107; "Diary" of, 108, 131-32; and Hardie, 109; alcalde of San Jose, 147; and Constitutional Convention, 177, 182, 184-85; swears in governor, 188; later life and death of, 190-91.

Disturnell, John: map of Alta California, illustration, 10: "Map of Mexico," 11

Dörnte, Charles, 197

Duels, 83, 169, 189

Durkin, Anthony, 160

Ellis, Alfred, 181

Family groups, aboard transports, 56, 212-13

Filibusters, 206-7, 210 n.29

First Regiment of New York Volunteers, The (Clark), 241-43

Fish Market Reporter (shipboard newspaper), 8-9, 13 n.8, 66

Folsom, Joseph L., 70, 83, 98, 189, 219; to mines with Mason, 132; in U.S. Army, 145; and Central (or Long) Wharf, 212; and Leidesdorff estate, 213-14; death of, 214

Fourgeaud, Victor, 227

Frémont, John Charles, 7, 188

Freund, Henry, 150

Frisbie, Eleazar, 135, 211, 219

Frisbie, John B., 40, 60, 134-35; 211, 219; on Mexican War, 5; on Naglee, 83, 217; and Constitutional Convention, 180, 182; business career of, 217-18; "Reminiscences" of, 253

Frisbie & Co., 211

Giffin, Guy J., 242

Gilbert, Edward, 98, 157; joins regiment, 60; on volunteers' motivation, 60-61; as journalist, 60,

161-62, 189; in San Francisco
Guards, 160; and Constitutional
Convention, 178, 180; elected
delegate, 181; elected congress-
man, 187; and Calif. statehood,
188; fatal duel with Denver,
189; tribute to, 189
Gold, discovery of, 125, 131-32
"Gold fever," 132-33
Governors Island (New York),
41; regiment encamped on,
illustration, 42
Graham, Will Hicks, 169
Grambs, Frederick C., 72
Gray, James A., 188
Greeley, Horace: opposition to
regiment, 46-47
Green, Alfred A., 169, 213
Griffin, John S., 227
Guadalupe Hidalgo, Treaty of: and
Disturnell map, 11; *projet* signed,
132; terms of, 134-35
Gwin, William M., 181, 188, 204

Halleck, Henry W., 90, 105, 183, 187
Hammond, R. P., 226
Hardie, James A., 70, 101, 109, 135,
145
Harris, Stephen C., 55, 165
Harrison, Edward H., 157-60, 212
Hewlett, Palmer B., 29, 212
Hollingsworth, John McHenry, 101,
117, 133, 143; motivation of,
62-63; "Journal" of, 80; to mines
with Stevenson, 137; delegate to
Constitutional Convention, 181,
186; departure from Calif., 192;
later life of, 193
Houghton, Sherman O., 237
Hounds, 202-5, 243, 245
Howard, W. D. M., 160, 165, 181,
204, 213, 218
Hubbard, George C., 162, 165, 167
Huefner, William, 219
Huxley, J. Mead, 219

Hyde, George, 178

Indians, 99-100, 110-11, 122-23
Isabella, 111

Jewett, William S., 189; 223
Johnson, Ira, 157-58
Jones, Thomas ap Catesby: seizes
Monterey, 20; suspended from
service, 152 n.13
Journal-keeping, 80
Journalists, among volunteers, 8, 13
n.8, 60, 148-49, 161-62, 167-68,
174 n.24, 190-91, 194 n.9, 235-
36

Kearney, Denis, 149
Kearny, Stephen W., 71, 133; and
"Army of the West," 26; informed of volunteer regiments,
27; arrives in Calif., 89-90;
named military governor, 91;
creates military districts, 101;
ordered to occupy Lower Calif.,
101; relinquishes command to
Mason, 102; departure from
Calif., 102; Benton's opinion of,
179
Kelly, Phillip, 81-82
Kemble, Edward C., 161-62
Ketchum, Thomas E., 111, 147-48

Lancey, Thomas Crosby, 32, 34 n.17
Larkin, Thomas Oliver, 8, 18, 22 n.4
Lawson, John, 198-99
Leavenworth, Thaddeus M., 165,
204, 224; as San Francisco
alcalde, 107, 159, 171-72
Lee, Cornelius R. V., 169
Leidesdorff, William A., 213
Lemon, George Frank, 167, 219
Linton, James, 210 n.29
Lippitt, Francis J., 52, 55-56, 187,
189, 204, 219; in Santa Barbara,
119-25; San Francisco Legisla-

tive Assembly, speaker of, 166; delegate to Constitutional Convention, 180-81; in Constitutional Convention, 185-87; in Civil War, 192; *Reminiscences* of, 192

Livermore, Abiel Abbott: on Manifest Destiny, 4-5

Loo Choo, 74, 96-97

Los Angeles *Southern Californian*, 190

Los Angeles Star, 168, 190

Love Life of Brig. Gen. Henry M. Naglee, The (Schell), 215-17

Lynch, James, 61, 124

Lynch, Joseph P., 201

Lynch, Patrick, 219

McDonald, Alexander C., 206

McDougal, John, 187

McVickar, John, xv-xvi, 236; illustration of, 51

Magee, Henry, 28-29

Magee, John, 28

Mail service, regimental, 119

Manigest Destiny, xvi, 5-6, 37-38, 60, 247-48; defined, 3-4; *New York Herald* editorial on, 49-50

Marcy, William G., 56, 70, 145-46; Secretary of Constitutional Convention, 184

Marcy, William L.: requisitions volunteers, 15-16, 23, 26; orders Kearny to Calif. 26; authorizes Stevenson's Regiment, 29-30; operating orders to Stevenson, 71; Polk letter to, 72

Marsh, John, 8

Mason, Richard B., 115, 133; as military governor, 102, 105; orders Naglee's arrest, 112; commends Stevenson, 115-16; to mines, 132; on desertion, 135; orders regiment discharged, proclaims

peace, 135; relieved of command, 170-71; Benton's opinion of, 179

Massett, Stephen C., 226-27, 231 n.6

Maxwell, William, 144

Merk, Frederick: on Manifest Destiny, 3, 12 n.1

Military commissions, 198; defined, ordered by Winfield Scott, 121

Military government, 155-72, 178-81; Benton on, 179-80; ends in Calif., 188

Moerenhout, J. A., 227

Mokelumne Hill, 143, 151

Mokelumne River, 143

Monroe Doctrine, 19

Monroe, James, 17, 31

Monterey: U.S. seizure of, 87-88; named Headquarters, Tenth Military Department, 91; Company I encamped at, illustration, 100; in 1847, illustration, 109; and Constitutional Convention, 180-81; 184-87

Morehead, Joseph C., 188, 206-7

Mormon Battalion, 30-31, 91; Marcy authorizes, 27; arrives in Calif., 90; enlistment expires, 101; departs for Utah, 116

Morrison, Roderick, 66, 160; "The Volunteer's Vision," 6-7; murder of, 150

Moscow, 98

Murray, Francis, 160

Murray, Robert, 145-46

Murray, Walter, 42-43, 56, 153 n.18; as Calif. journalist, 148-49; "Narrative of a California Volunteer," 253

Mustering out, 135-38

Mutiny: aboard *Susan Drew*, 81-83; threatened, aboard *Thomas H. Perkins*, 83; talk of, aboard *Loo Choo*, 83; in Santa Barbara, 120-22

Naglee, Henry M., 211, 219; conduct
on *Susan Drew*, 81-83; reputation
of, 82-83; 86 n.12, 217; Indian
campaigns of, 99-100; charges
of murder dismissed, 111-12,
138; and Constitutional Con-
vention, 178, 182; commands
Calif. Guard, 205; and Amer-
ican Theater, 213; business
career of, 214-15; and viticul-
ture, 214-15; 220 n.11; in Civil
War 215-17; letters of, to Mary
L. Schell, 215-17
Naglee, H. M. & Co., 214
Naglee & Sinton, 211, 214
Naglee Building, 214
New Orleans Picayune, 121
New York Commercial Advertiser, 74
New York Evening Post, 36, 47
New York Herald, 18, 36, 47, 49, 161,
168
New York Journal of Commerce, 36, 47
New York Morning Courier and Enquirer,
47, 179
New York of the Pacific, 224-28, 231
n.12
New York Sun, 18, 47
New York Tribune, 46-47
New York Volunteers, First Regi-
ment of: designation changed
from Seventh Regiment, 41, 48
n.10; reputation of, 202, 205,
242-46; sources of information
on, summarized, 246
New York Volunteers, Seventh Reg-
iment of: designated First
Regiment, 41, 48 n.10
Norris, John S., 210 n.29
Norton, Myron, 166, 170, 211; and
Constitutional Convention, 177-
78, 180; delegate to Constitutional Convention, 181, 184-85;
defense of Hounds, 204; in
Calif. Guard, 205; in Los
Angeles, 191-92

Ohio (U.S.S.), 137
Ord, Edward O. C., 90
O'Sullivan, James, 148-49

Pacific Squadron, 20-21
Palmer, Charles A., 64
Palmer, Cook & Co., 211, 215
Parker, R. A., 165
Parker, William C., 160, 211, 224,
231 n.13
Pearsall, Samuel W., 151
Pedrorena, Miguel, 184
Pendleton, George A., 137, 147-48
Penrose, George F., 79-80
Per Lee, Theron R., 160, 166-67,
188, 206
*Personal Adventures in Upper and
Lower California* (Ryan), 174
n.24
Pico, Pío, 88
Polk, James K.: war message to
Congress, 15; and Calif. acquisi-
tion, 16-21; letter to Marcy,
illustrated, 73
Popular justice: in San Jose, 199; in
mines, 199-200; in San Francisco
203-5, 243; Bancroft on, 204-5
Popular Tribunals (Bancroft), 202,
243-44
Power, Edward, 201-2
Power, John A., 201-2
Powers, Jack. *See* Power, John A.,
201-2
Preble (U.S.S.): convoy, 72
Printers. *See* Journalists
Pulis, John C., 170-71

Queen, James, 161, 194 n.9
Querétaro, Mexico, 135

Rancho Los Medanos, 224, 231 n.8
Reed family: murder of, 200
Regimental strength, xv-xvi, 233,
239 n.1
Regulators. *See* Hounds

Reid, Hugo, 184
Reminiscences of a Ranger (Bell), 191
Representative Citizens of Northern California, 151
Richardson, Charles, 210 n.29
Riley, Bennett: as military governor, 171; calls Constitutional Convention, 172, 181; relinquishes command, 188; and Calif. Guard, 205
Rio de Janeiro, 83-84
Roach, Thomas J., 111, 160, 165, 167
Roach, William, 207-8
Roberts, Samuel, 203-4
Robinson, Henry R.,: cartoon of regiment, 64-66
Royce, Josiah, 183, 205
Russ, Adolphus, 198, 212-13, 219
Russ, Augustus, 212
Russ, Charles, 198, 212-13
Russ, Christian, 198, 212
Russ, Henry, 212
Russ Building, 212
Russ family, 198, 211-13
Russ Gardens, 212
Russ house, illustrated, 94
Russ House (hotel), 212
Ryan, William Redmond: motivation of, 63-64; drawing, "On the Way to the Mines," 142; *Personal Adventures in Upper and Lower California*, 174 n.24

Sacramento, 171, 190
Sacramento Guards, 161
San Diego Illustrated Herald, 228-29
San Francisco: in 1846-1847, illustration, 94-95; population of, 1847, 91-92, 92 n.7; population of, 1848-1849, 158
San Francisco *Alta California*, 162, 164, 168-69, 187, 203, 211
San Francisco *California Star*, 91, 99, 160-61

San Francisco *California Star and Californian*, 161, 164, 178
San Francisco *Californian*, 136, 160-61
San Francisco *Examiner*, 32
San Francisco Guards, 159-61
San Francisco Legislative Assembly, 161-72, 173 n.15
San Luis Obispo Weekly Tribune, 149
San Pasqual, 90
Santa Barbara gun, 124-25
Schell, Mary L., 215-17
Schoolcraft, Henry A., 171, 178
Scott, Charles G., 210 n.29
Semple Robert, 184, 198
Shannon, William E., 29, 40; on Brazilian slavery, 84; reproved by Mason, 107; as alcalde of Sonoma, 147; delegate to Constitutional Convention, 182; introduces anti-slavery section, 285; compromises state boundary dispute, 190; death of, 190
Sherman, William T., 90, 105-6, 155-56, 226
Sinton, Richard H., 214
Sirey, James, 144
Sirrine, John J., 165
Six Months in the Gold Mines (Buffum), 167-68
Slacum expedition, 7
Slidell, John, 17
Sloat, John D., 20-21, 71, 87-89
Smith, Andrew J., 137
Smith, William H., 235
Snyder, Jacob, 219
Society of California Pioneers, The, 169, 218-29
Sonora Herald, 148
Soulé, Frank, 202, 243
Stearns, Abel, 118, 184, 191
Steele, Seymour, 56
Steuben County (New York), 27
Stevenson, Jonathan Drake, 29-31, 36, 115-16, 211, 223-32; selec-

tion of, for command, 29-31;
reports to Kearny, 93; to Monterey, 98; commands Southern
Military District, 101; ordered
to disband regiment, 135; mustered out, 137; in the mines,
143; and Constitutional Convention, 180, 182; and The
Society of California Pioneers,
219; photograph of, 225; marriage of, 228; legal practice of,
228-29; and Masonic Lodge,
224, 229, 232 n.17; as U.S.
Shipping Commissioner, 229,
232 n.16; *Memorial and Petition*
of, 231 n.12; death of, 229;
assessment of, 115-16, 224, 230
Stevenson, Matthew R., 69-70, 145
Stockton, Robert F., 89
Stockton Independent, 144
Susan Drew, 64, 74, 96; life aboard,
81, 84-85; mutiny aboard, 81-
83; military activity aboard, 85
Sutphen, William, 198
Sutter, John A., 99, 184
Sweden, 111

Tait, William G., 210 n.29
Taylor, Nelson: sails on *Brutus*, 80;
to mines with Stevenson, 137;
career after discharge, 144;
elected state senator, 188
Temple, R. E., 23
Tenth United States Military Department, California designated
as, 91
Texas, 17, 19, 25
Theall, Hiram W., 147, 149
Theatrical performances, 213, 220
n.4, 321 n.6
Third Artillery, Company F: arrival
in Calif., 90; officers of, 90;
strength of, 91; desertion from,
134
Thomas H. Perkins, 74; stores on, 70;

threat of mutiny aboard, 83;
military activity aboard, 85;
arrives in San Francisco, 86
Tompkins, Christopher, 90
Trist, Nicholas, 132
Turner, James, 84, 111
Two Years Before the Mast (Dana), 7

Uhrbrook, Henry, 207
U.S. Navy. *See* Pacific Squadron

Vallejo, Mariano G., 99, 136
Van Voorhies, William, 150, 164
Veeder, Peter G., 210 n.29
Vermeule, Thomas: sails on *Brutus*,
80; arrest in Los Angeles, 117;
court-martial, dishonorable discharge, 117-18; re-arrested, 133;
delegate to Constitutional Convention, 181; elected state
senator, 187-88; death of, 190
Vincent, Joshua S., 235-36; "Log-
Book" of, 8-9, 80; motivation of,
61-62; on Naglee, 82; and
Catholic Church, 109-10; death
of, 236
Volunteer journals, 252-53
"Volunteer's Vision" (Morrison), 6-7

Wadsworth, James C. L., 218-19
Walker, William, 207
Ward, James C., 159-60, 204, 212
Warren (U.S.S.), 137
War With Mexico Reviewed (Livermore),
4-5
West Point (military academy), 70-71
Whitehouse, Benjamin, 144
Wierzbicki, Felix P., 174 n.25
Wilkes expedition, 7
Williams, Edward, 137
Wilmot Proviso, 156
Women, aboard transports, 56
Wright, George W., 187
Wright, Silas, 23, 36